THE

PLANT CARE

MANUAL

STEFAN BUCZACKI

THE

PLANT CARE

MANUAL

The essential
guide to the
aftercare
of over 300
garden plants

CONRAN OCTOPUS

First published in Great Britain in 1992 by
Conran Octopus Limited
37 Shelton Street
London WC2H 9HN

British Library Cataloguing-in-Publication
Data
A catalogue record of this book is available
from the British Library

ISBN 1 85029 402 X

Senior Editor Sarah Pearce
Art Editor Helen Lewis
Consultant Editor David Joyce
Production Jill Macey
Editorial Assistant Jane Chapman

Illustrators:
Liz Pepperell (Plant portraits)
Vanessa Luff (Techniques)
Sarah Venus (Cover motif)

Typeset by Servis Filmsetting Ltd,
Manchester

Printed by Bath Press Colourbooks,
Great Britain

Cover produced and printed by
Harveys Ltd, Midlothian

Where measurements are given
for plants the height is given first,
followed by the spread.

CONTENTS

Introduction

This book is a guide to looking after the plants in your garden, and its principal purpose is to ensure that you obtain the most from them by feeding, watering, pruning and otherwise caring for them in the best possible way. Since problems often arise as a result of mistakes in the choice of plants for particular locations, I have also provided some information on the requirements of certain varieties and guidance on how to plant them. Each chapter deals with a different category of plants – shrubs, climbers, herbaceous perennials and so on – and discusses the care and treatment relevant to each group. Sometimes my advice may differ from that given in other gardening books, but my recommendations are based on personal experience and the procedures I suggest are those that I have found most successful. In the few instances where I discuss plants that I have not grown myself, never having gardened in the appropriate conditions, I have taken the advice of fellow gardeners whose opinions I respect.

In order to cater for gardens over as wide a geographical area as possible, I generally refer in my recommendations to seasons rather than individual months. For gardeners in Britain and Western Europe, I interpret winter as December to February, spring as March to May, summer as June to August, and autumn as September to November.

In discussing specific plants, I begin in every case with their site and soil requirements because inappropriate conditions are so often the cause of problems. The characteristics of all soils are defined by their texture and their structure. There is little you can do to alter the texture, which results from the relative proportions of sand, silt and clay particles present. A high percentage of minute clay particles makes for a 'heavy' soil, which is slow to warm up in spring but then retains heat well. It is rich in nutrients but poorly aerated, so root penetration is difficult and slow. Because of the close compaction of the clay particles, a heavy soil is poorly drained and may even become waterlogged at certain times of the year. By contrast, a 'light' soil has a high proportion of large sand particles and drains easily, thus losing both water and nutrients (by inference, plants will require feeding more frequently); it

warms up quickly in spring so growth may start early, but it cools down quickly too, meaning that the growing season may be short.

If you cannot alter fundamentally the texture of the soil, you can do a great deal to change its structure, which results from its 'pore and crumb' composition. A well-structured soil consists of the right balance between pores, for aeration and drainage, and solid matter, the crumbs, containing nutrients. The extent to which soil particles bind together to form crumbs with pore spaces in between depends on the presence of the natural glue-like substances contained in organic matter. Paradoxically, therefore, both a heavy, waterlogged clay and a light free-draining sand will be improved by the addition of organic material.

Watering and feeding are crucially important; very few plants will give of their best without the addition of some fertilizer to supplement that naturally available in the soil. I have, however, tried to keep matters as simple as possible, and I don't expect your garden shed to house a complete range of different blends of fertilizer to suit the individual requirements of every plant. Most of my recommendations can be satisfied with the following products: a balanced general purpose fertilizer such as fish, blood and bone (organically based) or Growmore (artificial), bonemeal, a proprietary rose fertilizer, and a soluble or liquid fertilizer with a high potash content. For a few plants growing on alkaline soils, a fertilizer containing sequestered iron will help to control leaf yellowing (chlorosis).

I am a great believer in mulching, which I consider to be one of the most important of all gardening tasks. An organic mulch applied once or preferably twice each year will serve the dual roles of keeping the soil moist and of suppressing weed growth. And the best source of organic mulching material is the compost bin. Composting is an essential part of good gardening practice, and it also provides a means of recycling most garden and household waste. A compost shredder will render even woody material suitable for composting.

The scope of *The Plant Care Manual* is confined to medium- and long-term plants, some of which, like trees and shrubs, retain an aboveground woody framework whereas others die down to a rootstock or some underground storage organ such as a bulb, corm, tuber or rhizome. Trees and shrubs will often require pruning, and correct pruning technique is usually the key to their success as garden plants. I have therefore devoted a substantial part of the book to this aspect of plant care, and a good set of pruning tools should be high on your list of garden equipment. It makes sense to buy the best quality secateurs you can afford (preferably both the anvil variety for hard, woody material, and the scissor or by-pass type for softer stems), loppers and a curved pruning saw.

But with the best will and the best management in the world, things sometimes go wrong. Pruning may be inadequate, pests and diseases may strike, or you may simply have inherited problems in taking over a garden whose plants have been neglected. This is where my troubleshooting advice may help because in many – perhaps in most – cases plants can be rejuvenated and rescued; you need to know what to do, how drastic your treatment can be, and when it should be undertaken. Pest and disease problems could fill a book on their own, but it is useful to be able to recognize the really common ones and know how to respond. It is worth saying, however, that while no husbandry will eliminate every problem, a well-fed, well-watered plant growing in optimum conditions will be the most likely to recover.

In most of the chapters I have given brief descriptions of the best ways to propagate the plants discussed. This is partly because I believe perpetuating your stock by this means is one of the most satisfying aspects of plant care, but also because in many cases rejuvenation (either on a regular basis or as a way of troubleshooting) can be achieved by way of cuttings, division or seeds.

Detailed information on plant propagation is available elsewhere, but the methods that I have advocated require no specialized equipment. Softwood, semi-ripe and hardwood cuttings simply take advantage of the growth stages through which plant stems pass in the course of a year. Softwood cuttings are generally taken early in the growing season, semi-ripe as the tissues begin to toughen and the stems become springy, and hardwood (from shrubs or trees) generally when the plant is dormant in winter. Any cutting bearing leaves must be kept in a moist atmosphere (such as a covered propagator or closed frame) in order to minimize moisture loss until it has formed roots.

Softwood and semi-ripe cuttings should usually be cut to a length of 10–15cm/4–6in, the cut being made just below a nodal point (where leaves emerge). The lowest few leaves should be pulled off and then, once the cuttings have formed roots, they should be potted on, the plants hardened off and left in their pots for at least a year before they are planted out in the garden. There is a good deal of mythology attached to the taking of semi-ripe cuttings with a 'heel' of old wood at the base, but for none of the subjects described in this book have I found that it makes any difference.

Leafless, hardwood cuttings of deciduous plants can be placed in a shaded spot in the open garden; they are generally the easiest type to take successfully although the slowest to root, sometimes requiring as much as eighteen months. Hardwood cuttings can be longer than other types, up to 20–30cm/8–10in.

A few plants are propagated by root cuttings. These are taken in winter when the plant is dormant, since they necessitate digging it up first. Short pieces of healthy root should be pushed vertically to their full length into pots of compost and incubated in the usual way.

Other means of propagation include layering, which is a useful method for those, mainly evergreen, shrubs and climbers that are otherwise difficult to root. It consists of anchoring into the soil a low-hanging branch while it is still attached to the parent plant. Division is a simple technique applicable only to non-woody plants. It is best done in autumn or spring, and comprises lifting an old-established plant clump with a fork and separating it into sections. The clump should be split into several pieces and only those vigorous parts from the periphery of the old clump retained.

Relatively few of the plants in this book are readily propagated by seed. With those for which it is recommended, sowing into a soil-based compost in pots in spring in either a cold greenhouse or a cold frame will usually yield satisfactory results, although germination may sometimes be slow and erratic and several months may elapse before you see anything.

For every entry I have indicated approximate growth rates and ultimate sizes. Clearly, such factors vary from site to site but I have tried to give information based on more or less ideal growing conditions, the conditions, in fact, in which each type of plant *should* be grown.

COMMON PLANT PROBLEMS

This is a simple guide to the recognition and treatment of the commonest and most import-ant plant pest and disease problems. There are, of course, thousands of others but only those listed here are likely to give rise to any real concern – and then only in a minority of cases. I have listed all these under the relevant plant entries, together with a brief indication of their commonest symptoms and, where appropriate, their treatment. This chart should always be read in conjunction with the plant entries since some of the problems are specific to certain types of plant. It can be extremely frustrating trying to match the symptoms of a particular disease to something seen on a plant on which the problem doesn't occur.

In many instances, a problem can be kept in check by following simple procedures of garden husbandry or hygiene, but for certain pests and diseases a chemical spray is the only realistic answer. I haven't hesitated, therefore, in sug-gesting the use of chemicals that are officially approved for use in gardens, but I do stress that they must always be applied strictly in accord-ance with the manufacturer's directions.

PROBLEM	RECOGNITION	TREATMENT
Adelgids	Woolly white sap-sucking insects on needles and shoots.	Spray with malathion insecticide.
Aphids	Infestation of green, black, grey or brownish sap-sucking insects.	Spray with any contact insecticide.
Bacterial canker	Gum oozes from bark; branches die back.	If symptoms persist, fell the tree.
Birds	Buds removed, flower petals torn, fruit removed.	Use appropriate scarers/repellents or netting – remember all birds are legally protected.
Black spot	More or less circular dark brown or black spots, often with accompanying leaf yellowing.	Spray with proprietary fungicide; a specific fungicide-insecticide mixture will also control aphids.
Box sucker	See Scale insects.	
Bulb, corm, tuber and rhizome rots	Plants fail to flower or grow feebly; underground storage structure may be soft and mouldy.	Destroy affected plants.
Canker	More or less rounded, sunken lesion on bark, usually with die-back of shoot beyond the lesion.	No treatment possible but badly diseased branches should be cut off.

PROBLEM	RECOGNITION	TREATMENT
Capsid bugs	Irregular tattering of leaves and/or bumps on fruit.	No treatment possible.
Codling moth	Fruit damaged inside along the core; a maggot often present within.	Use proprietary yellow moth traps.
Coral spot	Tiny pinkish spots on bark, often with some die-back of the shoot.	Cut out and destroy affected parts.
Die-back	Shoot dies from tip downwards, the tissue death gradually extending into previously healthy parts.	Cut out affected parts.
Eelworm	Vague symptoms but plants develop in stunted form, often in groups.	Grow plants on a different area of soil.
Fireblight	Blossom dies and foliage appears damaged as if scorched by fire.	Destroy affected plants.
Flea beetle	Leaves close to soil level perforated with masses of tiny holes.	Dust proprietary soil insecticide around plants.
Fruit rots	Fruits decay, either when still on the plant or shortly after picking. Mould growth may be present.	No treatment possible.
Fungal leaf spots	Large or small, regular or irregular lesions on leaves, often displaying some concentric patterning.	With few exceptions (see Black spot), no treatment is necessary.
Gall	Irregular warty growth on stems or leaves.	Cut out and destroy affected parts.
Grey mould	Fluffy grey mould associated with tissue decay and sometimes with die-back of shoots.	Spray with systemic fungicide or sulphur; destroy badly affected parts.
Honey fungus	Plant shows die-back and poor growth; toadstools and black strands may be present at stem base.	Seek specialist diagnosis before felling suspect trees.

Common Plant Problems

PROBLEM	RECOGNITION	TREATMENT
Leaf attacking insects	Pieces eaten from leaves, either at centre or margins; no slime trails present.	No treatment necessary.
Leaf-blister mite	Small, irregular dark brown blisters.	Collect and destroy affected leaves.
Leaf miner	Wavy tunnels visible *inside* leaf tissues.	Collect and destroy affected leaves.
Lily beetle	Pieces eaten from leaves and other parts; bright red insects present.	Spray insects with any contact insecticide.
Mildew	Dusty white covering on leaves, buds, flowers or other parts.	Spray with systemic fungicide or sulphur.
Narcissus fly	Flowers fail to form; tunnelling, often with maggots present, in bulbs.	Destroy affected plants.
Nut weevil	Small holes in nuts with contents destroyed.	No treatment possible.
Peach leaf curl	Leaves distorted and at first covered with dusty white covering, later turning red.	Spray with copper-containing fungicide as leaves open and again as they drop.
Pear midge	Young fruitlets drop prematurely and contain tiny yellowish maggots.	Collect and destroy affected fruits.
Plum fruit moth	See Codling moth.	
Red spider mite	Foliage turns brown or bronze, usually accompanied by fine cobwebbing within which are masses of minute brownish mites.	No treatment possible; if infestation is severe and persistent destroy affected plants.
Root decay fungi	See Honey fungus.	
Rust	Leaves and sometimes other parts have tiny black or brightly coloured dusty lesions.	Spray with proprietary fungicide, such as propiconazole, sold specifically for rust control.

Common Plant Problems

PROBLEM	RECOGNITION	TREATMENT
Sawfly	Leaves stripped; caterpillar-like insects may be present.	If insects are present, spray with contact insecticide.
Scab	Crusty lesions on fruit, leaves and/or stems.	Spray with benomyl in spring and then three times fortnightly.
Scale insects	Tiny, limpet-like sap-sucking insects accompanied by sticky honeydew.	Spray with systemic insecticide.
Silver leaf	Foliage turns silvery and branches die back.	Cut off dead branches and wait to see if tree recovers; if not, fell and destroy it.
Slugs	Leaves and other tissues eaten; slime trails present.	Use proprietary slug pellets or other proven remedy.
Snails	See Slugs.	
Thrips	Surface of flowers and/or leaves minutely speckled.	No treatment possible.
Tulip fire	Plants distorted, yellowish leaf spots, buds fail to form properly.	Destroy affected plants.
Water lily beetle	Furrows and small holes in upper leaf surfaces.	Wash off beetles with hose.
Whitefly	Tiny, white, moth-like insects, often accompanied by sticky honeydew.	Spray weekly with contact insecticide.
Wood decay fungi	Bracket-like fungal growth on stem.	No treatment possible but be aware that the tree may be physically unsound.
Woolly aphid	White, woolly tufts with small insects within.	Spray with tar oil wash in winter.
Virus	Numerous symptoms: the commonest are irregular leaf mottling and overall small size.	No treatment possible, but do not propagate from affected plants and destroy any that are badly affected.

SHRUBS

Principles of Care

I consider shrubs to be the most important plants in the modern garden. By selecting carefully from the vast number of deciduous and evergreen varieties available, it is possible to have attractive flowers, foliage, bark, buds and overall shape all year round. There are appropriate varieties for almost any soil and site conditions, although, as with other types of permanent (perennial) plants, relatively few are suitable for growing in deep shade. And while shrubs in general are rather more adaptable than herbaceous perennials, the commonest reason for failure is that no account has been taken of soil preference.

It is true that many shrubs will give perfectly acceptable results for several years with almost no attention at all, but feeding during the early part of the season with a general purpose or rose fertilizer (the former for foliage and the latter for flowering varieties) will bring clearly recognizable benefits. If you feed shrubs twice a year, in late spring and in summer, they will do even better, and I find it sad that many gardeners regard this as unnecessary; in my opinion it brings enormous rewards for very little effort. The addition of a moisture-retaining and weed-suppressing organic mulch early in the spring will also be beneficial. The stout woody framework of both trees and shrubs often causes gardeners to overlook the fact that they require as much protection from competing weeds, especially when young, as do any other plants. And when shrubs are planted in lawns or long grass it is important to leave an area of bare soil approximately 1m/3ft in diameter around the base, on which mulch and fertilizer can be applied. While a spring mulch is most important for moisture retentiveness, a mulch applied around the base of the plant in autumn will give valuable frost protection.

Few shrubs require staking unless they are to be trained in standard form (see page 18). Evergreen varieties will generally benefit from a protective screen of hessian or similar material during the first winter after planting, especially in colder areas. A winter screen will also allow the more tender wall-trained shrubs to be grown in colder regions.

Many shrubs (see Table), with the few important exceptions of those intolerant of dry conditions, make excellent subjects for growing in containers; this method is especially suitable for tender varieties as it allows them to be moved into a sheltered spot in the winter. Large containers that cannot be moved can be insulated by packing around them pieces of expanded polystyrene or similar material during periods of severe frost. In general, soil-based John Innes No. 3 potting compost should be used for container-grown shrubs; for rhododendrons, azaleas and camellias, however, a specially formulated acid (so-called ericaceous) compost should be used instead. The overall care, including pruning, outlined for shrubs in the open garden is equally applicable to those grown in containers, but here it is especially important to feed twice during the summer, to pay careful attention to watering and mulching, and not to allow the compost to dry out. With correct feeding and mulching, the compost need not be replaced, but re-potting may be necessary once or twice at, say, three-year intervals, until the plant reaches its mature size. Given this care, there is no reason why a shrub in a container shouldn't live as long and productively as one in the open garden.

SHRUBS PARTICULARLY SUITABLE FOR GROWING IN CONTAINERS

Abutilon	Hebe
Buxus	Laurus
Callistemon	Lavandula
Calluna	Potentilla
Camellia	Prunus (Portugal laurel)
Choisya	Rhododendron (including azalea)
Daphne	Rosmarinus
Erica	Skimmia
Fatsia	Thymus
Fuchsia	Dwarf conifers

SHRUBS PARTICULARLY SUITABLE FOR TRAINING AGAINST A WALL

Abutilon	Escallonia
Callistemon	Forsythia
Camellia	Fremontodendron
Ceanothus	Garrya
Chaenomeles	Jasminum
Cotoneaster	Pyracantha
Cytisus (battandieri)	

Pruning cuts

THE CORRECT CUT To prune most effectively, cut the plant stem just above a bud that faces away from the centre of the bush: about 5mm/¼in away from it is sufficient. Slant the cut downwards at a gentle angle away from the bud.

PRUNING

Countless shrubs survive for many years in gardens without ever being pruned. This may be because the species or variety will grow and bloom without any need for pruning; indeed, in a few instances, pruning would be detrimental. But most plants are unable to fulfil their real potential without it. Pruning is simply the deliberate removal of parts of a plant in order that the remaining parts will benefit. This benefit may derive from a more appealing shape, from increased flower or leaf production, from better light and air penetration, or from diseased parts being cut away. The operation can take several forms and in order that you may make best use of advice regarding specific types of shrub, I must clarify certain general pruning principles.

Shrubs are almost always pruned by removing parts of their shoots, a general term that includes all the woody growth, be it part of the main stem or the branches arising from the stem. Pruning cuts are always made just above a bud, usually an outward-facing bud (one positioned on the outer side of the plant); if there is no convenient bud, or pair of buds, cut back to just above the junction with the parent shoot. It is a general maxim that when you cut off the end of a shoot, the buds further down the stem (whether flower buds or leaf buds) are stimulated. If you regularly cut away the shoot tips, a more attractively compact, bushy or more floriferous plant will result. Within limits, the more severely you prune a sparse hedge, for example, the more it will thicken. In due course, however, the increased branching can produce a rather congested mass of growth, and it may be necessary to undertake some thinning out by cutting away a proportion of

the shoots completely and allowing light and air to penetrate to the centre of the plant.

The task of pruning flowering shrubs will be made simpler and more logical if it is related to the flowering habit and flowering time of the plant. Shrubs produce flowers from buds borne essentially in one of two ways, either on woody shoots that developed during the same season as the flowers, or on shoots that developed in the previous or earlier seasons. Most shrubs that flower on older wood do so before midsummer: the shoots and buds are ready to burst into life from the start of the season. On the other hand, most shrubs that flower on the current season's wood do so after midsummer: the plant must wait until the new crop of flower buds has had time to develop and mature. By waiting until after a shrub has flowered before pruning it you will ensure that you don't miss a season's blossoming.

Another general maxim is that shrubs flowering before midsummer should be pruned immediately after flowering is over, whereas those that flower later may either be pruned immediately or left until early in the following spring. The latter approach has the advantage in colder areas of leaving some additional frost protection on the plant in the form of the bare

Deadheading

REGULAR DEADHEADING Encourage most plants, and particularly repeat-flowering plants such as modern roses, to produce further flowers by regularly removing the dead heads. Cut the stem just above the first leaf that has a fat, healthy bud in its apex. This will then shoot to produce a new flower.

Understanding a shrub

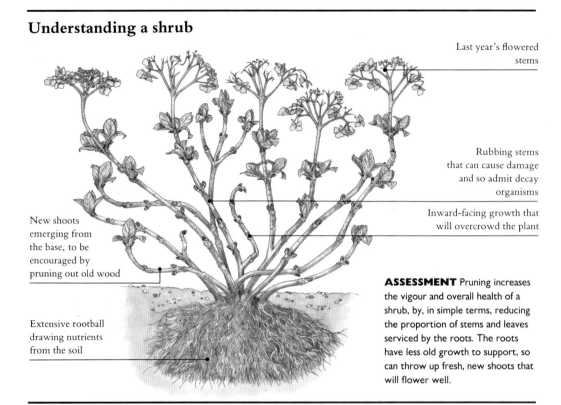

Last year's flowered stems

Rubbing stems that can cause damage and so admit decay organisms

Inward-facing growth that will overcrowd the plant

New shoots emerging from the base, to be encouraged by pruning out old wood

Extensive rootball drawing nutrients from the soil

ASSESSMENT Pruning increases the vigour and overall health of a shrub, by, in simple terms, reducing the proportion of stems and leaves serviced by the roots. The roots have less old growth to support, so can throw up fresh, new shoots that will flower well.

framework of shoots that will trap warm air. In general, too, shrubs that flower in the first half of the year require fairly light pruning (the shoots are cut back only a little) whereas those that flower later in the year usually require harder pruning (a rather greater proportion of each shoot is cut back).

While the specific method of pruning advocated for each type of shrub is described under the individual plant entries, there are a number of guidelines which apply to pruning in general that are worth stating here. Many flowering shrubs (roses in particular) benefit from being pruned on a three-year renewal cycle. This entails cutting back to soil level one third of the oldest shoots each year and ensures a constant supply of vigorous new growth.

I have mentioned the importance of cutting away any obviously diseased or damaged shoots, and this should be a routine procedure in spring, once the new leaves have begun to burst. It will then be evident which parts have been killed by winter frost and these should be pruned away, cutting into a few centimetres of the living shoot at the base. (A useful way to check the viability of shoots is to scratch the bark with your thumbnail. If the tissue beneath appears fresh and green, it is living; if it is pale green or brown, it is moribund; and if dark brown, it is dead.) The presence of disease in a shoot is often revealed by feeble leaf development and some coloured fungal growth on the bark; the salmon pink pustules of the coral spot fungus are among the commonest (see page 9).

Shrubs with variegated foliage are popular and attractive but many are apt to produce 'reverted' shoots with leaves of a uniform green. These all-green shoots are more vigorous than the variegated ones and will gradually take over, and it is important to cut them out as soon as they appear.

Shrubs that are commonly grown against walls in a more or less two-dimensional shape (see pages 14, 83 and overleaf) should of course have any shoots pointing directly towards or directly away from the wall cut away. But they also benefit from spur-pruning (see overleaf), in which the side-shoots arising from the main framework are cut back to within about 10cm/4in of their bases each year to produce short shoots termed 'spurs'. This operation helps to encourage the production of flowers in

Light and hard pruning

New shoot growth that will produce the next season's flowers

Buds further down the stems will now shoot into growth

AFTER LIGHT PRUNING To prune a shrub lightly, cut back each flowered stem by roughly one third, cutting to a pair of strong buds, or to a bud facing away from the centre of the plant. Remove diseased or rubbing stems. Keep the centre open and airy by, if necessary, cutting out up to one third of the stems completely every three or four years.

AFTER HARD PRUNING Cut back all the stems to buds as close to the base as possible. Vigorous new shoots arising from the base can be lightly cut back to a bud to stimulate further growth, or left alone. Where there are no buds near the base, or only very few, cut the stems back to the lowest strong bud, and cut out completely up to one third of the least healthy stems. Then feed and mulch the plant well to rejuvenate it and prompt new shoot growth.

neat clusters rather than spaced along elongated branches, which may be acceptable for a free-standing plant but can look very untidy in a confined space against a wall.

On wall-trained shrubs, just as with climbers, growth in girth during the course of a season can result in ties cutting into the bark or soft tissue of the shoots, so all ties must be checked and re-tied annually.

Many gardening books include information on root pruning to reduce the vigour of large shrubs. This book doesn't, because I consider it a difficult operation likely in many species to lead to suckering. It is best left, in the rare instances where it is beneficial, to an expert; although I have given some information on the root pruning of trees which may be relevant (see page 196).

Wall training shrubs

SPUR PRUNING This pruning method encourages flowers in neat clusters all along the stems. Every year at pruning time cut back all the side-shoots on the main stems to a bud that is within about 10cm/4in of the base of the shoot.

Cut back the leader to stimulate growth on the left side

Train in a shoot horizontally to form a new arm

Spur prune side-shoots growing vertically

WALL TRAINING (*Pyracantha*) Prune wall-trained shrubs regularly to keep them in shape. In early spring remove any shoots facing directly into or away from the wall. Tie down horizontally the main arms, and spur prune all the side-shoots on them. Tie in the vertical leader, or stimulate growth further down by cutting it off at a bud.

Remove shoots growing into or away from the wall

TRAINING A STANDARD

There is one method of pruning that is applicable to a considerable number of shrub types and yet is not as widely recognized as it deserves to be. This is the training of a multi-stemmed shrub into a form with only a single stem. Such a plant is called a standard. The technique offers a most attractive alternative to buying a plant grafted on to the single stem of a different variety, and it achieves a similar result. Select a single, strong vertical shoot on a young plant, preferably one close to its centre. Cut back the remaining shoots to soil level and tie the stem to a stake. Remove the side branches on the chosen shoot close to soil level. As the shoot elongates, tie it higher up the stake and continue to remove the side branches low down. Gradually, as the crown develops, remove side branches further up the stem to create an attractive, well-shaped plant. Once it has reached the desired height, cut back the leading shoot to encourage further bushiness in the crown. The method is applicable to most multi-stemmed shrubs, but it is particularly successful for some of the willows, some cotoneasters and *Buddleja alternifolia*.

When a shrub or climber is grown against a wall we take for granted that a permanent framework is left each year and pruning is restricted to the side-shoots. But a somewhat similar technique, analogous to training a standard, can be used with some free-standing shrubs such as *Buddleja davidii* and *Cotinus coggygria*. Instead of pruning them to the base, a framework of chosen size can be left, much as a single stem remains with the standard. Advice to prune to a point 'above soil level' should then be interpreted as 'above the framework'.

Training a standard (*Buddleja alternifolia*)

1 TRAIN THE PLANT VERTICALLY Select a strong stem on a young plant and remove all others. Stake the stem.

2 REMOVE SIDE-SHOOTS As the plant grows upwards, remove all the side-shoots on the lower part of the stem, and rub out the buds in the apices between shoots and stem. Leave the top 25cm/10in of the plant untouched: this will form the head.

3 DEVELOP THE HEAD Once the plant has reached about 2m/6½ft in height, pinch out the leading shoot to encourage the head to develop. Thereafter prune standards of *Buddleja alternifolia* every year after flowering, by lightly tipping back the flowered shoots, and removing one or two of the oldest shoots to encourage new growth. In autumn trim away any wayward shoots.

TROUBLESHOOTING

Any long-lived plant with a permanent above-ground structure runs the risk of developing problems through physical injury, disease, sheer neglect, or a combination of all three. Shrubs, tough as many of them may be, are no exception and from time to time they present gardeners with problems regarding both diagnosis and treatment if they are to be given a new lease of life. In most instances, rejuvenation is perfectly possible and it is relatively rare that a plant must be discarded, but it is important to recognize the problem and to know both the correct remedy and the correct time of year at which to perform it.

The most common cause of problems is simple neglect: a plant in need of regular pruning has not been pruned; it has not been fed; or weeds or other plants have been allowed to grow too close and compete with it.

Frequently all three types of neglect go hand in hand, and the result is poor performance in the production of flowers or foliage, which is generally pale and small. It may also result in 'legginess' – long, spindly shoots bare of leaves or flowers. It is surprising how often familiarity seems to breed a lack of awareness in gardeners regarding the condition of their own plants. Because they see a plant day after day they fail to appreciate that it could in fact be achieving

Troubleshooting: pruning

Flowers carried away from centre of the plant

Weak growth from old age or lack of nutrients

Shoot die-back on snags left by poor pruning

Poor, weak foliage

Lack of new shoots emerging from the base

Bare leggy stems, with no buds

ASSESSMENT Tired shrubs in need of rejuvenation are always easy to identify: flowering will be poor, and the plant's stems will be sparse for much of their length. There will probably be a mass of crossing stems, and lots of weak growth cluttering up the centre. Intelligent pruning will stimulate the root system to throw up plenty of healthy new growth which can then be cared for.

▶ **CUTTING BACK TO THE BASE** Some plants will tolerate being cut hard back to within a few inches of the base, cutting to just above buds if possible, otherwise to bare stems. Feed, water and mulch well, and protect new shoot growth from slugs and snails.

far better results, and it is only when they come across the same species in another garden that they recognize the defect. A simple way to check a shrub's performance is to look at the shoot tips and see the amount of growth that has occurred in each season; if the amount of new growth is declining, especially on a plant only five or six years old, it is likely that something is amiss.

Frost damage, which is easy to recognize, takes the form of browning of the most vulnerable parts of a plant – the shoot tips, buds and any newly opened or young leaves. Direct evidence of garden pests can generally be detected in traces of their activity – in leaves with holes or tattering, or small holes in woody tissues. Disease symptoms tend to be more nebulous,

but among the most common on above-ground parts are fairly regular spots or blotches on leaves, or coloured, more or less powdery mould or pustules. Below-ground effects of fungal attack on roots are usually manifested by wilting or dying back from the tips of the shoots (since these are the parts furthest from the roots, they suffer first from an interrupted water supply). If you suspect disease on the roots, and particularly if the soil is waterlogged or poorly aerated, dig into the soil near the plant to allow inspection of parts of the root system. Blackening of the youngest and finest roots is a good indication of fungal decay.

While specific pest and disease problems may require specific remedies (see pages 8–11), a number of general first-aid procedures can be

Two-year rejuvenation of a shrub

◄ **SPRING, 1ST YEAR** The shrub opposite has here had one third of its stems cut back to the base. The remaining stems have been lightly cut back, but it is best to leave them largely untouched: trimming back stimulates the stems to branch, whereas the plant will be stronger if new growth can be encouraged from the base. The plant must now be fed, watered and mulched well.

New growth on old stems

► **ASSESSMENT, 2ND SPRING** The plant has thrown up some new stems, and the old stems have produced new growth too. The new shoots from the base should be left untouched, but the oldest third of the stems can now be cut out completely; in this case four old stems remain, and one can be cut out.

Stem to be removed

New growth from base

Old stems for removal the next year

◄ **AFTER PRUNING, 2ND SPRING** One old stem has been removed, and with careful feeding, watering and mulching the plant will throw up further new shoots from the base. In the third spring, the plant should be strong enough for the remaining old stems to be cut out. Adopting a two- or three-year cycle to rejuvenate old shrubs will reduce the shock to the plant.

Principles of Care

Moving an established shrub

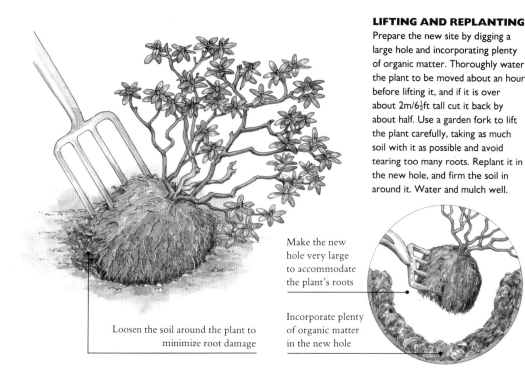

LIFTING AND REPLANTING
Prepare the new site by digging a large hole and incorporating plenty of organic matter. Thoroughly water the plant to be moved about an hour before lifting it, and if it is over about 2m/6½ft tall cut it back by about half. Use a garden fork to lift the plant carefully, taking as much soil with it as possible and avoid tearing too many roots. Replant it in the new hole, and firm the soil in around it. Water and mulch well.

Make the new hole very large to accommodate the plant's roots

Loosen the soil around the plant to minimize root damage

Incorporate plenty of organic matter in the new hole

undertaken with any plant that is failing to thrive, and these are best carried out in spring. Weed growth or other competing vegetation should be cleared away over an area of approximately 1m/3ft in diameter and the soil well forked over, a dressing of general purpose fertilizer forked in, the whole well watered, and a mulch of organic matter applied over the surface. Remedial pruning should then be carried out unless I have indicated in the individual plant notes that a particular variety will not respond to it. With a few exceptions, pruning should be spread over two or even three years, each time cutting back half or one third of the branches to about 10cm/4in above soil level. In a few cases (again, indicated in the individual entries), shrubs can be cut back completely to soil level in one operation.

If poor growth and performance are simply the consequence of the shrub having been planted in an inappropriate position, or if it is quite impossible to limit the plant's size in a confined space by pruning, moving it offers the best solution. While large shrubs can be moved, there is no simple rule-of-thumb method of ensuring that a move will be successful. Magnolias in particular have a reputation for being difficult to re-establish once moved, but even they can be transplanted if the operation is done carefully and at the optimum time. In my experience, early spring, before growth has really recommenced, is the best time of year to move both deciduous and evergreen species. The essence of a successful move is to disturb the roots as little as possible, lifting the plant with a large ball of soil and ensuring that it is transferred and replanted without delay. Its new position must be carefully prepared with plenty of organic matter and a sprinkling of bonemeal first, and the plant watered very thoroughly for some time after the move until it is well established and growing strongly.

If poor growth is the result of the plant having been placed in inappropriate soil, the remedy may be more difficult as few gardens offer a range of soil types and it is as likely to fail in the new place as in the old. The only realistic option, if the plant is not too large, is to try growing it in a container filled with an appropriate soil-based compost.

HEDGES

HEDGES

A hedge is simply a group of shrubs (or occasionally trees), planted in a row and treated as a single entity. The plants must be placed close enough together to produce a continuous barrier with no gaps within about five or six years. Only certain shrub and tree species are suitable as hedging for they must be amenable to clipping and able to develop new shoots from fairly old wood.

SHRUBS FOR HEDGING

Berberis	*Ligustrum*
Buxus	*Lonicera nitida*
Cotoneaster	*Pittosporum*
Escallonia	*Prunus laurocerasus*
Euonymus japonicus	*Pyracantha*
Forsythia	*Rhamnus* (deciduous)
Fuchsia	*Ribes*
Hippophaë	*Rosmarinus*
Lavandula	*Symphoricarpos*
Laurus nobilis	*Tamarix.*

TREES FOR HEDGING

Chamaecyparis/Cupressus/ × Cupressocyparis

Crataegus	*Taxus*
Fagus	*Thuja*
Ilex	*Tsuga.*

HEDGE MANAGEMENT

Apart from a few species grown as flowering hedges, where the primary purpose is decorative rather than the creation of a barrier, there are certain fairly general rules about hedge maintenance. Gardeners differ widely in the way they manage hedging plants but my practice is never to prune any new hedge until late in its first spring, at least one year after planting. Then as an annual routine I cut back one third (or two thirds on very vigorous types) of the leading shoot. This will encourage bushiness through the development of well-branched side-shoots. Once the lateral growth has begun to exceed the desired width, these side-shoots should be lightly trimmed, and when the leading shoots have reached the desired height, normal top and side trimming may begin, cutting back each year to the pre-selected level. Unless you have a very good eye, you will find sight lines of string attached to wooden stakes will make it easier to cut straight edges. It is nearly always impossible to clip a hedge as accurately as you can prune a free-standing shrub, and it is pointless to try to cut back to points just above buds. Indeed it is a feature of the species that have proved themselves successful as hedging plants that their buds appear close together or are not prone to dying back from pruning cuts made between buds.

Bear in mind the general principle that pruning stimulates growth (see page 15): while a weak hedge can be improved by a hard trim,

Trimming a hedge

◀ **EVERGREEN HEDGE** Trim often to give a neat uniform appearance. If you don't trust your eye, establish a cutting line by pushing canes into the soil and tying string tautly around them. Trim the top flat, but slope the sides outwards at the base – called a 'batter'. Light will then reach the base of the hedge and ensure even density.

▶ **ORNAMENTAL DECIDUOUS HEDGE** At the appropriate trimming time, give hedging shrubs such as forsythia a light all-over trim.

Filling gaps in a hedge

▶ **ASSESSMENT** A hedge that is struggling to produce even, dense growth may need infilling with new plants. At an appropriate spot along the hedge, cut back the existing plants to make a gap in which you can work. With a sharp-edged spade or secateurs, slice down through the existing roots to make a planting hole.

◀ **INFILLING WITH NEW PLANTS** Incorporate plenty of organic matter in the base of the planting hole, and fork it in well. If the soil is very heavy, work it well to loosen it and add grit to improve drainage. Plant in good container-grown specimens of new plants, planting two if the hole is big enough. Water and mulch well in the following growing seasons, and trim appropriately to give a dense hedge.

the less you prune the really vigorous hedging species, such as Lawson or Leyland cypress, the less pruning they require.

Details of the time and frequency of trimming are given under the individual entries for the hedging species listed.

It is a curious fact that while most gardeners recognize the value of feeding and mulching free-standing shrubs, they very seldom do so for hedges. Yet they too, certainly in the early stages, will develop better and more rapidly if they are similarly cared for.

HEDGE TROUBLESHOOTING

Hedges are as likely to be neglected and over-grown as other shrubs and can in many cases be similarly rejuvenated. Those that have grown too tall or too wide commonly present problems and it must be said that with most conifers, and certainly with cypresses, almost nothing can be done; they will not regenerate

from old wood and if cut back there will be no new growth to cover the bare base. It is for this reason that I stress the importance of trimming gradually as the plant develops in order to encourage bushiness. I have no solution to offer the owner of a grossly overgrown coniferous hedge but to suggest that it should be removed and a fresh start made.

Those plants that I consider the best hedging species (most notably yew, beech and, to a lesser extent, box and tsuga) will, however, regenerate satisfactorily even when very over-grown. Irrespective of their present dimensions, cut back an overgrown hedge in spring to a height and width that is about halfway between the existing size and the desired size. Feed it well, and the following year cut it again to the size you want.

Gaps can sometimes be remedied by a combination of general cutting back and of wiring side branches across the gap (see opposite).

Troubleshooting: hedges

FILLING GAPS If the coverage of an evergreen is gappy or unsatisfactory, wiring can improve it substantially. At clipping time leave plenty of shoots around the gaps untrimmed. When the shoots are long enough, bend them down and wire them over the gap criss-cross fashion. Trim the ends lightly to stimulate growth, and feed the hedge well. The wires will quickly disappear into the foliage. The following season clip right over the repair as normal.

GAPS AT THE BASE Hedges that have become bare and leggy at the base are a common sight. At clipping time leave plenty of shoots low down on the hedge untrimmed, and let them elongate significantly. When they are long enough, pull them down and fix them securely, either pegging them into the ground or wiring them to the hedge stems. Trim the shoots with secateurs until dense growth has been restored, then clip the hedge as normal.

COMPLETE REJUVENATION Some hedges, particularly beech, become sparse and weak growing, or completely overgrown. If the plant is one that can be cut back very hard, it may be possible to rejuvenate the hedge by cutting it hard back on one side, right to the main stem. Feed, water and mulch well. In the following year if the hedge is recovering strongly, or in the year after that if recovery is sluggish, cut the other side back similarly.

Abutilon – Buddleja

Abutilon × suntense

Aucuba japonica

Abutilon

A fairly large genus with species that range in habit from annuals to trees. The shrubs include both evergreen and deciduous forms with mainly bell-shaped blue, white, red or occasionally yellowish summer flowers in varying sizes. They are only suitable for milder areas (or conservatories) but make very good plants for large containers if these can be moved under protection in winter.

Soil Humus-rich, well drained.

Situation Full sun or light shade, close to a south- or south-west-facing wall or other protection except in very mild, especially coastal areas.

Watering and feeding Mulch in autumn and spring. Feed with a balanced rose or similar potash-rich fertilizer in mid-spring and again around midsummer. Allow dormant plants in containers to become fairly dry in winter.

Pruning Cut back any frost-damaged shoots at least 15cm/6in into sound wood to just above a good bud in spring. Straggly, more or less climbing forms such as *A. megapotamicum* may be pruned more severely, cutting back the previous season's growth by two thirds in spring. The stems will need tying in to supports.

Common problems Frost damage; red spider mite and whitefly can be troublesome in warm summers.

Propagation Semi-ripe cuttings in early autumn.

Troubleshooting Established plants may show a tendency to become straggly. This is best combated by cutting out the oldest shoots, cutting back the remainder by about two thirds, and then routinely cutting back the previous season's growth by about half each spring.

Size The smallest of the common abutilons are the hybrids such as 'Kentish Belle', which reaches about 1.5 × 1.5m/5 × 5ft in four to five years, although others such as 'Ashford Red' and 'Canary Bird' tend to be larger and similar to the *A. × hybridum* varieties (about 2.5–3 × 2.5–3m/8–10 × 8–10ft). *A. × suntense* is more vigorous and will reach 5 × 3m/16 × 10ft in five years; *A. vitifolium* is of similar speed of growth but more upright, attaining 4 × 2.5m/13 × 8ft; the lax *A. megapotamicum* is almost a short climber, reaching about 3 × 3m/10 × 10ft over the same timespan.

Aucuba

The evergreen spotted laurel, *A. japonica*, is one of the most undervalued of garden shrubs. In the best forms, it has most attractive foliage and berries and is tolerant of conditions in which very few other plants will survive.

Soil Any, including acid, highly alkaline and very dry.

Situation Light to very deep shade, intolerant of full sun. The only shrub I know that will grow beneath beech trees.

Watering and feeding Mulch in autumn and spring. Feed with a balanced general fertilizer in mid-spring.

Pruning None necessary.

Common problems A blackening of the young shoot tips, for which I do not know the reason.

PROPAGATION Semi-ripe cuttings in summer or hardwood cuttings in winter.

TROUBLESHOOTING Overgrown plants may be cut back to within 30–45cm/1–1½ft of soil level and will regenerate.

SIZE 1–1.5 × 1–1.5m/3–5 × 3–5ft after five years (depending very much on the growing conditions); about 4 × 3.5m/13 × 11ft after fifteen years.

Berberis BARBERRY

A very large and valuable genus of deciduous and evergreen more or less spiny shrubs, with generally small leaves and small, yellow, orange or almost reddish flowers in clusters. Many forms have attractive berries. The common species are all hardy, and some make excellent prickly hedges.

SOIL Almost any, provided it is not very heavy or waterlogged.

SITUATION Sun or partial shade; full sun produces the best flowers. A few of the evergreen types benefit from some wall protection in colder areas.

WATERING AND FEEDING Mulch in autumn and spring. Feed with a balanced rose or similar potash-rich fertilizer in mid-spring, and again around midsummer.

PRUNING Not normally necessary when grown as a shrub. When grown as a hedge, clip once in early autumn, cutting the sides fairly hard but the leading shoots only lightly until the required height is reached.

COMMON PROBLEMS None.

PROPAGATION Semi-ripe cuttings in early autumn, hardwood cuttings in winter, or by layering.

TROUBLESHOOTING Old and straggly bushes can sometimes be rejuvenated by thinning in spring, taking out some stems at or near ground level. Significant cutting back of the shoots should only be done on plants used for hedging.

SIZE There are a few dwarf forms such as *B. thunbergii* 'Atropurpurea Nana' which are unlikely to exceed about 60 × 60cm/2 × 2ft, but most of the common varieties will attain about 3 × 3m/10 × 10ft after seven or eight years. Among commonly available types, *B.* × *carminea*, *B. jamesiana*, *B.* × *lologensis* (although not all of its varieties) and some forms of *B. thunbergii* have an arching habit and will grow taller, up to about 5m/16ft in ten years.

Buddleja

A genus of deciduous or occasionally evergreen, fairly large shrubs or almost small trees, most with large clusters of tiny, often fragrant flowers from midsummer onwards according to type. The colours range from white through yellow to red, blue and purple, and one species in particular, *B. davidii*, is especially prized for its attractiveness to butterflies.

SOIL Almost any, provided it is not very heavy or waterlogged. *B. davidii* is notably lime tolerant and best in a slightly poorer soil than other types will tolerate.

SITUATION Full sun.

Berberis thunbergii 'Rose Glow'

Buddleja – Calluna

Buddleja alternifolia

WATERING AND FEEDING Mulch in autumn and spring. Feed with a balanced rose or similar potash-rich fertilizer in mid-spring, and again around midsummer.

PRUNING Varies significantly between species. *B. davidii* should have all shoots cut back to about 15cm/6in above soil level at the end of the winter. Alternatively it may be grown on a permanent framework of stems up to 1m/3ft above ground level, in which case annual pruning should be to cut back to about 15cm/6in above this main stem.

B. alternifolia grown as a normal shrub should have the flowering shoots cut back to their base after the blooms have faded and the oldest shoots cut out at the same time, but is more attractively trained as a standard (see pages 18–19). When grown in this way, cut back the flowered shoots as above, and to maintain the attractive weeping habit cut out any wayward shoots in autumn and again after flowering.

Other species may have old wood cut back and any necessary shaping done after flowering.

COMMON PROBLEMS Normally none, although capsid bugs can cause leaf tattering.

PROPAGATION Semi-ripe cuttings in late summer, hardwood cuttings in winter.

TROUBLESHOOTING Old and straggly bushes are scarcely worth rejuvenating for new stock will establish easily and quickly. Most of the larger species, such as *B. globosa*, are naturally lax and straggly and for this reason not suited to small gardens.

SIZE *B. davidii*, pruned annually, should never exceed about 4 × 4m/13 × 13ft. Other species will attain about 5m/16ft in five years, although the tree-like *B. colvilei* may be taller still. On *B. alternifolia* trained as a standard, routine pruning becomes difficult if the plant is allowed to grow taller than about 2.5m/8ft.

Buxus BOX

This is one of the most useful evergreen hedging plants, and it can also make a useful specimen shrub either for shaping as topiary or, especially with the variegated forms, for foliage appeal.

SOIL Almost any, provided it is not very heavy or waterlogged; valuably lime tolerant.

Buxus microphylla

SITUATION Sun or partial shade; tolerant of exposure to fairly cold winds.

WATERING AND FEEDING Mulch in autumn and spring. Apply a balanced general purpose fertilizer in early spring.

PRUNING None necessary. When grown as a hedge or for topiary, clip twice a year, first around midsummer and again in early autumn; or clip once only in late summer, although this will give a tidy appearance for a shorter time.

COMMON PROBLEMS Sap-sucking box sucker and aphids can distort shoot tips and form sticky honeydew.

PROPAGATION Hardwood cuttings in late autumn.

TROUBLESHOOTING Old and straggly bushes can be rejuvenated to some extent by cutting hard back in spring, but take care not to cut too far into old wood or the plant may not produce new

Buxus sempervirens

shoots. It is best to do the job in stages, cutting back to about 60cm/2ft above the old wood first, to see if new growth is stimulated, then cut further the following year if desired.

SIZE The small-leaved *B. microphylla* will attain about 3 × 4m/ 10 × 13ft after many years. The common *B. sempervirens* will very slowly grow to about 5–6m/16–20ft but the varieties 'Handsworthiensis' and 'Suffruticosa' will barely reach a third of this. Variegated forms will remain more or less dwarf.

Callistemon BOTTLEBRUSH

The evergreen *C. citrinus* is one of the relatively few Australian shrubs to be hardy in Britain, although it is reliable only in mild and coastal areas. It is scarcely a beautiful plant overall, but its individual red (or occasionally yellow) flowers are striking for their bottlebrush-like form.

SOIL Fertile, light, free-draining.

SITUATION Full sun, preferably with the protection of a south- or south-west-facing wall.

WATERING AND FEEDING Mulch in autumn and spring. Apply a balanced rose or similar potash-rich fertilizer in mid-spring, and again around midsummer.

PRUNING None necessary, but cut out any frost-damaged shoots in spring.

COMMON PROBLEMS None, apart from frost damage.

PROPAGATION Semi-ripe cuttings in late summer.

TROUBLESHOOTING Old and straggly bushes can be rejuvenated to some extent by cutting hard back in spring, but bottlebrush shrubs usually look straggly, so you may be unable to improve the appearance as much as you might wish.

SIZE 2 × 1.5m/6½ × 5ft after five years and perhaps double this after twenty years.

Callistemon citrinus

Calluna LING, HEATHER

Calluna is one of the two common evergreen heather genera (see also *Erica*) used in gardens, with a very large number of summer-flowering varieties all derived from the species native to Britain, *C. vulgaris*.

SOIL All varieties must have acid, free-draining, humus-rich soil.

SITUATION Partial shade is tolerated but much the best results are achieved in full sun.

WATERING AND FEEDING Heathers require abundant moisture, although they are intolerant of waterlogged conditions. Mulch the plants in autumn and spring. Apply a balanced rose or similar potash-rich fertilizer in mid-spring, and again around mid-summer. One of the best mulches is chopped pine needles; in common with most acid-loving shrubs, heathers prefer plant-derived composts to animal manures.

PRUNING Use shears to cut off dead flower heads, cutting fairly hard to just above the old wood. It is preferable to wait until spring to do this, for the dead heads can be most attractive through the winter.

Calluna vulgaris 'Peter Sparkes'

Calluna – Ceratostigma

REJUVENATING HEATHERS
Old plants of *Calluna* and *Erica* tend to become brown, woody and sparse at the centre. In spring clip the plant hard with shears, then mound some good garden soil over the centre (above). During that growing season the plant will send up fresh new rooted shoots (above right). Leave these plantlets to grow on where they are, or if they are very crowded replant them elsewhere.

COMMON PROBLEMS None, although the centre of old plants may die out (see above).

PROPAGATION 5–6cm/2–2½in long semi-ripe cuttings in late summer; or by layering.

TROUBLESHOOTING When the centre of an old plant becomes brown and woody, it may be possible to rejuvenate it by shearing hard back in spring and placing a mound of soil over the centre (see above). Natural layers should form with fresh new shoots.

SIZE In general, heathers attain their maximum size – most species attain 30 × 30cm/1 × 1ft – and optimum appearance after about five or six years, and most are best replaced after eight or nine years. There are a few dwarf forms, such as 'Pygmaea', which barely attain 15 × 15cm/6 × 6in, and a few more spreading ones, such as 'Sir John Charrington' and 'Robert Chapman', which will reach 40 × 50cm/15 × 20in or more.

Camellia

One of the most highly prized of all evergreen shrubs, having rich, glossy foliage and beautiful flowers, of which the best may be single, double or semi-double and pink, red, occasionally white, or mixtures of the three. There are also a few yellowish-flowered varieties, in my view of dubious appeal. The soil conditions for all camellias are critically important.

SOIL All varieties must have acid, free-draining, humus-rich soil.

SITUATION Partial sun or shade, with some protection from wind and cold. Camellias grow best beneath the shade of other shrubs and trees in a naturally peaty soil, but they are also successful grown in an acid compost in containers.

WATERING AND FEEDING Mulch in autumn and spring; apply a balanced rose or similar potash-rich fertilizer in mid-spring, and again around midsummer. One of the best mulches is chopped pine needles; in common with most acid-loving shrubs, they prefer plant-derived composts to animal manures. Even on naturally acid soil, they will benefit from an application of sequestered iron in spring.

PRUNING None required although wayward shoots that affect the overall shape of the plant can be cut out after flowering.

COMMON PROBLEMS Frost damage, scale insects giving rise to sooty mould development, leaf chlorosis and bud drop. The latter is usually caused by sudden changes in temperature or some drying out of the soil.

PROPAGATION Semi-ripe cuttings in autumn, or leaf-bud cuttings in early spring.

Camellia reticulata

TROUBLESHOOTING Old and misshapen bushes can sometimes be restored by hard pruning but the resulting plant is unlikely ever to achieve its original beauty.

SIZE Although several species of *Camellia* have been involved in the development of modern varieties, most have similar, fairly slow growth rates and will reach their ultimate size of about 3–4 × 2–3m/10–13 × 6½–10ft after fifteen or twenty years.

Ceanothus

Ceanothus is much prized for its unusual blue flowers, there being few other easily grown shrubs with this colour. There are late summer and autumn-flowering deciduous types, and evergreen forms, some of which flower in early summer and some in late summer and autumn. Although their pruning differs, both deciduous and evergreen varieties have similar requirements and are always best in milder or more sheltered gardens.

SOIL Rich, light, free-draining.

SITUATION Full sun, with some protection from cold winds; the evergreen species, which are less hardy than the deciduous types, are especially intolerant of exposure to cold winds.

WATERING AND FEEDING Mulch in autumn and spring. Feed with a balanced rose or similar potash-rich fertilizer in mid-spring, and again around midsummer.

PRUNING Evergreen varieties grown as free-standing plants require little more than the cutting out of dead shoots and tidying up after flowering. When the early-flowering evergreen types are grown as wall shrubs, they should be pruned harder after flowering, to within three buds of the previous season's growth. Deciduous varieties should be pruned hard in spring, again to within three buds of the previous season's growth.

COMMON PROBLEMS The foliage of evergreen species is prone to winter browning, and the buds of early-flowering types to damage by late frosts. On all types, leaf chlorosis and scale insects can occasionally be troublesome.

PROPAGATION Semi-ripe cuttings in summer (evergreen varieties), or hardwood cuttings in winter (deciduous varieties).

TROUBLESHOOTING After severe frost damage, especially on evergreen types, cut back at least 30cm/1ft into unaffected wood, even if this means cutting back almost to soil level.

SIZE The most vigorous evergreen forms, such as *C. arboreus* 'Trewithen Blue', on a good site may reach up to 8 × 8m/26 × 26ft after ten years or so, although most will barely reach half this size. The deciduous varieties tend to be smaller, reaching about 2.5 × 2.5m/8 × 8ft in the same time.

Ceratostigma   SHRUBBY PLUMBAGO

There are only two or three species of *Ceratostigma*, all equally valuable for their hardiness, small size and electric-blue flowers late in the summer.

SOIL Tolerates almost any provided not very heavy or waterlogged, but performs noticeably better in rich, free-draining soil.

Ceanothus impressus

Ceratostigma – Cornus

Ceratostigma willmottianum

SITUATION Tolerant of light shade but always best in full sun.

WATERING AND FEEDING Mulch in autumn and spring. Apply a balanced rose or similar potash-rich fertilizer in mid-spring, and again around midsummer.

PRUNING Routinely cut back all shoots to just above soil level in mid-spring.

COMMON PROBLEMS None.

PROPAGATION Semi-ripe cuttings in late summer.

TROUBLESHOOTING *C. plumbaginoides* is a rather creeping species and can become invasive – I have had it well established in a lawn – so its lateral extension needs limiting with a spade. Resist the temptation to treat it like a herbaceous perennial and dig it up to divide, for it re-establishes very slowly.

SIZE For *C. plumbaginoides*, see above; *C. willmottianum* spreads little and after annual pruning reaches a height of about 60cm–1m/ 2–3ft with each year's growth.

Chaenomeles JAPANESE QUINCE

The ornamental quinces are deciduous spring-flowering shrubs with apple-like blossom and fruits that can be cooked as substitutes for real quinces. They are most usually trained as wall shrubs, although some varieties are really too spreading for this and are better grown as free-standing shrubs.

SOIL Almost any, provided it is not very heavy or waterlogged; the plants tend to suffer from leaf chlorosis on alkaline soils.

SITUATION Tolerates some shade but the flowers are always best in full sun. Although usually grown against a wall, it doesn't really need shelter in most areas.

WATERING AND FEEDING Mulch in autumn and spring. Feed with a balanced rose or similar potash-rich fertilizer in mid-spring, and again around midsummer.

PRUNING On wall-trained plants, cut back the previous season's growth to two or three buds from the base after flowering, and cut out any shoots growing directly towards or away from the wall. If space is very confined, the plant may be spur pruned after flowering by cutting back the side-shoots to 3–4cm/1½in from their bases; the stubs that remain form the spurs. On free-standing plants, thin out overcrowded shoots (the centre very easily becomes congested) and cut back the previous season's growth by about one third after flowering.

COMMON PROBLEMS Leaf chlorosis; fireblight; irregular leaf patterning caused by viruses.

PROPAGATION Semi-ripe cuttings in late summer.

TROUBLESHOOTING Old bushes become very woody and misshapen and are scarcely worth rejuvenating, especially when they have been trained against a wall.

SIZE Varieties derived from *C. japonica* reach about 1 × 2m/3 × 6½ft after seven or eight years; those derived from *C. speciosa* reach about 3 × 4m/10 × 13ft after ten years; while those from the hybrid *C.* × *superba* achieve about 1.5 × 2m/5 × 6½ft in the same time, but there are more and less vigorous, and also more and less upright, forms in both of the latter species, so select carefully.

Chaenomeles × *superba*

Choisya MEXICAN ORANGE

This popular evergreen shrub is grown both for its foliage and flowers, although the golden form, *C. ternata* 'Sundance', is much more of a foliage plant.

SOIL Most, although best on fairly rich, well-drained soil, preferably not strongly alkaline.

SITUATION Full sun with shelter, especially for the golden form.

WATERING AND FEEDING Mulch in autumn and spring. Feed with a balanced rose or similar potash-rich fertilizer in mid-spring, and again around midsummer.

PRUNING Cut out the oldest one third of the shoots in mid-spring, after flowering.

COMMON PROBLEMS Frost damage; leaf chlorosis.

PROPAGATION Semi-ripe cuttings in late summer.

TROUBLESHOOTING None usually needed, although if necessary the stems can be cut hard back after flowering.

SIZE *C. ternata* will reach $2-3 \times 2-3m/6\frac{1}{2}-10 \times 6\frac{1}{2}-10ft$ after about eight or ten years; 'Sundance' about two thirds of this size.

Cistus ROCK ROSE

The rock roses are plants of the Mediterranean, and their bright colours and patterns are only an option for those whose garden can reproduce that region's hot dry conditions. Although strictly classed as sub-shrubs, they are in many ways more akin to herbaceous perennials.

SOIL Light, free-draining, moderately rich to poor.

SITUATION Full sun, shelter from cold winds; good in mild, coastal gardens.

WATERING AND FEEDING Mulch in autumn and spring. Feed with a balanced general purpose fertilizer in mid-spring, and again after midsummer. Take care not to overwater.

PRUNING Trim very lightly in spring to remove any shoots damaged in winter. Disturb the plants as little as possible; they resent being dug up or transplanted.

COMMON PROBLEMS None.

PROPAGATION Semi-ripe cuttings in summer, hardwood cuttings in winter, the species from seed.

TROUBLESHOOTING Not likely to be necessary where conditions are appropriate.

SIZE Most varieties will attain a height and spread of about $1 \times 1m/3 \times 3ft$ within three years.

Cornus DOGWOOD

The deciduous shrubby dogwoods form a distinct group of varieties of two main species grown for their foliage and attractively coloured stems. These species are *C. alba* and *C. stolonifera*, and they are deliberately kept small by pruning. There are two other common shrubby foliage species (*C. florida* and the creeping *C. canadensis*), and several attractive larger species that form small trees (see page 204).

Choisya ternata

Cistus × corbariensis

Cornus – Cotoneaster

Cornus alba 'Sibirica'

SOIL Most; several of the varieties are tolerant both of heavy waterlogged clay and light sandy conditions.

SITUATION Partial shade but will tolerate full sun. *C. canadensis* is best in some shade.

WATERING AND FEEDING Mulch in autumn and spring. Feed with a balanced general purpose fertilizer in mid-spring, and again around midsummer.

PRUNING To obtain the brightly coloured young shoots that are the principal appeal of *C. alba* and *C. stolonifera*, cut all shoots back to about 20cm/8in above soil level in mid-spring every year. *C. florida* and *C. canadensis* require no pruning.

COMMON PROBLEMS None.

PROPAGATION Hardwood cuttings in winter.

TROUBLESHOOTING None needed.

SIZE *C. alba* varieties grown for their stems will be kept to about $1.5 \times 1m/5 \times 3ft$ by annual pruning, but the yellow-stemmed *C. stolonifera* 'Flaviramea', even with pruning, will reach $2m/6\frac{1}{2}ft$ in height and spreads extensively. *C. florida* will reach $4 \times 4m/13 \times 13ft$ after ten or twelve years; *C. canadensis* is a ground-cover plant, reaching $20cm \times 3m/8in \times 10ft$ in the same time.

Cotinus SMOKE BUSH

C. coggygria is grown equally for its feathery flowers and attractive, rounded deciduous foliage, particularly appealing in the purple-coloured forms, *C.c.* 'Foliis Purpureis' and 'Royal Purple'.

SOIL Most, but best in humus-rich, slightly moist conditions.

SITUATION Tolerates partial shade but the purple of the coloured foliaged forms tends to be paler there and the flowers only develop satisfactorily in full sun.

Cotinus 'Flame'

WATERING AND FEEDING Mulch in autumn and spring. Feed with a balanced rose or other potash-rich fertilizer in mid-spring, and again around midsummer.

PRUNING None needed, but from time to time cut out the oldest branches in spring to induce new growth. For the best leaves on forms with good foliage (although at the expense of flowers), cut all the stems back to soil level, or to a low framework of permanent stems, in spring.

COMMON PROBLEMS None.

PROPAGATION Layering; difficult to establish from cuttings.

TROUBLESHOOTING None needed.

SIZE After about fifteen years may reach 5–6 × 5–6m/16–20 × 16–20ft, but slows down after attaining about half this size.

Cotoneaster

A large genus of very useful evergreen and deciduous shrubs with foliage, some flower and much fruiting appeal. The treatment of the various types differs in some respects and I shall therefore divide them into four groups:

    1 Low- to medium-growing deciduous
    2 Low- to medium-growing evergreen
    3 Tall deciduous
    4 Tall evergreen.

SOIL All groups are very tolerant of most soils; group 2 will tolerate poor soils.

SITUATION Full sun to medium shade (all groups). Some forms are very successful against north- or east-facing walls.

WATERING AND FEEDING Mulch in autumn and spring. Apply balanced rose or similar potash-rich fertilizer in mid-spring and again around midsummer.

PRUNING GROUPS 1 AND 2 None, other than occasional shaping and to keep within limits. When growing group 2 types as a hedge, clip twice, first around midsummer and again in early autumn; or clip once only in late summer, although this will give a tidy appearance for a shorter time.

GROUP 3 None; if used as hedging plants trim to give a very light shaping in spring.

GROUP 4 None, but some may usefully be trained. For instance, *C. floccosus* is excellent when trained against a wall, while *C. × watereri* 'Rothschildianus' can be trained on a single stem to make a fine standard plant for winter appeal (see pages 18–19).

COMMON PROBLEMS All are prone to fireblight disease.

PROPAGATION Semi-ripe cuttings in late summer or hardwood cuttings in winter.

TROUBLESHOOTING None usually needed. Old and woody plants can sometimes be rejuvenated by cutting back to just above the old wood in spring, although the plants may never regain their best shape.

SIZE GROUP 1 Notably slow growing, reaching about 1.5 × 3m/ 5 × 10ft after eighteen or twenty years.

GROUP 2 Horizontal types such as *C. horizontalis* will reach 60cm × 3m/2 × 10ft after about fifteen years; taller forms, such as

Cotoneaster horizontalis

Cytisus battandieri

that usually called *C*. 'Hybridus Pendulus', about 1.5 × 3m/5 × 10ft in the same time (although this is often sold grafted as a standard).
GROUP 3 Will reach about 4 × 4m/13 × 13ft in twenty years.
GROUP 4 Will reach 5–7 × 5–7m/16–23 × 16–23ft after about twenty years (and about the same height if trained as a standard).

Cytisus BROOM

This is one of three important genera of deciduous or evergreen, spring-flowering shrubs referred to as brooms, *Genista* and *Spartium* being the others. They are distinctive for their yellow, white or red pea-like blossom, although they fail miserably if their soil and situation requirements are not carefully considered.
SOIL Intolerant of heavy, wet, clayey soils, and rarely successful in highly alkaline conditions.
SITUATION Full sun. *C. battandieri* will benefit from some wall protection.
WATERING AND FEEDING Mulch in autumn and spring. Feed with a balanced rose or other potash-rich fertilizer in mid-spring, and again around midsummer.
PRUNING None.
COMMON PROBLEMS None, although leaf chlorosis may occur in strongly alkaline conditions.
PROPAGATION Semi-ripe cuttings in early summer.
TROUBLESHOOTING Most species and varieties are short-lived or, at least, become woody and leggy after ten to fifteen years. They will not regenerate from old wood and should be replaced.
SIZE Varies considerably. The tallest species, *C. battandieri*, reaches about 6 × 6m/20 × 20ft after eighteen or twenty years; the more or less ground-covering types, such as *C.* × *kewensis*, only about 50cm × 1.5–2m/1½ × 5–6½ft after five or six years. Over the same timespan the intermediate varieties of *C.* × *praecox* grow to about 1.5 × 2m/5 × 6½ft, and the slightly more vigorous *C. multiflorus*, and the varieties of *C. scoparius*, about 3 × 2m/10 × 6½ft.

Daphne

Daphnes are evergreen or deciduous, mainly low-growing shrubs, popular principally for their intensely perfumed winter or early spring flowers. They thrive in situations that suit few other flowering shrubs, but some species are rather tender.
SOIL Deep, rich, moist, well drained, preferably slightly acidic.
SITUATION Preferably light or medium shade; most will tolerate full sun but the perfume seems to be more apparent in a cool, more shady woodland situation.
WATERING AND FEEDING Mulch in autumn and spring. Apply a balanced rose or other potash-rich fertilizer in mid-spring, and again around midsummer.
PRUNING None.
COMMON PROBLEMS None.
PROPAGATION Semi-ripe cuttings in early or mid-summer. Some species, most notably *D. mezereum*, may strike with difficulty and should be layered.

Daphne tangutica

TROUBLESHOOTING None needed. Old plants which become leggy and woody are best replaced.
SIZE All remain fairly small and after about ten years reach their maximum height, which ranges from about $50 \times 80\text{cm}/1\frac{1}{2} \times 2\frac{1}{2}\text{ft}$ for *D. blagayana* to about $2 \times 1\text{m}/6\frac{1}{2} \times 3\text{ft}$ for *D. odora*.

Deutzia

A widely admired pink- or white-flowered deciduous shrub with few detracting features; nevertheless it has never really achieved the popularity that it deserves.
SOIL Moist, fairly rich, usually good on chalky soils, but always intolerant of dryness.
SITUATION Full sun to light shade, preferably with some shelter from cold winds.
WATERING AND FEEDING Mulch in autumn and spring – this is very important as the plant is prone to suffer injury from drought. Feed with a balanced rose or similar potash-rich fertilizer in mid-spring, and again around midsummer.
PRUNING Cut back the oldest third of the shoots to soil level in spring, after flowering.
COMMON PROBLEMS None.
PROPAGATION Semi-ripe cuttings in summer or hardwood cuttings in winter.
TROUBLESHOOTING Oversized or straggly plants can usually be rejuvenated by cutting back the shoots to soil level in spring, staging the operation over a period of two years.
SIZE Will reach about $2 \times 1\text{m}/6\frac{1}{2} \times 3\text{ft}$ after five years and up to $4 \times 4\text{m}/13 \times 13\text{ft}$ after sixteen to eighteen years.

Deutzia × elegantissima

Elaeagnus

Deciduous or evergreen, medium-sized shrubs, grown principally for their attractive foliage. None of the forms are truly spectacular, but all are easy to obtain and grow. I always think of them as being among the real 'workhorses' of the shrub garden.
SOIL Almost any, but generally least successful in very dry or very alkaline conditions.
SITUATION Tolerates some shade, but always best in full sun.
WATERING AND FEEDING Mulch in autumn and spring. Feed with a balanced general purpose fertilizer in mid-spring, and again around midsummer.
PRUNING None, although some types can be lightly trimmed as hedging in late spring.
COMMON PROBLEMS None.
PROPAGATION Semi-ripe cuttings in summer or hardwood cuttings in winter.
TROUBLESHOOTING None needed, although old plants which become leggy and woody will usually regenerate if cut back hard in late spring. If variegated forms produce any all-green shoots, these must be cut out promptly.
SIZE All will reach about $3–4 \times 3–4\text{m}/10–13 \times 10–13\text{ft}$ after fifteen to eighteen years.

Elaeagnus pungens 'Maculata'

Mixed heather border
Erica carnea

Escallonia 'Apple Blossom'

Erica HEATHER

One of the two common evergreen heather genera (see also *Calluna*) used in gardens, including a very large number of varieties with white, pink or red flowers and, sometimes, coloured foliage. They are usefully divided into the winter- and spring-flowering forms derived principally from *E. carnea* and *E. × darleyensis*, and the summer-flowering types derived from *E. cinerea* and other species, because the soil conditions necessary differ between the two groups.

SOIL All winter-flowering heathers (*E. carnea* and *E. × darleyensis*) are tolerant of alkaline soils, provided they are moist and organic. All other varieties must have moist, acid conditions.

SITUATION Partial shade is tolerated, but much the best results are achieved in full sun.

WATERING AND FEEDING Heathers require abundant moisture, although they are intolerant of waterlogged conditions. Mulch in autumn and spring. Apply a balanced rose or similar potash-rich fertilizer in mid-spring, and again around midsummer. One of the best mulches is chopped pine needles, and in general heathers prefer plant-derived composts to animal manures.

PRUNING Use shears to cut off dead flower heads in spring, cutting lightly and not very close to the old wood.

COMMON PROBLEMS None, although the centre of old plants may die out (see below).

PROPAGATION 5–6cm/2–2½in long semi-ripe cuttings in late summer or layer.

TROUBLESHOOTING When the centre of old plants becomes brown and woody, it may be possible to rejuvenate them from natural layers: see *Calluna*, page 30.

SIZE In general, heathers attain their maximum size and optimum appearance after about five or six years. They are best replaced after eight or nine years. Some, most notably the varieties of *E. carnea*, are best considered as slow-growing ground-cover plants, each reaching about 15 × 80cm/6in × 2½ft (usually planted in groups for best effect). Others form small clumps, and the most vigorous types, such as *E. vagans* 'Mrs D. F. Maxwell' or some forms of *E. erigena* or *E. terminalis*, will reach about 80 × 80cm/2½ × 2½ft, or even more.

Escallonia

An invaluable evergreen plant for milder, especially coastal areas, both as a free-standing shrub or a flowering hedge.

SOIL Tolerant of most, although generally least successful in highly alkaline conditions.

SITUATION Full sun to moderate shade, but flowers less satisfactorily in shade.

WATERING AND FEEDING Mulch in autumn and spring. Feed with a balanced rose or other potash-rich general fertilizer in mid-spring, and again after midsummer.

PRUNING When grown as a free-standing shrub none is necessary, apart from the removal of frost-damaged shoots in spring;

once established, the plant will benefit from the cutting back of the oldest third of the shoots in spring to stimulate new growth. When grown as a hedge, clip twice, first around midsummer and again in early autumn.

COMMON PROBLEMS None, apart from some frost damage.

PROPAGATION Semi-ripe cuttings in summer or hardwood cuttings in winter.

TROUBLESHOOTING Overgrown or frost- and cold-damaged plants may be cut back to within 30–45cm/1–1½ft of soil level, and will even regenerate after being cut back to just a few centimetres above soil level, although they will take up to three years to resume flowering and normal vigour.

SIZE Up to 2 × 2m/6½ × 6½ft after five to seven years, and about 4 × 4m/13 × 13ft after twenty years.

Euonymus

Deciduous or evergreen, medium-sized foliage shrubs; a genus that includes some of the most useful and easy to grow variegated evergreens. In every garden there should be at least one representative of this genus.

SOIL Almost all.

SITUATION Tolerates moderate shade, but most varieties are best in full sun. *E. japonicus* is a useful coastal plant, being tolerant of salt spray.

WATERING AND FEEDING Mulch in autumn and spring. Apply a balanced general purpose fertilizer in mid-spring, and again around midsummer.

PRUNING Normally none, although ground-covering varieties of *E. fortunei* benefit from having upright shoots cut back in spring or early autumn. *E. japonicus* can be grown as a hedge; clip it twice, first around midsummer and again in early autumn; or clip once only in late summer, although this will give a tidy appearance for a shorter time.

COMMON PROBLEMS Mildew on *E. japonicus*.

PROPAGATION Semi-ripe cuttings in summer or hardwood cuttings in winter.

TROUBLESHOOTING None needed.

SIZE The ground-covering evergreen *E. fortunei* will attain about 60cm × 2.5m/2 × 8ft after fifteen years. The evergreen *E. japonicus* will reach about 3 × 3–4m/10 × 10–13ft; the deciduous *E. europaeus* about 4 × 6.5m/13 × 22ft, and *E. alatus* about 2 × 4m/6½ × 13ft.

Euonymus fortunei 'Aurea Marginata' and 'Argentea Marginata'

Fatsia

This handsome species looks like a house plant but in fact is a fairly tough and very useful evergreen shrub for difficult sites.

SOIL Tolerates most, but best on moist, rich organic soils.

SITUATION Always best in medium or deep shade and with some shelter in cold areas; intolerant of full sun.

WATERING AND FEEDING Mulch in autumn and spring. Feed with a balanced general purpose fertilizer in mid-spring, and again around midsummer.

Fatsia japonica

Forsythia × intermedia
'Spectabilis'

PRUNING None needed.

COMMON PROBLEMS None.

PROPAGATION Leaf-bud cuttings in summer.

TROUBLESHOOTING None needed, but plants that have grown too large may be cut back hard and will regenerate successfully.

SIZE Will attain about 4 × 4m/13 × 13ft in about sixteen years.

Forsythia

Deciduous shrubs that light up gardens everywhere with their yellow and golden spring flowers. They are among the easiest grown and most popular of all shrubs, but the pruning still commonly causes confusion to gardeners.

SOIL Almost any, provided it is well drained and fairly deep; they are prone to wilt on shallow soil.

SITUATION Full sun; even in partial shade, the flowering is greatly impaired. *F. suspensa* is very successful when trained against a wall; *F. × intermedia* forms a good ornamental hedge.

WATERING AND FEEDING Mulch in autumn and spring. Feed with a balanced rose or similar potash-rich fertilizer in mid-spring, and again around midsummer. Take special care not to allow the plants to dry out while in flower.

PRUNING Free-standing shrubs are best pruned at least once every two or three years by cutting back the oldest third of the shoots to ground level immediately after flowering. Any overcrowded shoots should be removed at the same time. Plants trained against a wall should be clipped back hard immediately after flowering. When grown as a hedge, clip once, lightly, shortly after flowering.

COMMON PROBLEMS None; a slightly disfiguring gall that commonly appears on the shoots is harmless.

PROPAGATION Semi-ripe cuttings in late summer, or hardwood cuttings in winter.

TROUBLESHOOTING Old, congested and woody plants can sometimes be rejuvenated by cutting the shoots back to soil level in spring. The work should be staged, cutting back one third of the shoots in each of three successive years. If the plant is very old it is better replaced.

SIZE Varies slightly between varieties. Most (including the old *F. × intermedia* 'Spectabilis', which I still consider the best) will reach about 3 × 1.5m/10 × 5ft after five years and then 4 × 3m/13 × 10ft after fifteen, but *F. suspensa* is taller and more lax (sometimes called the climbing forsythia), whereas the low, spreading 'Arnold Dwarf' barely exceeds 1 × 2m/3 × 6½ft in five years.

Fremontodendron

Two or three species of evergreen or semi-evergreen shrubs with the most striking, large buttercup-yellow flowers; the colour is derived, however, not from the petals but the sepals. I suspect that their reputation for being very tender is not really justified for, given some wall protection, they have survived exceedingly cold winters in my own garden.

SOIL Almost any, provided it is well drained and preferably fairly deep; they are tolerant of alkalinity.

SITUATION Full sun or very light shade. The shelter of a wall is almost essential for they are very lax and, even in a mild area, don't make successful free-standing plants.

WATERING AND FEEDING Mulch in autumn and spring. Apply a balanced rose or similar potash-rich fertilizer in mid-spring, and again around midsummer.

PRUNING None normally necessary, apart from cutting back any stems damaged by frost; if trained against a wall in a fairly confined area, the plant may be spur pruned by cutting back the sideshoots after flowering to about 4cm/1½in from their bases (the stubs that remain form the so-called spurs).

COMMON PROBLEMS None.

PROPAGATION Softwood cuttings in early summer.

TROUBLESHOOTING The plant has a reputation for being short-lived and there is no doubt that apparently healthy specimens will suddenly die back without warning. This may happen to individual branches as well, which should then be cut back to 13cm/5in above their base, or above the junction with the main stem.

SIZE Attains about $3 \times 3m/10 \times 10ft$ after five years, but plants that survive long enough can be at least $8 \times 6m/26 \times 20ft$ after twenty years.

Fremontodendron 'California Glory'

Fuchsia

In mild or coastal areas, the fuchsia is a hardy shrub that makes a good hedge. Elsewhere, it is a tender perennial to be taken in and out of the garden more like a pelargonium. I have included them all here, but distinguish where treatment differs.

SOIL HARDY FUCHSIAS Almost any, provided it is well drained. TENDER FUCHSIAS Treat as for hardy forms; when grown in containers they generally fare best in soil-based compost.

SITUATION Full sun or very light shade.

WATERING AND FEEDING HARDY FUCHSIAS Mulch in autumn and spring. Apply a balanced rose or similar potash-rich fertilizer in mid-spring, and again around midsummer. TENDER FUCHSIAS Follow a regime for container plants giving a liquid fertilizer with high potash content once a week.

PRUNING HARDY FUCHSIAS In areas where significant damage from frost is unlikely, none is necessary. Where some frost damage is normal, either cut back in spring to at least 15cm/6in beyond damaged shoots, or cut back to ground level in spring. When grown as a hedge, clip once in autumn or early spring, cutting the sides fairly hard but the leading shoots only lightly until the required height is reached. TENDER FUCHSIAS None normally necessary while growing outdoors. If plants are overwintered in containers under cover, cut back by at least two thirds in autumn, before taking indoors.

COMMON PROBLEMS Whitefly; greenfly.

PROPAGATION Softwood cuttings in summer or early spring.

TROUBLESHOOTING Very old and woody hardy plants can be rejuvenated by cutting hard back in spring.

Fuchsia 'Mrs Popple'

Fuchsia – Hamamelis

Garrya elliptica

SIZE Varies, depending on variety. The most popular hardy varieties used for hedging are forms of *F. magellanica*, especially 'Riccartonii', which, if unpruned, in mild areas will grow quickly to reach 1.5 × 1.5m/5 × 5ft after about ten years. Tender varieties are much smaller but it is important to choose one appropriate for your needs; the trailing, cascading or basket varieties should be used for hanging baskets and window boxes, the upright types for other containers and for open ground planting.

Garrya   TASSEL BUSH

G. elliptica, the single species, is a fairly hardy evergreen, although it is almost always grown as a wall shrub for the appeal of its elongated winter catkins. It can be grown as a free-standing bush but is likely to be browned by cold winds.

SOIL Almost any, provided it is not prone to waterlogging. Like all wall shrubs, the plant will benefit from a fairly high content of moisture-retaining organic matter.

SITUATION Full sun or medium shade, although the production of catkins is always best in sun.

WATERING AND FEEDING Mulch in autumn and spring. Feed with a balanced rose or similar potash-rich fertilizer in mid-spring, and again around midsummer.

PRUNING None normally necessary, although wall-trained plants growing in a confined space will be kept tidier by having the previous season's shoots cut back to 10cm/4in above their bases immediately after flowering.

COMMON PROBLEMS Coral spot.

PROPAGATION Semi-ripe cuttings in summer or hardwood cuttings in winter.

TROUBLESHOOTING None normally necessary. Very old or diseased wood should be cut hard back in early spring.

SIZE Attains about 3 × 2m/10 × 6½ft after five years, and about 5 × 4m/16 × 13ft after eighteen or twenty years.

Genista

A genus of attractive, mainly yellow-flowered spring- or summer-blooming deciduous shrubs. Some species are known as brooms, others as gorse and yet others as greenweeds. Some forms possess greatly reduced leaves and appear almost to have leafless green stems. All are hardy.

SOIL Almost any, but highly intolerant of waterlogging.

SITUATION Full sun.

WATERING AND FEEDING Mulch in autumn and spring. Feed with a balanced rose or similar potash-rich fertilizer in mid-spring, and again around midsummer.

PRUNING Inadvisable.

COMMON PROBLEMS None.

PROPAGATION Semi-ripe cuttings in summer or hardwood cuttings in winter.

TROUBLESHOOTING None normally necessary. Old and badly shaped plants should be replaced.

Genista lydia

SIZE The largest species, *G. aetnensis*, forms a small spreading tree, reaching about 2.5 × 2.5m/8 × 8ft after five years and up to 5 × 5m/16 × 16ft after twenty. Other species are unlikely to exceed about 1m/3ft in height and one, *G. lydia*, is lower growing still and forms good ground cover.

Hamamelis WITCH HAZEL

Witch hazels, a small group of deciduous shrubs or almost small trees, are greatly prized for their spidery yellow or red flowers that appear on the leafless branches in winter. They are very demanding in their soil and site requirements and prone to damage by hard winter frosts.

SOIL Rich and preferably acid, although they are tolerant of soils around neutral provided there is a high organic matter content. Intolerant of waterlogging or heavy clay.

Hamamelis mollis 'Superba'

SITUATION Light shade or full sun.

WATERING AND FEEDING Mulch in autumn and spring. Feed with a balanced rose or similar potash-rich fertilizer in mid-spring, and again around midsummer.

PRUNING None.

COMMON PROBLEMS None.

PROPAGATION Almost impossible from cuttings but layering is usually successful.

TROUBLESHOOTING None normally necessary. Witch hazels will not regenerate satisfactorily from old wood.

SIZE Slow growing in its early stages, reaching about 1.5 × 1.5m/ 5 × 5ft after five years, but ultimately up to 5 × 4m/16 × 13ft after eighteen to twenty years.

Hebe 'Midsummer Beauty'

Hebe

A large group of evergreen shrubs characterized by dense inflorescences of white or bluish flowers, the shrubby relatives of *Veronica*. Types with normal leaves include 'Carl Teschner' and 'Midsummer Beauty'; the whipcords have conifer-like foliage, exemplified by *H. ochracea*, *H. o.* 'James Stirling', and *H. cupressoides*. Few broadleaved species are sufficiently hardy, however, to be relied upon outdoors in any except mild or coastal areas.

SOIL Light, free-draining, intolerant of waterlogging.

SITUATION Full sun.

WATERING AND FEEDING Mulch in autumn and spring. Feed with a balanced rose or similar potash-rich fertilizer in mid-spring, and again around midsummer.

PRUNING Lightly trim normal-leaved varieties in spring to encourage new shoot development. The whipcord species should not be pruned.

COMMON PROBLEMS Leaf spotting, shoot die-back.

PROPAGATION Semi-ripe cuttings in summer, or layers.

TROUBLESHOOTING Plants that are badly frost damaged or otherwise seriously misshapen should be cut back almost to soil level in spring.

SIZE There are two main groups of normal-leaved hebes: the low-growing ground-cover forms such as *H. pinguifolia*, which reach their full size of about 30cm × 1m/1 × 3ft after five years; and the popular taller shrubs which attain about 1 × 1m/3 × 3ft after a similar time and then slowly reach 1.5–2 × 2–3m/5–6½ × 6½–10ft in fifteen to twenty years. The whipcords will reach their ultimate height and spread of 45 × 75cm/1½ × 2½ft over about five years.

Hibiscus

The hardy species is the deciduous *H. syriacus*; its flowers have shorter trumpets than those of the popular evergreen conservatory and house plant species, and flowers in white, blue, mauve or pink. They are not hardy enough for cold areas and even in favoured localities, flower buds will be harmed by late frosts in some seasons.

SOIL Light, rich, free-draining, intolerant of waterlogging.

SITUATION Tolerates light shade or full sun, preferably with a little shelter.

WATERING AND FEEDING Mulch in autumn and spring. Apply a balanced rose or similar potash-rich fertilizer in mid-spring, and again around midsummer.

PRUNING None necessary, although on well-established plants the previous season's shoots may be shortened by up to half in spring, to encourage a bushy habit.

COMMON PROBLEMS None.

PROPAGATION Semi-ripe cuttings in summer.

TROUBLESHOOTING None normally necessary.

SIZE Reaches about 1 × 1m/3 × 3ft after five years and in favoured areas may attain about 3–4 × 3–4m/10–13 × 10–13ft after sixteen to eighteen years.

Hibiscus syriacus

Hippophaë SEA BUCKTHORN

A very familiar plant to coastal gardeners from its natural habitat on sand dunes, but scarcely known elsewhere. It is a useful screening and winter-berrying shrub in appropriate conditions, but is always best in maritime areas.

SOIL Light, free-draining, tolerant of fairly high alkalinity.

SITUATION Full sun, tolerant of exposure and salt spray.

WATERING AND FEEDING Mulch in autumn and spring. Feed with a balanced rose or similar potash-rich fertilizer in mid-spring, and again around midsummer.

PRUNING None. When grown as a hedge, clip once two or three weeks after midsummer, and again in early autumn.

COMMON PROBLEMS None, although a failure to form berries commonly occurs because the sexes are on different plants; both male and female are required for fruiting.

PROPAGATION Difficult to propagate from cuttings, and normally grown from seed.

TROUBLESHOOTING None normally necessary, but very old and woody plants may regenerate if cut back hard into the old wood in spring.

SIZE Reaches about $2 \times 2m/6\frac{1}{2} \times 6\frac{1}{2}$ft after five years and ultimately $6 \times 6m/20 \times 20$ft after about fifteen years.

Hippophaë rhamnoides

Hydrangea

One of the most useful groups of deciduous flowering shrubs, with one related common climber (see page 91). Hydrangeas may grow inadequately or produce flowers of the wrong colour if the soil and site do not meet their requirements.

SOIL Rich, moist but not prone to waterlogging. Hydrangeas are tolerant of acidity and alkalinity but the flower colour of many popular mop-heads and some lace-cap varieties will vary with soil conditions. To obtain the desirable blue, acid soil must be used; any lime present will turn them red. A proprietary 'blueing powder' will help to correct this but is never as successful as growing the plants on a naturally acidic soil.

SITUATION Light shade; most varieties are tolerant of exposure and salt spray.

WATERING AND FEEDING Mulch in autumn and spring. Apply a balanced rose or similar potash-rich fertilizer in mid-spring, and again around midsummer.

PRUNING Most species and varieties require none, with the following exceptions. On established plants of the mop-head and lace-cap varieties of *H. macrophylla*, cut out up to one third of the oldest or weakest non-flowered shoots each year, in late spring, to a few centimetres above soil level. At the same time, cut off dead flower heads, cutting back to a strong pair of new leaves. Similarly cut back any frost-damaged shoots. Prune *H. paniculata* in mid-spring, cutting back the previous season's growth to within three buds of the base.

COMMON PROBLEMS Leaf tattering caused by capsid bugs, powdery mildew in hot summers.

Hydrangea (lacecap)

Hydrangea – Kerria

Hypericum olympicum

PROPAGATION Semi-ripe cuttings in late summer.

TROUBLESHOOTING Old, woody or winter-damaged plants of most varieties will regenerate if cut back hard in mid-spring but flowering may be set back by one or two years.

SIZE Varies according to species, although most types, including the mop-head and lace-cap varieties of *H. macrophylla*, will fairly quickly reach about 1 × 1m/3 × 3ft and then eventually, after about fifteen years, reach 2 × 2–2.5m/6½ × 6½–8ft. Among other popular forms, *H. involucrata* is perhaps the smallest, eventually reaching about 1 × 1m/3 × 3ft, while *H. paniculata* is the largest, reaching about 4 × 4m/13 × 13ft in fifteen to eighteen years.

Hypericum   ST JOHN'S WORT

A genus of evergreen and deciduous flowering shrubs, grown for their yellow-orange flowers and, in the case of the very popular *H. calycinum*, as a very tough ground cover.

SOIL Almost any, *H. calycinum* especially being tolerant of extremes of acidity, alkalinity and dryness.

SITUATION Most forms prefer light shade, although *H. calycinum* is tolerant of deep shade.

WATERING AND FEEDING Mulch in autumn and spring. Feed with a balanced rose or similar potash-rich fertilizer in mid-spring, and again around midsummer.

PRUNING Varies with species. *H. calycinum* and the varieties grown for their coloured foliage should be cut back to soil level in spring in every other year, to encourage vigorous new shoot growth. The varieties grown for flowers and fruit can be similarly treated but will in consequence remain fairly small; they are better pruned annually, in spring, cutting back the oldest one third of the shoots to soil level.

COMMON PROBLEMS Rust.

PROPAGATION Semi-ripe cuttings in summer or hardwood cuttings in winter. *H. calycinum* produces abundant suckers, which are readily removed and replanted.

TROUBLESHOOTING Old, woody or neglected plants will regenerate if cut back hard in early spring.

SIZE Most forms grow fairly slowly to reach about 1 × 1m/3 × 3ft after ten years, but *H. calycinum* is vigorous and will reach about 30cm × 1m/1 × 3ft after three or four years.

Jasminum

There are two common and popular outdoor jasmines: the yellow-flowered, winter-blooming *J. nudiflorum* and the white-flowered, fragrant, summer jasmine, *J. officinale*. The latter is rather more tender, and is often classed as a climber but although its shoots are certainly lax, I always think it is better considered as a wall shrub. Both are excellent plants although not all gardens suit them equally.

SOIL Almost any, especially for *J. nudiflorum*, which will tolerate rather poor conditions. *J. officinale* is less tolerant of extremes of dryness or waterlogging.

Jasminum nudiflorum

SITUATION Full sun to light shade; *J. nudiflorum* is the more shade-tolerant of the two. *J. officinale* must have some shelter from cold winds and will disappoint in cold, exposed gardens.

WATERING AND FEEDING Mulch in autumn and spring. Feed with a balanced rose or similar potash-rich fertilizer in mid-spring, and again around midsummer.

PRUNING *J. nudiflorum*: when it is grown free-standing, I prefer to cut back the oldest third of the stems to ground level every spring, but leave the previous season's flowered shoots. When trained against a wall, I treat it like a hedge and clip it hard immediately after the flowers fade. *J. officinale*: cut back the long, whippy shoots by up to two thirds in mid-spring.

COMMON PROBLEMS None. Winter cold may damage shoots; cut out in mid-spring.

PROPAGATION Semi-ripe cuttings in summer.

TROUBLESHOOTING Old, woody or neglected plants will usually regenerate if cut back hard in early spring.

SIZE *J. nudiflorum* will reach about 1.5 × 1.5m/5 × 5ft after five years and about twice this after twenty. *J. officinale* is roughly twice as fast growing and vigorous, ultimately reaching as much as 10 × 10m/33 × 33ft, although it is much better pruned back to limit this potential.

Kalmia CALICO BUSH

The exquisitely beautiful, spring-flowering evergreen *K. latifolia* is a relative of rhododendrons and azaleas. It makes a good companion to them and requires very similar conditions. Unfortunately, if the natural garden soil is unsuitable, it doesn't in my experience grow well in a container.

SOIL Deep, rich, acid and moist.

SITUATION Full sun to light shade.

WATERING AND FEEDING Mulch in autumn and spring. Feed with a balanced rose or similar potash-rich fertilizer in mid-spring, and again around midsummer.

PRUNING None needed.

COMMON PROBLEMS None.

PROPAGATION Hardwood cuttings in winter.

TROUBLESHOOTING None normally necessary.

SIZE Fairly slow growing: reaches about 1.5 × 1.5m/5 × 5ft after five years, twice this after about fifteen years.

Kerria JEW'S MALLOW

Perhaps the easiest and least demanding flowering garden shrub, the deciduous, yellow spring-flowering *K. japonica* has the merit of an upright habit, almost like a raspberry cane.

SOIL Almost any; tolerant of dryness and waterlogging, acidity and alkalinity.

SITUATION Full sun to moderate shade.

WATERING AND FEEDING Mulch in autumn and spring. Apply a balanced rose or similar potash-rich fertilizer in mid-spring, and again around midsummer.

Kalmia latifolia

Kerria japonica 'Pleniflora'

Kerria – Leycesteria

Laurus nobilis

PRUNING Cut back the oldest third of the shoots to soil level, immediately after flowering.
COMMON PROBLEMS None.
PROPAGATION Semi-ripe cuttings in late summer, hardwood cuttings in winter, or from rooted suckers.
TROUBLESHOOTING None normally necessary.
SIZE Fast growing, reaching its ultimate height of about 2.5–3m/8–10ft in under five years. It will then spread slowly to form a clump about 3m/10ft in diameter after twenty years.

Laurus SWEET BAY, BAY LAUREL

One of two evergreen shrubs popularly known as laurels, *L. nobilis* has been grown in gardens for centuries. It is almost the only large shrub routinely used as a herb but it is a valuable ornamental too; carefully clipped specimens in pots command very high prices. It is much tougher than it is often given credit for and, even when damaged, has great powers of regeneration.
SOIL Almost any, provided it is not very wet.
SITUATION Tolerates full sun to deep shade, but foliage is browned by exposure to cold winds.
WATERING AND FEEDING Mulch in autumn and spring. Feed with a balanced general fertilizer in mid-spring.
PRUNING None is necessary but plants can be clipped or pruned to shape in spring. When grown as a hedge, clip once in early autumn, cutting the sides fairly hard but the leading shoots only lightly until the required height is reached.
COMMON PROBLEMS Scale insect, leading to sooty mould.
PROPAGATION Semi-ripe cuttings in summer.
TROUBLESHOOTING Cold-damaged or overgrown plants may be cut back hard into the old wood, and will regenerate.
SIZE Reaches 1.5 × 1m/5 × 3ft after five years but left unpruned will become a tree of 12 × 9m/40 × 30ft after about 30 years.

Clipping lavender

AFTER FLOWERING Keep plants compact by shearing them over quite hard.

Lavandula LAVENDER

There are several species and numerous varieties of lavender and it is important to choose them carefully for the required purpose. Only the dwarf, compact varieties are suitable for hedging but some of these have very little scent.
SOIL Prefers a light, free-draining soil but will tolerate almost any provided it is not very wet.
SITUATION Full sun.
WATERING AND FEEDING Mulch in autumn and spring. Feed with a balanced rose or similar potash-rich fertilizer in mid-spring, and again after midsummer.
PRUNING None is necessary but a light trim in mid-spring will encourage a bushy habit and hard clipping after the flowers have faded – just cutting into the woody growth at the base of the flower spikes – will create the neatest appearance. When grown as a hedge, clip once immediately after flowering. If flowers are required for pot pourri, they must be cut just as they open fully.
COMMON PROBLEMS None.

PROPAGATION Semi-ripe cuttings in summer.

TROUBLESHOOTING Old and woody plants usually regenerate satisfactorily if cut back hard in spring, cutting about 5cm/2in into the woody tissue.

SIZE Dwarf hedging varieties will reach about 60 × 60cm/2 × 2ft in four years; taller types about 1 × 1m/3 × 3ft after ten years.

Lavatera MALLOW

A varied genus of plants that includes some popular bedding annuals and biennials as well as the varieties considered here. Of those seen most commonly, *L. olbia* (of which 'Rosea' is the best known) is shrubby and *L. thuringiaca* (of which 'Barnsley' is the most familiar) is herbaceous, but it is impossible to draw a hard and fast line between the two species. Their soil and site requirements are all similar and rather critical if the best results are to be achieved. Plants in the closely related genus *Malva*, also known as mallows, may be treated similarly.

SOIL Tolerant of a range of conditions from rich to moderately poor, but must be free-draining. Particularly successful in alkaline conditions. The commonest reason for failure is that the plants are growing in heavy clay or strongly acidic soil.

SITUATION Full sun to light shade with shelter from cold winds. Ideally suited to mild, coastal gardens.

WATERING AND FEEDING Mulch in autumn and spring. Feed with a balanced general purpose fertilizer in mid-spring, and again after midsummer.

PRUNING Prune in spring, preferably by cutting one third of the shoots back to just above soil level, then cutting the remainder into healthy wood about 30cm/1ft beyond the limits of any frost or cold damage; or cut the entire plant back to about 30cm/1ft above soil level.

COMMON PROBLEMS None.

PROPAGATION Semi-ripe cuttings in early summer or hardwood cuttings in winter.

TROUBLESHOOTING Overgrown, damaged or straggly plants can usually be rejuvenated by cutting them back to about 30cm/1ft above soil level in spring, and feeding well.

SIZE Up to 2–3 × 2–3m/6½–10 × 6½–10ft after five years without hard pruning; will attain about 1.5–2 × 1.5m/5–6½ × 5ft in a single season if pruned hard.

Lavatera olbia 'Rosea'

Leycesteria

A greatly underrated but valuable, hardy deciduous shrub that is tolerant of difficult sites and very useful for flower and foliage interest at the back of a border or in a slightly shady corner. *L. formosa* is the most common species.

SOIL Almost any, provided it is not highly alkaline.

SITUATION Full sun or medium shade.

WATERING AND FEEDING Mulch in autumn and spring. Apply a balanced rose or similar potash-rich fertilizer in mid-spring, and again after midsummer.

Leycesteria formosa

Leycesteria – Myrica

Ligustrum ovalifolium

Ligustrum ovalifolium 'Aureum'

Lonicera nitida 'Baggesen's Gold'

PRUNING Cut back all shoots to a few centimetres above soil level in early spring.

COMMON PROBLEMS None.

PROPAGATION Does not strike easily from cuttings, and is usually grown from seed.

TROUBLESHOOTING Old and neglected plants will usually regenerate satisfactorily if cut back to soil level in spring.

SIZE With annual pruning, will attain about $2 \times 1m/6\frac{1}{2} \times 3ft$ each season, after the first two years.

Ligustrum PRIVET

The evergreen Japanese privet (*L. ovalifolium*) is the hedging plant of the past. It still has its devotees, but there are now many better plants for the purpose. The golden variety justifiably remains popular as a specimen shrub.

SOIL Almost any, provided it is not highly alkaline.

SITUATION Full sun to fairly deep shade.

WATERING AND FEEDING Mulch in autumn and spring. Apply a balanced general fertilizer in mid-spring.

PRUNING No pruning is actually necessary, but privets will almost always require some shaping which can be done in spring. When grown as a hedge, clip several times starting just after the time when the last frost is likely to occur, and stop at the first autumn frost.

COMMON PROBLEMS Aphids, leading to sooty mould growth.

PROPAGATION Semi-ripe cuttings in midsummer or hardwood cuttings in winter.

TROUBLESHOOTING Old, woody and neglected plants usually regenerate if cut back hard into the old wood in spring.

SIZE In the unlikely event of never being pruned, privets will reach about $3 \times 3m/10 \times 10ft$ after five years and double this after sixteen to eighteen years.

Lonicera HONEYSUCKLE

Although *Lonicera* is best known as a genus of climbing honeysuckles, there are several evergreen and deciduous shrubby species, some very hardy and familiar, others more tender and less common but highly desirable.

SOIL Most, provided it is not very dry or waterlogged.

SITUATION Full sun to light shade.

WATERING AND FEEDING Mulch in autumn and spring. Feed with a balanced general fertilizer in mid-spring.

PRUNING No pruning is normally necessary with the deciduous types, although up to one third of the oldest shoots may be removed each spring to encourage new growth. The evergreen *L. nitida* may be treated similarly but is also often used as a hedge. In this case, clip several times starting just after the last frost and stopping at the first frost of autumn.

COMMON PROBLEMS None.

PROPAGATION Semi-ripe cuttings in midsummer or hardwood cuttings in winter.

TROUBLESHOOTING Old, woody and neglected plants can sometimes be rejuvenated if cut back hard in spring, but very old and misshapen plants are better replaced.

SIZE Most of the common deciduous and evergreen forms will reach about 1×2m/$3 \times 6\frac{1}{2}$ft after five years and about $2–3 \times 4$m/$6\frac{1}{2}–10 \times 13$ft after fifteen years. The major exception is the semi-evergreen *L. pileata*, which is a ground-cover plant eventually reaching about 1×4m/3×13ft.

Mahonia

The most familiar mahonia is *M. aquifolium*, one of the toughest of all evergreen shrubs and one that will grow, and even flower, almost anywhere. It has several larger-leaved relatives, more beautiful in bloom but also rather more tender.

SOIL Most will tolerate a wide range of soils but are least successful in very dry sites.

SITUATION *M. aquifolium* tolerates full sun to deep shade; the other species and varieties prefer very light shade, with some shelter from cold winds.

WATERING AND FEEDING Mulch in autumn and spring. Feed with a balanced rose or similar potash-rich fertilizer in mid-spring, and again after midsummer.

PRUNING No pruning is necessary on *M. aquifolium*, unless it is grown as a hedge. On *M. × media* 'Charity', *M. lomariifolia*, *M. japonica* and related plants, a more compact habit will be encouraged by cutting back non-flowering shoots by about one half in mid-spring, at least in the early years. If a tall plant is required to fill a sheltered corner, however, this will not be necessary.

COMMON PROBLEMS Rust on *M. aquifolium*.

PROPAGATION Very difficult to strike from cuttings, although semi-ripe wood in early summer may be successful; otherwise propagate by layering.

TROUBLESHOOTING Old, woody and neglected plants can sometimes be rejuvenated if cut back hard in spring but very old and misshapen plants are better replaced.

SIZE *M. aquifolium* reaches its maximum height of about $1–1.2$m/3×4ft within three or four years but then creeps slowly outwards, reaching about 3m/10ft ultimately. The other common species will reach about 1.5×2m/$5 \times 6\frac{1}{2}$ft after five years and $3–4 \times 3$m/$10–13 \times 10$ft after twenty, although hybrids such as 'Charity' may reach half as much again.

Mahonia × media 'Charity'

Myrica WAX MYRTLE, BAYBERRY

A variable but particularly useful genus of deciduous and evergreen shrubs or, in a few cases, small trees, that will grow in conditions too wet for most others. Their flowers are interesting if unspectacular, but the deciduous *M. gale*, the sweet gale or bog myrtle, has delightfully perfumed leaves, while the American species (the evergreen *M. californica*, *M. cerifera* known as the wax myrtle, and *M. pensylvanica*) bear characteristic, wax-coated fruits.

SOIL Wet, boggy, acidic; intolerant of alkalinity.

Myrica pensylvanica

Myrica – Paeonia

Nandina domestica

Situation Full sun or very light shade with shelter from cold winds; myricas are plants for mild areas.

Watering and feeding Mulch in autumn and spring unless growing in very boggy conditions with constant surface water. Feed with a balanced rose or similar potash-rich fertilizer in mid-spring, and again around midsummer.

Pruning Varies considerably between species. None is required for *M. gale* and may easily result in branch die-back. The two related American species, *M. cerifera* and *M. pensylvanica*, may be used as hedging or trained on single stems to form round-headed standards: in both cases clip in late spring and early autumn.

Common problems None.

Propagation Semi-ripe cuttings in early spring, or from seed.

Troubleshooting Old or damaged plants of all species except *M. gale* will regenerate if cut back to soil level, preferably spreading the work over two or three years. *M. gale* cannot be rejuvenated satisfactorily.

Size *M. gale* will reach its full size of about 1–1.5 × 1m/3–5 × 3ft after about eight years. Over about sixteen years, *M. pensylvanica* will attain roughly 3 × 2m/10 × 6½ft, *M. californica* 8–10 × 8m/26–33 × 26ft if grown in good conditions, and *M. cerifera* up to 10 × 10m/33 × 33ft in mild areas.

Nandina

A genus of one, more or less evergreen, bamboo-like species, grown principally for its foliage in cooler areas but with the added bonus of flowers and bright red fruits in mild climates.

Soil Tolerates most, although best on well-drained but moist, acidic soils.

Situation Full sun with shelter from cold winds.

Watering and feeding Mulch in autumn and spring. Feed with a balanced rose or similar potash-rich fertilizer in mid-spring, and again around midsummer.

Pruning It is sensible to cut away dead flowered or fruiting stems, and to cut back very old shoots to soil level in spring.

Common problems None.

Propagation By division in spring, or from seed.

Troubleshooting Damaged or overgrown plants may be cut back to soil level and should regenerate satisfactorily.

Size 1–1.2 × 1–1.2m/3–4 × 3–4ft after fifteen years.

Olearia   DAISY BUSH

One of the most familiar, popular and pretty of evergreen flowering shrubs for mild-climate gardens, but too tender to be of much use anywhere else unless it can be given good protection.

Soil Tolerates a wide range of soils but is always best in free-draining, rich and slightly acidic conditions.

Situation Full sun but with shelter from cold winds.

Watering and feeding Mulch in autumn and spring. Apply a balanced rose or similar potash-rich fertilizer in mid-spring, and again after midsummer.

Olearia macrodonta

PRUNING Once plants are established, cut back the oldest third of the shoots to soil level in late spring.

COMMON PROBLEMS None.

PROPAGATION Semi-ripe cuttings in summer or hardwood cuttings in winter.

TROUBLESHOOTING Old, woody and neglected plants can sometimes be rejuvenated if cut back hard in spring but very old and misshapen plants are better replaced.

SIZE In coastal gardens, attains about 1×1m/3×3ft after five years and 4×4m/13×13ft after eighteen to twenty years.

Pachysandra

A very low-growing, ground-cover shrub, useful for dry and difficult areas, although tolerant of a wide range of conditions.

SOIL Tolerates many but best on moist, rich, organic soils.

SITUATION Full sun to deep shade; a useful plant for moist areas under trees.

WATERING AND FEEDING Mulch in autumn and spring. Feed with a balanced general fertilizer in mid-spring.

PRUNING None necessary.

COMMON PROBLEMS None.

PROPAGATION Division (treat like a herbaceous perennial).

TROUBLESHOOTING Old and straggly plants may be rejuvenated by cutting them back to soil level in spring and applying both a mulch and a general fertilizer.

SIZE Slower growing than is often claimed, especially the variegated form, which can be very slow indeed. The normal species will attain about 20×80cm/8in $\times 2\frac{1}{2}$ft after five years and about 30cm $\times 2$m/$1 \times 6\frac{1}{2}$ft after fifteen or seventeen years, although as ground cover a large number of individual plants would be used.

Pachysandra terminalis 'Variegata'
Pachysandra terminalis

Paeonia   TREE PAEONY

The so-called tree paeonies are genuine shrubs, superb in flower in the right conditions. Sadly, some of the best forms tend to be rather scarce.

SOIL Tolerates a wide range provided it is not very heavy or waterlogged, but less successful in highly alkaline conditions.

SITUATION Full sun to light shade, although with some shelter from cold winds.

WATERING AND FEEDING Mulch in autumn and spring. Feed with a balanced rose or similar potash-rich fertilizer in mid-spring, and again after midsummer.

PRUNING None necessary or even advisable, as the plants may be seriously checked by it.

COMMON PROBLEMS None.

PROPAGATION Not possible. The true species are propagated from seed; some of the Chinese and Japanese varieties by grafting.

TROUBLESHOOTING None should be necessary, but dead or damaged branches should be cut back to their base. Many tree paeonies have such heavy double blooms that they may require staking during flowering time.

Paeonia delavayi lutea

Paeonia – Pittosporum

Philadelphus coronarius

Phlomis fruticosa

SIZE The modern Oriental varieties (which are grafted on to herbaceous paeony rootstocks), and the true species, including the exceptionally lovely *P. suffruticosa* as well as the more common *P. delavayi lutea*, will attain about 1.5 × 1.5m/5 × 5ft after ten to twelve years. *P. delavayi ludlowii* will eventually grow to about twice this size.

Philadelphus MOCK ORANGE

Also mistakenly known as syringa, philadelphus is among the most rewarding of deciduous, hardy summer-flowering shrubs.

SOIL Most, but succeeds best on more or less neutral, well-drained rich loams.

SITUATION Full sun to medium shade, although variegated and golden-leaved forms will scorch in full sun and cold winds.

WATERING AND FEEDING Mulch in autumn and spring. Feed with a balanced rose or similar potash-rich fertilizer in mid-spring, and again after midsummer.

PRUNING No pruning is necessary but all types benefit from cutting out the oldest third of the shoots after flowering.

COMMON PROBLEMS Aphids.

PROPAGATION Semi-ripe cuttings in summer or hardwood cuttings in winter.

TROUBLESHOOTING Old, congested and very woody plants can be rejuvenated by initiating the annual pruning outlined above.

SIZE The small shrubby forms, such as 'Manteau d'Hermine', are slow growing and will reach 70 × 70cm/2 × 2ft after about five years and slightly over 1m/3ft ultimately. Half as fast and large again is a slightly taller group, with 'Belle Etoile' the best known variety; the largest group, including 'Beauclerk', 'Virginal' and *P. coronarius* 'Aureus', will reach 1.5 × 1m/5 × 3ft after five years and 3–4 × 3–4m/10–13 × 10–13ft after sixteen to eighteen years.

Phlomis JERUSALEM SAGE

Great, gaunt and ungainly it may be, yet many gardeners love the Jerusalem sage for its whorls of flowers in pastel shades. They are undeniably plants of the sun.

SOIL Light, free-draining.

SITUATION Full sun.

WATERING AND FEEDING Mulch in autumn and spring. Feed with a balanced general purpose fertilizer in mid-spring, and again after midsummer.

PRUNING Cut out damaged or overcrowded shoots in spring.

COMMON PROBLEMS None.

PROPAGATION Division in spring, semi-ripe cuttings in summer, hardwood cuttings in winter, or from seed.

TROUBLESHOOTING None normally necessary but very woody and unkempt plants may regenerate if up to one third of the shoots are cut back to just above soil level in spring.

SIZE The common, true Jerusalem sage, *P. fruticosa*, will reach 1.2 × 1m/4 × 3ft after three years, although there are related and slightly smaller species.

Photinia

One of the few genera of evergreen (or in a few instances, deciduous) shrubs in which the primary appeal derives from the colour of the young shoots in spring, for flowering is unusual in gardens.

SOIL Most, but succeeds best on acidic soils, and generally unsuccessful with any alkalinity.

SITUATION Full sun to light shade; requires some shelter from cold winds.

WATERING AND FEEDING Mulch in autumn and spring. Feed with a balanced general fertilizer in mid-spring.

PRUNING None necessary.

COMMON PROBLEMS None.

PROPAGATION Semi-ripe cuttings in summer.

TROUBLESHOOTING Rarely necessary, but old plants will usually respond well to being cut back hard in spring.

SIZE Up to 1.5 × 2m/5 × 6½ft after five years, 5 × 4m/16 × 13ft after twenty years.

Pieris

Like *Photinia*, some varieties of the evergreen genus *Pieris* are grown principally for the colour of their young shoots, but others are worth having for their delicate tresses of cream spring flowers. Although the plant is hardy, the young shoots can be damaged by late frosts and the soil and site requirements are fairly exacting.

SOIL Moist, rich, acidic; will not flourish in very dry conditions and is intolerant of any alkalinity.

SITUATION Light shade; requires some shelter from cold winds.

WATERING AND FEEDING Mulch in autumn and spring. Feed with a balanced rose or similar potash-rich fertilizer in mid-spring, and again after midsummer.

PRUNING None necessary.

COMMON PROBLEMS None.

PROPAGATION Semi-ripe cuttings in summer or by layering.

TROUBLESHOOTING None necessary.

SIZE Varies slightly but most varieties will attain 60cm–1m × 1m/2–3ft × 3ft after about five years, and perhaps double this after eighteen or twenty years.

Photinia davidiana

Pittosporum

A delightful and delicately foliaged evergreen, much beloved of flower arrangers but with rather exacting requirements if it is to be really successful.

SOIL Fairly rich, free-draining, suitable for most soil types but rather intolerant of high alkalinity.

SITUATION Full sun or light shade with some shelter from cold winds; very successful in maritime areas.

WATERING AND FEEDING Mulch in autumn and spring. Feed with a balanced general fertilizer in mid-spring.

PRUNING None necessary, but can be trimmed as a hedge: clip twice, first around midsummer and again in early autumn.

Pieris japonica 'Pink Delight'

Pittosporum – Pyracantha

COMMON PROBLEMS None, apart from frost damage.

PROPAGATION Semi-ripe cuttings in late summer.

TROUBLESHOOTING None normally necessary, but overgrown or very woody plants regenerate if cut back to about 30cm/1ft above soil level in spring. Very large plants are best treated in two stages: cut back to about 1.5m/5ft in the first year and then back to 30cm/1ft in the following year, if they have satisfactorily produced new shoots.

SIZE The commonest varieties, including the popular 'Garnettii', will reach about 1.5–2 × 1m/5–6½ × 3ft in favourable, mild areas after five years, and about 6 × 2.5–3m/20 × 8–10ft after twenty.

Pittosporum tenuifolium

Potentilla

Among the most useful and adaptable of free-flowering, small deciduous shrubs. They are suitable for most gardens, provided care is taken in siting them.

SOIL Preferably light and free-draining; intolerant of waterlogging or high alkalinity.

SITUATION Full sun; potentillas flower much less satisfactorily in even light shade.

WATERING AND FEEDING Mulch in autumn and spring. Feed with a balanced rose or similar potash-rich fertilizer in mid-spring, and again after midsummer.

PRUNING None necessary, but most varieties usually produce more flowers and maintain a more effective, neater shape if the oldest one third of the shoots are regularly cut back to just above soil level each spring.

COMMON PROBLEMS None.

PROPAGATION Semi-ripe cuttings in late summer or hardwood cuttings in winter.

TROUBLESHOOTING Old, overgrown or very woody plants will usually regenerate satisfactorily if cut back to just above soil level in spring, although the task is better staged over two or three years. Very large and neglected plants are best replaced. Even young potentillas look dead or moribund in winter and there is a temptation to cut them back hard in the belief that they have suffered frost damage. Always wait until the buds have burst (which in some varieties may be quite late), as this will reveal those parts that have truly been killed back.

SIZE Varies considerably. Some dwarf or almost ground-covering varieties, such as *P. fruticosa* 'Manchu', will slowly reach about 20 × 75cm/8in × 2½ft, but most of the common bush varieties will reach about 1.2 × 1.2m/4 × 4ft after eight or nine years.

Potentilla fruticosa 'Elizabeth'

Prunus

Most of the *Prunus* varieties and species grown in gardens are tree-sized (see pages 214 and Tree Fruit) but there are a few important types that are classed as shrubs: the cherry laurel, *P. laurocerasus*, a one-time favourite hedging plant; the Portugal laurel, *P. lusitanica*, used as a specimen shrub and for topiary; and some dwarf, flowering forms.

Pittosporum – Pyracantha

Prunus mume 'Beni-chidori'

SOIL Almost any, although *P. glandulosa*, *P. laurocerasus* and *P. tenella* are less successful in strongly alkaline conditions.

SITUATION Full sun or light shade; laurels, except cherry and Portugal laurels, will tolerate deep shade, one of their chief merits.

WATERING AND FEEDING Mulch in autumn and spring. Feed with a balanced general fertilizer in mid-spring.

PRUNING The laurels do not require any pruning but can be cut to shape as necessary and, if required, clipped as hedges or specimens. When that is the case, clip once in early autumn, preferably with secateurs to avoid disfiguring the large leaves. Among the dwarf, flowering species, only *P. × cistena*, *P. glandulosa* and *P. triloba* require or indeed tolerate pruning. Between one third and one half of the shoots should be cut back by about half, immediately after flowering.

COMMON PROBLEMS Peach leaf curl and mildew will affect some species but laurels are generally trouble free.

PROPAGATION Laurels and some other varieties may be propagated from semi-ripe cuttings, in early summer, but a few of the flowering species are notoriously tricky.

TROUBLESHOOTING Old, overgrown or very woody laurels will usually regenerate satisfactorily if cut back to just above soil level in spring. This may also be successful on varieties tolerant of pruning; others, such as *P. mume*, are best replaced.

SIZE Unpruned, cherry laurel will reach 3 × 3m/10 × 10ft after five years and 8–10 × 8m/26–33 × 26ft after eighteen or twenty. Portugal laurel and *P. mume* will attain a little over half these sizes, while the remaining species will reach about 1 × 1m/3 × 3ft after five years, and double this ultimately.

Pyracantha FIRETHORN

Popular and hardy, ornamental evergreen shrubs, grown in part for their blossom but more importantly for their red, orange or yellow berries, which are retained well into the winter when birds allow. They are often grown as wall shrubs.

SOIL Almost any, although intolerant of high alkalinity.

Pyracantha – Rhododendron

Pyracantha rogersiana

SITUATION Full sun to fairly deep shade, although with increasingly fewer flowers and fruits, the greater the shade.

WATERING AND FEEDING Mulch in autumn and spring. Feed with a balanced rose or similar potash-rich fertilizer in mid-spring, and again after midsummer.

PRUNING None required when grown as a free-standing specimen. When grown as an informal hedge, clip twice, first around midsummer and again in early autumn. When grown as a wall shrub, shape plants by cutting as hard back as necessary in very early spring.

COMMON PROBLEMS Fireblight; scab sometimes disfigures the fruits and causes them to drop.

PROPAGATION Semi-ripe cuttings in summer.

TROUBLESHOOTING Misshapen or overgrown plants will generally respond to being cut back hard in early spring, although flowering and fruiting will be reduced for one or two seasons.

SIZE About 2 × 1.5m/6½ × 5ft after five years, 4 × 3–4m/13 × 10–13ft after about twenty years.

Rhamnus BUCKTHORN

Not the most familiar of ornamental shrubs, but the buckthorns have much to commend them. In milder gardens, the variegated evergreen forms can be most appealing.

SOIL Almost any, although the evergreen forms are intolerant of waterlogging.

SITUATION Light to moderate shade, with effective shelter from cold winds.

WATERING AND FEEDING Mulch in autumn and spring. Feed with a balanced general fertilizer in mid-spring.

PRUNING None required, although evergreen forms may be lightly trimmed to shape in spring. Deciduous forms may be used in informal hedges: clip twice, the first time two or three weeks after midsummer, the second in early autumn; or clip once only in late summer, although this will give a tidy appearance for a shorter time.

COMMON PROBLEMS None.

PROPAGATION Semi-ripe cuttings in late summer or hardwood cuttings in late winter.

TROUBLESHOOTING None normally necessary.

SIZE Will attain 2×1.5m/$6\frac{1}{2} \times 5$ft after five years, up to 5×4m/16×13ft after sixteen to eighteen years.

Rhododendron

The largest and most valuable group of evergreen flowering shrubs in appropriate soil conditions, although some species and varieties are much hardier than others. I also include here those species and varieties generally known as azaleas, some of which are evergreen and some deciduous.

SOIL Acidic, organic, moist but not prone to waterlogging. Intolerant of any alkalinity.

SITUATION Light to moderate shade; azaleas are generally more tolerant than rhododendrons of full sun. Many rhododendrons will thrive only in mild areas and, in general, it is the larger, tree-like species and varieties and those with very large leaves that are among the most tender.

WATERING AND FEEDING Mulch in autumn and spring. Apply a balanced rose or other potash-rich fertilizer in mid-spring, and again after midsummer. The mulch is best made from acidic material such as chopped conifer needles. Although many rose and similar fertilizers contain bonemeal, its slightly alkaline nature will not harm these or other acid-loving plants.

PRUNING None required, although careful removal of dead flower heads improves the appearance of plants and encourages new flower buds to develop. This operation is, however, all but impossible on very large plants or on an extensive collection.

COMMON PROBLEMS None, although bud blast sometimes occurs. This fungal disease spread by insects causes the buds to shrivel and bear tiny black, pinhead-like structures. If possible, affected buds should be collected and destroyed. Leaf spotting is also common, although seldom serious.

PROPAGATION Very difficult, other than by layering.

TROUBLESHOOTING None normally necessary, although old plants will often regenerate after being cut back hard into the old wood in spring, with the operation staged over three years.

SIZE Varies widely from dwarf, rock garden shrubs such as *R. impeditum* to species that in mild areas can become multi-stemmed trees 20m/65ft tall. Carefully check the label when buying plants, especially if you live in a favourable mild climate, and be prepared to increase the predicted ultimate size by about half as much again, as there is a tendency for some nurseries to underestimate the growth of rhododendrons.

Rhamnus cathartica

Azalea 'Merlin'

Rhus glabra 'Laciniata'

Rhus SUMACH

The deciduous stagshorn sumach is sometimes classed as a small tree, although in most gardens it normally attains only large shrub size. It is grown essentially for its vivid autumn foliage colours but unfortunately has a stark winter appearance and a habit of suckering, especially if its roots are damaged or disturbed.

SOIL Any.

SITUATION Full sun or light shade.

WATERING AND FEEDING Mulch in autumn and spring. Apply a balanced general fertilizer in mid-spring.

PRUNING None required, although plants can be cut back to ground level each spring to stimulate the production of new shoots with larger than normal leaves.

COMMON PROBLEMS None.

PROPAGATION Semi-ripe cuttings in summer, hardwood cuttings in winter, or from suckers.

TROUBLESHOOTING None normally necessary, although old plants will regenerate after being cut back to about 45cm/1½ft above soil level in spring.

SIZE Without pruning, the stagshorn sumach (*R. typhina*) will attain about $2 \times 2m/6\frac{1}{2} \times 6\frac{1}{2}$ft after five years and around $6-7 \times 5m/20-23 \times 16$ft after eighteen to twenty years.

Ribes FLOWERING CURRANT

The deciduous and reliably hardy, spring-blooming flowering currants have an ability to grow in most situations, but their ultimate size is not always fully appreciated. They also have a valuable and slightly more tender evergreen relative in *R. speciosum*, the fuchsia-flowered gooseberry.

SOIL Will tolerate most, although generally least successful in very dry conditions.

SITUATION Full sun or light shade; *R. speciosum* requires some shelter and is best grown as a wall shrub.

WATERING AND FEEDING Mulch in autumn and spring. Feed with a balanced rose or similar potash-rich fertilizer in mid-spring, and again after midsummer.

PRUNING Cut out the oldest one third of the shoots in spring, after flowering, to prevent the plants from becoming leggy and unkempt. *R. speciosum* will generally require lighter pruning, and in most areas this may only mean cutting out those parts killed by winter cold. When flowering currants are grown as an informal hedge, clip once lightly, shortly after flowering.

COMMON PROBLEMS Aphids.

PROPAGATION Semi-ripe cuttings in summer or hardwood cuttings in winter.

TROUBLESHOOTING Old and overgrown plants can usually be rejuvenated by cutting back hard to just above soil level in spring, spreading the work over two spring seasons.

SIZE Most forms, including the popular *R. sanguineum* 'Pulborough Scarlet', will attain about $1.5 \times 1.5m/5 \times 5$ft after five years and about $2.5 \times 2.5m/8 \times 8$ft after twelve or fifteen years.

Ribes sanguineum

Romneya TREE POPPY

The deciduous Californian tree poppy is another of those mis-named plants, a shrub called a tree but having much in common with a flowering herbaceous perennial. It is undeniably lovely with huge white flowers, but will not be successful if the soil is wrong – although it can become too vigorous once established in good conditions.

SOIL Moist, rich, acid or alkaline; *Romneya* will not tolerate a clay soil or one prone to waterlogging.

SITUATION Full sun.

PRUNING Cut back to soil level in early spring.

COMMON PROBLEMS None.

PROPAGATION Root cuttings in winter; one of the classic plants for this method of propagation and always given to horticulture students to practise on.

TROUBLESHOOTING None should be necessary; old and over-grown plants may be divided in spring.

SIZE The tree poppy will attain 1m/3ft in height but spreads somewhat invasively and can become 2–3m/6½–10ft across after ten or fifteen years.

Romneya coulteri

Rosa ROSE

As a group, roses are justifiably the most popular of all garden plants. But they do comprise a large number of sub-groups, and while their soil and site requirements are fairly similar, their ultimate sizes and the manner in which they are best pruned differ considerably. Most of the sub-groups include some climbing forms but these are described separately (see pages 93–5).

SOIL Although tolerant of a wide range of soil types, they will always be most successful in a rich, moisture-retentive soil, but this could range from an organic loam to a heavy clay. Light soils will produce good roses provided large quantities of organic matter are incorporated. Roses are least successful on very acidic soils, while in very alkaline conditions they may suffer from severe leaf chlorosis.

SITUATION Full sun or light shade; some varieties in almost all groups are successful in deeper shade. Others, most notably the tea roses and some of the less common species, are more tender and require shelter from cold winds. Overall, the rugosas and rugosa hybrids are the most tolerant of exposure.

WATERING AND FEEDING Mulch in autumn and spring. Feed with a balanced rose or similar potash-rich fertilizer in mid-spring, and again after midsummer.

PRUNING Varies considerably between groups although, on all varieties, any very long and whippy shoots that are not to be used to form part of the permanent framework should be cut back by about half in autumn, to minimize damage caused to the plant's overall stability by winter gales. Most garden roses are grafted on to rootstocks of different varieties, chosen for their rooting rather than flowering attributes. Suckers may arise from these below soil level and must be pulled away promptly.

Rosa

HYBRID TEAS In spring, cut back any damaged shoots to soil level, cut out any very feeble or spindly shoots, and then cut back all remaining shoots by approximately half, cutting slightly less for vigorous, strongly growing varieties and slightly more for weaker growing ones.

FLORIBUNDAS In spring, cut out one third of the shoots to soil level, cutting out principally the oldest but also removing any diseased or damaged ones. Then cut back the remaining shoots by

Roses: pruning hybrid teas

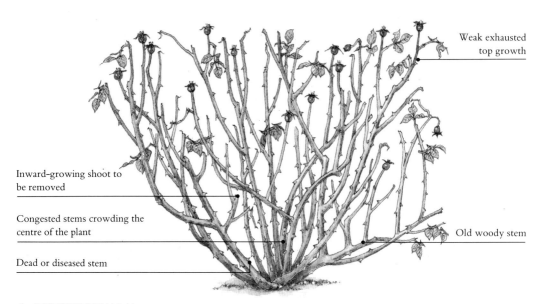

Weak exhausted top growth

Inward-growing shoot to be removed

Congested stems crowding the centre of the plant

Old woody stem

Dead or diseased stem

▲ **ASSESSMENT** Hybrid tea roses are vigorous plants, and at pruning time in spring will look a mass of tangled stems. They can be pruned hard, to stimulate plenty of new growth on which the summer's flowers will be borne.

▶ **AFTER PRUNING** Cut back to soil level no more than one third of the shoots, removing any showing signs of damage from rubbing or disease, and those that look feeble or spindly. This will leave about two thirds of the stems: cut these back to tiny pink buds low down on the stem and facing away from the centre of the plant. For vigorous varieties cut to a bud about half way up the stem; for weaker varieties prune harder, to a bud about a third of the way up.

Bud facing away from the centre of the plant

Stems cut back by about two thirds

Shoots removed to soil level

approximately one third, cutting by slightly less for vigorous, strongly growing varieties, and by slightly more than a third for weaker growing ones.

SHRUB ROSES Although this is a highly diverse group, including, among the more familiar types, rugosas, albas, damasks, noisettes, bourbons, musks, centifolias, a number of species or seedlings derived from them, and a few so-called ground-cover or procumbent varieties, they may all be treated similarly. Little

Roses: pruning floribundas

Tangled mass of exhausted top growth

Old stem to remove

Congested centre to the plant

Bud facing away from the centre of the plant

Stems cut back by about one third

Some stems removed to soil level

▲ **ASSESSMENT** Floribundas produce their flowers in clusters, so at pruning time in spring there will be a tangled mass of top growth. The aim of pruning is to remove all this tired growth, and stimulate new growth from the base.

▶ **AFTER PRUNING** Cut back to soil level one third of the stems, removing the oldest and any showing signs of damage. Cut the remaining shoots back to buds that face away from the plant's centre, and are about two thirds of the way up the stem. Cut strong varieties back by slightly less, and weaker ones by slightly more.

Rosa

pruning is needed although, every two or three years, the oldest shoots or any that are damaged or diseased should be pruned to soil level to stimulate the production of new growth. Any abnormally long shoots that were cut back in the autumn (see page 61), should also be pruned to soil level in the spring. It is important not to leave shoots only partially cut back on shrub roses, as this will result in an unsightly proliferation of twiggy growth. Shrub roses should not be dead-headed after the flowers have faded as, in many instances, they produce very attractive hips in the autumn. The old fruits will drop, shrivel or be eaten by birds during the winter and, as there are usually so many of them, it is only worth cutting off the more unsightly dead heads in spring.

Roses: pruning shrubs

◄ **ASSESSMENT** Shrub roses produce the most beautiful effect if they are pruned as little as possible. Don't even deadhead in late summer, for many varieties produce attractive hips. Either leave these to drop off naturally, or deadhead in spring. The result will be a graceful and elegant bush, with plenty of healthy stems growing directly from the base, and little twiggy top growth. Occasionally remove the oldest stems, as shown below.

► **AFTER PRUNING** Every two or three years in spring, encourage the plant to produce healthy new growth from its base by removing about a quarter to a third of the stems. Cut back to soil level those stems whose brown colour suggests they are old and exhausted, and any stems with signs of damage or disease. Leave the top growth untouched, although the plant can be deadheaded if you prefer.

Roses: troubleshooting

Branching, twiggy top growth

Poor foliage

Old, exhausted woody stem

Crossing stems

Weak growth from the base

▲ **ASSESSMENT** This shrub rose shows the results of poor pruning in the past: the stems have been repeatedly cut back to remove the top growth, so the plant has produced branching, twiggy growth at the tops of the stems, but little new shoot growth from the base. Its exhausted stems have bowed under the weight to unbalance its shape. Flowering is good, but the foliage is poor due to inadequate feeding and mulching. Remedial pruning needs to be combined with careful feeding, watering and mulching.

◀ **AFTER PRUNING, 1ST SPRING** The oldest stems have all been removed, and the weak shoots from the base cut out. The remaining stems are left untouched. Depending on the vigour of the plant, between one and two thirds of the stems can be removed in the first pruning.

▶ **AFTER PRUNING, 2ND SEASON** The initial pruning and feeding will throw up new shoots from the base. At the second pruning time, another old stem can be cut out completely, and the plant progressively renewed.

Rosa – Salix

Rosa 'Alec's Red'

Rosmarinus officinalis

MINIATURES These scaled-down versions of floribundas or hybrid teas require less true pruning and more of a tidying up in spring. They are all slightly more prone than their larger counterparts to frost damage and, inevitably, there will be some dead shoots to be cut out in spring. Their growth also tends to be more congested and so, at the same time, the twigs may be thinned out. Some varieties tend to produce long flowering shoots, and these should be cut back to a bud just above soil level, after the flowers have faded in autumn.

STANDARD AND HALF-STANDARD ROSES These are artificial productions comprising a selected variety grafted at the desired height on the stem of a rootstock. They should be pruned as described for the variety, except that pruning back 'to soil level' should be read as pruning back to the point of grafting.

COMMON PROBLEMS Mildew; aphids; black spot; rust.

PROPAGATION Hardwood cuttings in early winter, although it must be said that these are often very difficult to strike from hybrid teas and floribundas.

TROUBLESHOOTING Old and overgrown plants can often be rejuvenated by cutting back the shoots to just above soil level, in spring; spread the work over three seasons so that no more than one third of the shoots is cut out at any one time. Although there are some notable and fine very old rose specimens, they are generally plants that have been tended throughout their lives and my feeling is that a neglected rose more than eight or ten years old is best replaced.

SIZE Enormously variable, so check label descriptions. As a general guide, most roses will attain their final height in three to five years (allowing for pruning of those for which it is needed). Miniatures reach about $30 \times 30cm/1 \times 1ft$, hybrid teas and floribundas about $1m \times 80cm/3 \times 2\frac{1}{2}ft$, and shrub roses about $1.5–2 \times 1.5m/5–6\frac{1}{2} \times 5ft$, but there are larger and smaller varieties in all of these groups.

Rosmarinus ROSEMARY

Although usually grown as a herb for culinary use, rosemary also makes a most useful evergreen foliage shrub. It is tolerant of a wide range of conditions, and is particularly attractive and useful as a low hedge.

SOIL Will tolerate most, although never very successful in waterlogged or very highly alkaline conditions.

SITUATION Full sun or very light shade.

WATERING AND FEEDING Mulch in autumn and spring. Feed with a balanced general fertilizer in mid-spring.

PRUNING Cut out the oldest one third of the shoots in spring. When grown as hedges, clip twice, first around midsummer and again in early autumn.

COMMON PROBLEMS None.

PROPAGATION Semi-ripe cuttings in early summer.

TROUBLESHOOTING Overgrown plants can usually be rejuvenated by cutting back hard to just above soil level, spreading the work over two consecutive spring seasons.

SIZE Most varieties will attain their ultimate height of about 1.5 × 1.5m/5 × 5ft after five or seven years, but there are a few lower-growing forms, the best known being the dark-blue-flowered *R. officinalis* 'Severn Sea'.

Rubus FLOWERING BRAMBLE

Although most of the hardy deciduous *Rubus* species and varieties in gardens are grown for their soft fruit, there are a few worthy of including where space permits for their flowering and ground-covering attributes.

SOIL Will tolerate most soils, although most species suffer from nutrient deficiencies in strongly alkaline conditions and are fairly intolerant of dryness.

SITUATION Light to moderate shade, although will tolerate full sun and deeper shade.

WATERING AND FEEDING Mulch in autumn and spring. Feed with a balanced rose or other potash-rich fertilizer in mid-spring, and again after midsummer.

PRUNING Varies with species. Those such as *R. cockburnianus*, grown for their white stems, should be cut back to soil level in early spring. The ground-covering *R. tricolor* needs no pruning. Those types grown principally for their flowers, such as the popular *R.* Tridel 'Benenden', should have the oldest third of the shoots cut back to soil level each spring.

COMMON PROBLEMS None.

PROPAGATION Semi-ripe cuttings in summer or hardwood cuttings in winter.

TROUBLESHOOTING Old and overgrown plants of all types can usually be rejuvenated by cutting back hard to just above soil level in spring.

SIZE With the pruning regime suggested, *R. cockburnianus* will reach about 3 × 3m/10 × 10ft after five years. Unpruned, *R. tricolor* will soon reach its ultimate height of about 75cm/2½ft and will spread to about 3–4m/10–13ft after twelve years. *R.* 'Benenden' will reach about 1 × 1m/3 × 3ft after five years and 3 × 3m/10 × 10ft after fifteen years.

Rubus cockburnianus

Salix WILLOW

There are numerous deciduous willows suitable for growing as garden shrubs; a few larger species make good trees (see page 216), while others are most inappropriate for any garden use. Tolerant of a wide range of conditions, they are particularly useful for heavy and wet sites.

SOIL Will tolerate most, although particularly successful in wet or even waterlogged soils.

SITUATION Full sun to moderate shade.

WATERING AND FEEDING Mulch in autumn and spring. Feed with a balanced rose or other potash-rich fertilizer in mid-spring, and again after midsummer.

PRUNING Varies with species. Many willows require no pruning. This applies to all of the dwarf species, such as *S.* 'Boydii', the

Salix helvetica

low-growing types like *S. lanata* and *S. helvetica* (even when grown grafted atop an upright stem as a standard), and to larger species grown for their overall form, foliage effect and catkins, such as *S. fargesii* and *S. gracilistyla* and its form 'Melanostachys'. The latter species, however, does respond well to hard pruning to keep the plants manageable, and other common and popular species that benefit from pruning are *S. exigua*, *S. irrorata* and *S. udensis* (previously *S. sachalinensis*). All of these should be pruned to about 30cm/1ft above soil level every three years, in early spring. This will produce the attractively coloured shoots that will then gradually fade between prunings.

COMMON PROBLEMS Many species suffer from leaf-attacking insects and fungal leaf spots, which may cause some disfigurement as the summer progresses.

PROPAGATION Hardwood cuttings in winter, layers or suckers; willows root more readily from cuttings than any other shrub.

TROUBLESHOOTING Old and overgrown plants of all types will regenerate extremely well if cut back hard to just above soil level in spring.

SIZE Varies greatly, so check label descriptions. The genus includes prostrate forms like *S. repens* (2m/6½ft spread after five years); small, slow-growing shrubs such as *S. helvetica* (80 × 80cm/ 2½ × 2½ft after five years), and robust, vigorous species such as *S. gracilistyla* 'Melanostachys' (2.2 × 2m/7 × 6½ft after five years).

Sambucus ELDER

The hardy, deciduous elderberry, *S. nigra*, is scarcely a worthy garden plant in its wild state but it has some selected foliage forms and a related species, *S. racemosa*, that with careful pruning make most attractive garden shrubs.

SOIL Almost any, including wet and dry sites.

SITUATION Light shade; tolerant of moderate shade, but golden-foliaged varieties tend to be scorched in full sun.

WATERING AND FEEDING Mulch in autumn and spring. Apply a balanced general fertilizer in mid-spring.

PRUNING There are two options. If the oldest one third of the shoots is pruned to soil level each year, in spring, the plants will reach a greater height but the leaves will be generally less attractively coloured and smaller. By cutting all the shoots back to soil level each spring, the best foliage will be obtained but the plants will remain much smaller.

COMMON PROBLEMS Aphids.

PROPAGATION Semi-ripe cuttings in late summer or hardwood cuttings in winter.

TROUBLESHOOTING Old and overgrown plants of all types regenerate successfully if they are cut back hard to just above soil level in spring.

SIZE With complete annual pruning, all forms will reach about 2 × 1m/6½ × 3ft each year. With partial pruning, they will attain a maximum of about 3–4 × 2m/10–13 × 6½ft. Unpruned, *S. racemosa* will reach about 6 × 4m/20 × 13ft after twenty years, and *S. nigra* about half as tall again.

Sambucus racemosa 'Plumosa Aurea'

Santolina COTTON LAVENDER

Often seen in the herb garden but makes a useful silver-foliaged small shrub for other places too, provided the dry and sunny conditions so beloved of Mediterranean plants can be supplied. It is sometimes grown as an ornamental border plant, and makes an interesting change from the more familiar dwarf box.
SOIL Light, free-draining.
SITUATION Full sun or very light shade.
WATERING AND FEEDING Mulch in autumn and spring. Feed with a balanced general fertilizer in mid-spring.
PRUNING Trim lightly with shears in late spring, cutting just a few centimetres above the base of last year's growth.
COMMON PROBLEMS None.
PROPAGATION Semi-ripe cuttings in summer.
TROUBLESHOOTING Old plants are best replaced; as with most shrubby herbs, the effective life is only four or five years.
SIZE Within five years, will attain about 50×75cm/$1\frac{1}{2} \times 2\frac{1}{2}$ft.

Santolina pinnata neapolitana 'Edward Bowles'

Sarcococca SWEET BOX

Also known as Christmas box, these are among the lesser known of the easily grown and widely available garden shrubs. They are worthy of much wider note for their fragrant winter flowers.
SOIL Organic and fertile soil is required but they are tolerant of acidity and alkalinity.
SITUATION Full sun to moderate shade.
WATERING AND FEEDING Mulch in autumn and spring. Feed with a balanced rose or other potash-rich fertilizer in mid-spring, and again after midsummer.
PRUNING None necessary.
COMMON PROBLEMS None.
PROPAGATION Semi-ripe cuttings in late summer, hardwood cuttings in winter, or by suckers.
TROUBLESHOOTING If old plants become congested and flowering diminishes, cut back the oldest third of the shoots to about 10cm/4in above soil level after flowering in spring.
SIZE *S. confusa* is a slow-growing dwarf species that will attain about 1×1m/3×3ft after fifteen years. *S. hookeriana* will reach this in half the time and ultimately grow to about 2×2m/$6\frac{1}{2} \times 6\frac{1}{2}$ft.

Senecio

One of the most widely grown of all evergreen garden shrubs, the yellow-flowered and greyish-leaved 'daisy bush' is too often neglected and allowed to become unkempt and straggly. Although a very indulgent plant, it really looks its best in gentler climates. The most popular variety is still often called *S. greyi*, although its more correct names are *S.* 'Sunshine' or, more recently, *Brachyglottis* 'Sunshine'.
SOIL Tolerates most provided it is not cold or waterlogged.
SITUATION Full sun to very light shade; the plant is tolerant of salt spray and is therefore a useful seaside plant.

Sarcococca confusa

Senecio – Spartium

Senecio greyi

WATERING AND FEEDING Mulch in autumn and spring. Feed with a balanced rose or similar potash-rich fertilizer in mid-spring, and again around midsummer.

PRUNING Trim lightly with shears in spring to maintain an attractive and compact shape.

COMMON PROBLEMS None.

PROPAGATION Semi-ripe cuttings in summer.

TROUBLESHOOTING Straggly and misshapen plants, provided they are not very old and woody, can generally be rejuvenated if cut back to about 45cm/1½ft above soil level in spring.

SIZE Will grow fairly swiftly to reach about 1–1.5 × 1–1.5m/ 3–5 × 3–5ft after four or five years.

Skimmia

Skimmias are extremely popular and widely grown small, ever-green, berrying shrubs with specific soil and site requirements.

SOIL Always best in moist, organic acid soil; intolerant of dryness and of impoverished or alkaline conditions, which result in small, yellowed foliage.

SITUATION Light to moderate shade; in full sun, the foliage yellows most unattractively.

WATERING AND FEEDING Mulch in autumn and spring. Feed with a balanced rose or other potash-rich fertilizer in mid-spring, and again after midsummer.

PRUNING None necessary.

COMMON PROBLEMS Leaf chlorosis, as described above. A fail-ure to form berries almost always arises because for most varie-ties, separate male and female plants need to be grown in close proximity to each other.

Skimmia japonica 'Rubella'

PROPAGATION Semi-ripe cuttings in late summer or hardwood cuttings in winter.

TROUBLESHOOTING If old plants become congested and flowering diminishes, cut back the oldest third of the shoots to about 10cm/4in above soil level immediately after flowering.

SIZE All varieties likely to be grown in gardens are slow growing and attain their ultimate height of 1–1.5 × 1–1.5m/3–5 × 3–5ft after about twelve or fifteen years.

Sorbus

All except one of the common *Sorbus* species grown in gardens will eventually reach tree size (see page 217) but the exception, *S. reducta*, is a worthy and attractive, deciduous, suckering species with foliage, blossom and fruiting appeal.

SOIL Almost all.

SITUATION Full sun or light shade.

WATERING AND FEEDING Mulch in autumn and spring. Apply a balanced rose or other potash-rich fertilizer in mid-spring, and again after midsummer.

PRUNING None necessary.

COMMON PROBLEMS None.

PROPAGATION From suckers.

TROUBLESHOOTING None normally necessary, but old or overgrown plants can be rejuvenated by cutting hard back to just above soil level in spring.

SIZE Slow growing and spreading, reaching about 25 × 50cm/10in × 1½ft after five years and about 75cm × 2m/2½ × 6½ft after sixteen to eighteen years.

Sorbus reducta

Spartium SPANISH BROOM

A one-species genus as far as gardens are concerned, *S. junceum* is a summer-flowering yellow broom, relatively easy to grow but sharing the same soil and site requirements as the other related broom genera *Cytisus* and *Genista*.

SOIL Light, free-draining, tolerant of high alkalinity but not of waterlogging.

SITUATION Full sun or light shade. Like several other shrubby members of the pea family, its tolerance of salt spray makes this an excellent plant for coastal gardens.

WATERING AND FEEDING Mulch in autumn and spring. Feed with a balanced rose or other potash-rich fertilizer in mid-spring, and again after midsummer.

PRUNING None.

COMMON PROBLEMS None.

PROPAGATION Difficult from cuttings; semi-ripe cuttings in summer are the only ones worth trying.

TROUBLESHOOTING None normally necessary; old and overgrown plants are best replaced.

SIZE Reaches about 2 × 1m/6½ × 3ft after six or eight years and twice this eventually, although plants this large are likely to be leggy and unattractive and are best replaced.

Spartium junceum

Spiraea × arguta

Spiraea

A large genus of hardy deciduous shrubs, suitable for a wide range of sites and grown principally for their feathery spring and summer flowers. They are commonly described as 'small' but many will eventually grow fairly tall and be wide spreading.

SOIL Almost all, although generally least successful in highly alkaline conditions.

SITUATION Full sun or light shade.

WATERING AND FEEDING Mulch in autumn and spring. Feed with a balanced rose or other potash-rich fertilizer in mid-spring, and again after midsummer.

PRUNING Varieties that flower before midsummer should be pruned immediately after flowering, by cutting back the oldest third of the shoots to soil level. Forms that flower after midsummer should have all shoots pruned to about 20cm/8in above soil level in early spring.

COMMON PROBLEMS None.

PROPAGATION Semi-ripe cuttings in summer or hardwood cuttings in winter.

TROUBLESHOOTING None normally necessary but overgrown plants can be rejuvenated by cutting all shoots back to just above soil level in spring; this is most successful on late-flowering varieties. With spring-flowering types, the operation is best spread over two or three years.

SIZE There are a few relatively dwarf forms, such as *S. × bumalda*, which will attain about 1 × 1m/3 × 3ft after ten years, but most, including the popular bridal wreath, *S. × arguta*, will reach this in half the time, and 2–2.5 × 2–2.5m/6½–8 × 6½–8ft after fifteen or twenty years.

Stephanandra

A genus with two familiar, hardy and easy to grow yet rather different, deciduous species worthy of a place in most gardens for their foliage: *S. incisa* (most usually seen in its variety 'Crispa'), and *S. tanakae*, which has the added attraction of winter stems the colour of mahogany. The former is one of the best and most underappreciated of deciduous, moderately vigorous, groundcover shrubs.

SOIL Almost all, provided not very dry.

SITUATION Full sun or light shade.

WATERING AND FEEDING Mulch in autumn and spring. Feed with a balanced general fertilizer in mid-spring.

PRUNING None necessary for *S. incisa* 'Crispa'. On *S. tanakae*, cut the oldest third of the shoots to soil level each spring, to encourage the production of the young brown shoots in winter.

COMMON PROBLEMS None.

PROPAGATION Hardwood cuttings in winter.

TROUBLESHOOTING None normally necessary but overgrown or, in the case of *S. incisa* 'Crispa', very congested plants can be rejuvenated by cutting some or all shoots back to just above soil level in spring.

Stephanandra tanakae

Size *S. incisa* 'Crispa' forms a dense ground-covering mound, about $50 \times 75cm/1\frac{1}{2} \times 2\frac{1}{2}ft$ after five years and $1–1.5 \times 1–1.5m/$ $3–5 \times 3–5ft$ after twenty years. *S. tanakae* will attain about $1.5 \times$ $1m/5 \times 3ft$ after five or seven years and perhaps $3 \times 2m/10 \times 6\frac{1}{2}ft$ after fifteen years, in good conditions.

Stranvaesia

One species and four or five varieties of a very attractive, hardy evergreen shrub, grown for the value of both its foliage and flowers. It is more accurately now included in the genus *Photinia*, but is still usually sold under its old name.

Soil Almost all, although least successful in dry conditions.

Situation Full sun or moderate shade.

Watering and feeding Mulch in autumn and spring. Feed with a balanced rose or other potash-rich fertilizer in mid-spring, and again after midsummer.

Pruning None required.

Common problems Fireblight, the very damaging disease that also affects fruit trees in the family Rosaceae; it is sensible not to plant stranvaesias in areas where there are commercial apple or pear orchards.

Propagation Semi-ripe cuttings in summer or by layering.

Troubleshooting Old and neglected plants may be rejuvenated by cutting back the oldest shoots to soil level in spring.

Size Reaches $2 \times 1.5m/6\frac{1}{2} \times 5ft$ after five years, and about $7 \times 4–5m/23 \times 13–16ft$ after twenty years.

Stranvaesia davidiana

Symphoricarpos SNOWBERRY

The hardy, deciduous snowberry is aptly named, for its large globular fruits are usually snow white and have the merit of hanging on the plant through much of the winter as birds seem largely to ignore them. It makes a useful informal hedging plant.

Soil Any, including very dry.

Situation Full sun to deep shade.

Watering and feeding Mulch in autumn and spring. Feed with a balanced rose or other potash-rich fertilizer in mid-spring, and again after midsummer.

Pruning None necessary for free-standing shrubs, although up to a third of the oldest stems can be cut back to soil level in spring to stimulate new growth. For hedges, clip twice, first around midsummer and again in early autumn.

Common problems None.

Propagation Semi-ripe cuttings in summer or hardwood cuttings in winter.

Troubleshooting Old and neglected plants may be rejuvenated by cutting them back to soil level in spring.

Size The commonest species, *S. rivularis* (now *S. albus laevigatus*), is a suckering and somewhat invasive plant that can reach $2.5 \times$ $3–4m/8 \times 10–13ft$ after fifteen years. But there are other species and varieties, including the popular *S. × doorenbosii* varieties with pink fruits, that only attain half this size.

Symphoricarpos × doorenbosii

Syringa – Ulex

Syringa 'Louis van Houtte'

Syringa LILAC

Lilacs are among the most familiar, hardy and trouble free of all deciduous flowering shrubs. In many sites they can attain the size of small trees, and for this reason, and because they are much less attractive when out of flower, they are unwise choices for small gardens. Almost all of the common varieties are derived from the species *S. vulgaris*, to which my remarks below refer, although there are many other attractive species and varieties, much less known and less widely available.

SOIL Always best in rich, organic soils and least successful in dry or highly alkaline conditions.

SITUATION Full sun or moderate shade.

WATERING AND FEEDING Mulch in autumn and spring. Feed with a balanced rose or other potash-rich fertilizer in mid-spring, and again after midsummer.

PRUNING As most lilacs are grafted on to wild lilac rootstock, suckers will arise and should be carefully cut away in spring and autumn. Lilacs can be left for many years without pruning but are always better if up to one third of the oldest or weakest shoots are cut back to their bases each year, in spring. The flower heads are most unattractive when they fade, and, if practicable, should be cut off after flowering – which is another good reason for routine annual pruning, as the job of dead heading is so much easier on a smaller plant.

COMMON PROBLEMS None.

PROPAGATION Semi-ripe cuttings in late summer.

TROUBLESHOOTING Old and overgrown plants may be rejuvenated by cutting back the oldest shoots to soil level and reducing the remainder by half in spring, although it will be two or three years before the plant returns to its full flowering potential.

SIZE Unpruned, reaches $1.5 \times 1m/5 \times 3ft$ after five years, and $5 \times 5m/16 \times 16ft$ after twenty years.

Tamarix TAMARISK

Deciduous shrubs with a very distinctive feathery appearance of both foliage and flower heads. Invaluable in areas that approximate to their natural coastal habitats, but prone to damage by cold winds in others.

SOIL Light, free-draining but fertile; especially intolerant of heavy, waterlogged conditions.

SITUATION Full sun or light shade; always best in mild maritime gardens where its tolerance of sea breezes and salt spray make it particularly invaluable.

WATERING AND FEEDING Mulch in autumn and spring. Apply a balanced rose or other potash-rich fertilizer in mid-spring, and again after midsummer.

PRUNING None necessary to encourage flowering but the plants then tend to become leggy and straggly. To avoid this, prune in spring. The varieties that bloom after midsummer should have all the old flowered shoots cut back hard, reducing their overall length by at least half. Spring-blooming types should be pruned

Tamarix pentandra

after they have flowered by cutting the oldest third of the shoots back by at least half. When grown as a hedge, either leave quite informal as a simple screen, with almost no clipping at all, or, for a more compact hedge, clip twice, first around midsummer and again in early autumn.

COMMON PROBLEMS None.

PROPAGATION Hardwood cuttings in early winter.

TROUBLESHOOTING Old and overgrown plants may be rejuvenated by cutting back up to one third of the oldest shoots to soil level and reducing the remainder by half, in spring.

SIZE If left unpruned, tamarisk will reach a height and spread of about 1.5×1.5m/5×5ft after five years, and about 4×4m/13×13ft after sixteen or eighteen years.

Thymus THYME

Thymes are most usually seen in the herb garden but they make attractive, small evergreen shrubs for other areas too, particularly where their fragrance can be appreciated – such as the rock garden, between paving stones and in wall crevices.

SOIL Light, free-draining and preferably alkaline; intolerant of heavy, waterlogged or strongly acid conditions.

SITUATION Full sun or very light shade.

WATERING AND FEEDING If grown as flowering ornamentals, mulch in autumn and spring. Feed with a balanced rose or other potash-rich fertilizer in mid-spring, and again after midsummer. If grown principally for culinary use, substitute a balanced general fertilizer, and apply it in spring only.

PRUNING Trim back dead flower heads with shears.

COMMON PROBLEMS None.

PROPAGATION Semi-ripe cuttings in summer.

TROUBLESHOOTING None necessary. After five or six years, old plants should be replaced.

SIZE Varies according to variety. Within their five- or six-year lifespan, the more vigorous bush forms, such as 'Silver Posie', will reach 25×20cm/10×8in; the creeping forms, such as 'Doone Valley', about 5×25cm/2×10in.

Thymus 'Doone Valley'

Ulex GORSE

To my mind, the deciduous, hardy gorse could be grown much more extensively in larger gardens. It is somewhat coarse in appearance but undeniably beautiful in flower, and it provides a most effective screen or barrier when mass planted; also, it is tolerant of a wide range of conditions.

SOIL Most types, but least successful in strongly acid conditions.

SITUATION Full sun or very light shade; requires shelter from very cold winds but highly tolerant of coastal wind.

WATERING AND FEEDING Mulch in autumn and spring. Feed with a balanced rose or other potash-rich fertilizer in mid-spring, and again after midsummer.

PRUNING None necessary.

COMMON PROBLEMS None.

Ulex europaeus 'Plenus'

Ulex – Vinca

Vaccinium myrtillus

PROPAGATION Semi-ripe cuttings in summer or hardwood cuttings in winter.

TROUBLESHOOTING Neglected plants may be rejuvenated by cutting them back to soil level after flowering. This is particularly worth doing, as the plant is not very widely stocked by garden centres and may be hard to replace.

SIZE Reaches 75cm × 1m/2½ × 3ft after five years, and about 2 × 3m/6½ × 10ft after fifteen years.

Vaccinium

If you have the correct conditions, the bilberry and its allies, including the blueberry, will thrive in your garden. The deciduous types will provide superb autumn colours and, in many instances, repay you with a fruit crop. Unfortunately they are fussy plants, and if you do not have precisely the right conditions, there is little point in trying to grow them.

SOIL Highly acid, moist, organic; a shortcoming in any of these respects will not be tolerated.

SITUATION Full sun or very light shade; the plants require shelter from very cold winds.

WATERING AND FEEDING Mulch in autumn and spring. Feed with a balanced rose or other potash-rich fertilizer in mid-spring, and again after midsummer.

PRUNING None necessary.

COMMON PROBLEMS None.

PROPAGATION Semi-ripe cuttings in early summer or hardwood cuttings in autumn.

TROUBLESHOOTING If plants become very woody and congested, they can usually be rejuvenated by cutting the old wood back to soil level in late winter.

SIZE Varies considerably and label information should be read carefully. The American highbush blueberry (*V. corymbosum*) will reach 1.5 × 1.5m/5 × 5ft after about ten years, whereas the bilberry, *V. myrtillus*, will never exceed a quarter of this.

Viburnum

A large genus of hardy evergreen and deciduous shrubs that includes some of the best medium and large species for gardens. They are suitable for most types of garden soil and site, and offer both flower and foliage appeal in return for relatively little effort or attention.

SOIL Almost any.

SITUATION Generally best in light shade but most are tolerant of full sun and slightly deeper shade.

WATERING AND FEEDING Mulch in autumn and spring. Apply a balanced rose or other potash-rich fertilizer in mid-spring, and again after midsummer.

PRUNING None necessary.

COMMON PROBLEMS None.

PROPAGATION Semi-ripe cuttings in early summer or hardwood cuttings in winter.

TROUBLESHOOTING Overgrown and congested plants are readily rejuvenated by cutting the oldest shoots back to soil level in late winter, but it is best if the operation is spread over three years to give the plant time to recover.

SIZE Varies considerably, although most viburnums eventually make fairly large plants. Check label descriptions in each instance, but most will reach about 1.5 × 1m/5 × 3ft after five years and around 3–5 × 3–4m/10–16 × 10–13ft after fifteen years. Notably lower and slower-growing types among common species are the evergreen *V. davidii* and the deciduous *V. carlesii* (which occurs in several named varieties); both forms will attain about 1.5–2 × 1.5–2m/5–6½ × 5–6½ft over the same timespan.

Viburnum plicatum 'Mariesii'

Vinca PERIWINKLE

One of the most useful groups of ground-cover shrubs for difficult sites – although the less vigorous types are also worth growing for their attractive foliage, which is supplemented by bright, usually blue, flowers.

SOIL Almost any, even when very dry.

SITUATION Generally best in light shade but tolerant of full sun and slightly deeper shade; the combination of dry soil and deep shade is one in which few other plants will thrive.

WATERING AND FEEDING Mulch in autumn and spring. Feed with a balanced rose or other potash-rich fertilizer in mid-spring, and again after midsummer. (It can be difficult to apply mulch once the plants are well established and forming an effective ground-covering carpet.)

Vinca major

PRUNING Use shears or a strimmer to cut *V. major* back to soil level every two or three years, in early spring. *V. minor* should be trimmed more lightly with shears at the same time.

COMMON PROBLEMS Rust disease can be serious on *V. major* but I have never known it so on *V. minor*.

PROPAGATION Semi-ripe cuttings in early summer, hardwood cuttings in winter, or from natural layers.

Vinca – Dwarf conifers

Weigela florida

TROUBLESHOOTING Overgrown plants are readily rejuvenated by trimming them back to soil level in spring, then providing mulch and a general fertilizer.

SIZE Both common species are fairly fast growing. Individual plants reach their ultimate size of about 50cm × 1m/1½ × 3ft for *V. major* and about 20 × 80cm/8in × 2½ft for *V. minor* in under five years, although few gardeners will grow individual plants as they are almost always mass planted for ground cover.

Weigela

Deciduous, spring- and summer-flowering shrubs tolerant of a wide range of conditions.

SOIL Almost any.

SITUATION Best in full sun but tolerates light shade.

WATERING AND FEEDING Mulch in autumn and spring. Feed with a balanced rose or other potash-rich fertilizer in mid-spring, and again after midsummer.

PRUNING None is really necessary but once plants are established, they will benefit from having the oldest third of the shoots cut back to their base each year after flowering.

COMMON PROBLEMS None.

PROPAGATION Semi-ripe cuttings in late summer, hardwood cuttings in winter.

TROUBLESHOOTING Old plants can be rejuvenated by pruning as outlined above, although the modern varieties are better than many of those planted fifteen or twenty years ago, so really old stock is best replaced.

SIZE The most popular weigela is 'Bristol Ruby', which will reach 1–1.5 × 1–1.5m/3–5 × 3–5ft after five years, and 2–2.5 × 2–2.5m/6½–8 × 6½–8ft after about fifteen years. Few others are likely to be larger than this and some, such as 'Newport Red', may be about three quarters of this height.

Bamboos

Bamboos are woody grasses. They comprise a huge group of plants in a huge range of sizes, among which the biggest and most attractive are often not hardy. Some of the hardy species are invasive and, overall, bamboos should be chosen and positioned with care.

SOIL Best in rich, moist loam but tolerate most provided it is not too dry or subject to waterlogging.

SITUATION Light to moderate shade but must have shelter from cold winds.

WATERING AND FEEDING Mulch in autumn and spring. Feed with a balanced general purpose fertilizer in mid-spring and again after midsummer. Take care not to allow the soil to dry out, particularly until the plants are well established.

PRUNING Thin out dead canes in spring by removing the oldest and most damaged; do not cut back the whole plant to soil level annually. Some bamboos flower regularly, some irregularly and some hardly ever, but in all cases, after flowering, cut back the old

Pleioblastus auricomus (Arundinaria viridistriata)

flowered stems. In some species, flowering seems to occur on all shoots at the same time and no leafy shoots are then produced. In such instances, the entire plant will have to be cut back to soil level and may in fact appear dead, but it will usually grow again the following year. While a few bamboos do die after flowering, this does not seem to occur with any of the common hardy types.

COMMON PROBLEMS None.

PROPAGATION Division in autumn or spring; use a spade to sever the roots, which on large plants can be very tough.

TROUBLESHOOTING Not likely to be necessary.

SIZE Varies widely between species; as a guide, although almost all bamboos extend laterally, the less vigorous hardy forms such as the dwarf varieties of *Pleioblastus auricomus* (previously *Arundinaria viridistriata*) will only reach about 75 × 40cm/2½ × 1½ft in three years, whereas the more vigorous species, such as *Drepanostachyum falconeri* (previously *Arundinaria falconeri*), can reach 10m/33ft in height and 2m/6½ft in spread after the same time.

Dwarf conifers

This is a large and heterogeneous group of plants comprising dwarf, or very slow-growing, variants of coniferous trees. They are grown in much the same way as more conventional shrubs and, as a group, are probably the most widely represented shrubs in gardens after roses. Their colours and overall growth habits can be useful in mixed plantings. They are adaptable to a wide range of conditions, although most share one or two drawbacks.

SOIL Most, although best on fairly rich, well-drained soil, preferably slightly acidic; least successful on highly alkaline or heavy waterlogged soils.

SITUATION Full sun or light shade; although some are tolerant of considerable exposure to low temperatures, almost all tend to be browned by cold or salt-laden winds.

WATERING AND FEEDING Mulch in autumn and spring. Apply a balanced general fertilizer in mid-spring.

PRUNING Not necessary, although all may be trimmed lightly in late spring or late summer to maintain a neat appearance. Some prostrate forms occasionally produce upright shoots, and these must be cut out.

COMMON PROBLEMS Red spider mite; cold wind damage; foliage browning from fungal root decay in wet soils.

PROPAGATION Almost impossible to strike from cuttings without a facility for misting.

TROUBLESHOOTING I am persuaded that broken, misshapen, browned or otherwise damaged plants should be replaced as they rarely regenerate and recover their shape satisfactorily.

SIZE Varies greatly with genus and overall habit. There are upright conical, globular, pyramidal or umbrella-shaped varieties, as well as horizontal and truly prostrate types. Read label information carefully and then allow for growth of at least half as much again. Also check if the plant is a genuine dwarf variety or, like the popular Korean fir, *Abies koreana*, merely a slow-growing one that will eventually become a tree.

Juniperus scopulorum 'Skyrocket'

Thuja plicata 'Collyer's Gold'

Juniperus horizontalis

Dwarf conifers

CLIMBERS

Principles of Care

There are few, if any, gardens that are not enhanced by some climbing plants. Not only do they increase the overall growing area, they also cover unsightly walls and other structures that are best concealed. They are in reality simply shrubs with weak stems which have adopted the habit of growing on some form of natural or artificial support, but this lifestyle does impose certain constraints.

SOIL AND SITE REQUIREMENTS

I can perhaps best describe in general terms the soil and site requirements for climbers by saying that the recommendations I make for shrubs apply even more strongly to climbers. Their habit of growing against a vertical support almost invariably means that they will be growing in soil that is drier than that in the open garden. Extra attention must therefore be given to watering and mulching, not only for the general well-being of the plants but also to ensure that there is no premature drop of flowers or fruit.

Where a climber is supported by another plant it will inevitably be competing with its host not only for water but also for nutrients. Compensation must therefore be made by watering regularly in summer and by applying fertilizer assiduously at the suggested times. While I recommend general purpose or rose fertilizers, a liquid feed is also beneficial in cases where the soil is especially dry and a solid formulation would merely lie on the surface.

Aspect is also of particular importance to climbers, especially those grown against walls, for the wall itself will on the one hand afford shelter from cold winds, but on the other cast shade. While a north-facing wall is often considered one of the harshest situations in the garden, in practice far more problems are likely to arise with climbers grown against east-facing walls, where the rapid thawing of frozen tissues early on spring mornings can cause considerable damage. Tender climbing plants will therefore almost always do better on a north-facing than an east-facing aspect.

Climbing plants can be grown in containers in just the same way as other shrubs, but the same constraints apply: they must be grown in a good soil-based compost and kept well watered, mulched and fed. The types of shrub that generally fare least satisfactorily in containers (mainly deep-rooting varieties) will similarly fare badly as their climbing counterparts; roses are the best and most important examples of this. Climbers are generally grown in containers because the ground in the chosen site is paved or otherwise covered. There are few instances, however, where a couple of slabs or a small area of concrete or tarmac can't be removed to allow the plant to be grown directly in the soil.

PRUNING AND SUPPORT

All the general comments that I have made concerning pruning of shrubs (see pages 15–16) are also relevant to climbers, but it is important to bear in mind that if a plant needs heavy pruning to restrict its size it is probably growing in the wrong place. I make a significant distinction between vigorous, straggly climbers that are best grown over a large support such as an old tree or a very large pergola, which need little if any pruning, and the less rampant varieties that, with a modest amount of pruning, can be trained over a small archway or wall-mounted trellis. Trying to grow a vigorous climber such as *Clematis montana* in a confined space, against a house wall for instance, is a recipe for problems, and you can do no better than learn from nature's example and grow them as they grow in the wild – allowing them free rein to scramble over a tree stump, a rock face or even a rough slope.

If a climber can't be pruned because it is too big, too inaccessible or so entangled with another plant that to prune would harm the other, leave well alone. Flowering may in due course be impaired and some dead growth may become apparent, but by removing as much dead material as possible and paying extra attention to feeding and watering you will probably achieve a more satisfactory result in the long term.

There is a widespread tendency among gardeners to use inadequate supports for climbers; trellises are usually far too feebly constructed and poorly fixed, wall nails too small and insufficiently anchored, and even training wires often too thin. Choose trellis that is held together with something rather stronger than tacks, and attach it to wooden battens in order to separate it from the wall surface and so allow the free circulation of air around the plant.

Supporting and training climbers

◀ **USING WIRES** Wires tied tautly between ring-headed screws offer permanent and unobtrusive means of support for climbing plants. The screws should be screwed into purpose-made wall plugs. Tie the plant stems on to the wires as they become robust enough. Either use string tied in a figure-of-eight so that the knot cannot rub the plant stem; or use proprietary metal ties.

▶ **USING TRELLIS** More decorative than wires, trellis is an effective means of support for less robust climbers. Always fix the trellis on to battens, so that it stands away from the wall: this ensures a good flow of air and reduces the chance of disease. Each year at pruning time cut out any shoots that have forced themselves behind the trellis.

▼ **TRAINING PLANTS** If left to themselves, most climbers would bear flowers only at the tips of their shoots. To encourage flowering along the full length of every stem, bend them down horizontally and tie them to the support. Buds will break into growth all along the stem.

Principles of Care

Free-standing structures

TRAINING THE PLANTS Climbing plants grown up pergolas or other free-standing structures need to have their stems trained down nearly horizontally to encourage flowering all along their length. While each shoot is still young and pliable, wind it around the upright and tie it in.

When supporting climbers on wires, choose the plastic-coated wire sold specifically for training (rather than for tying) and attach it to screw-pattern vine eyes plugged into the wall or, if necessary, to straining bolts. Check all the ties by which individual shoots are attached to the supports at least once each year. The girth of the stems of a vigorous climber can increase considerably during the course of a season and the tie that was loose one autumn can become a garotte by the next.

There is one important group of climbing plants, among which ivies are the best known, that require no artificial support for they have self-clinging aerial roots. While it is often said that ivy will damage brickwork, this is true only where bricks are crumbly or mortar is loose, as is often the case on old buildings, but it is worth pointing out that ivy can cause superficial if not structural damage to paint-work such as window frames.

Complaints are sometimes made because newly-planted, self-clinging climbers refuse to climb, but there is nothing abnormal in this and the plants must simply be left to their own devices.

I have mentioned the growing of *Clematis montana* over trees, and this is a perfectly acceptable practice with almost any climber, vigorous or not. But never try to grow a climber over a young, small or feeble tree as the host plant will suffer. As a general rule, a tree or large shrub about 5m/16ft tall will usually be robust enough to support any except the most aggressive of climbers.

Common problems

While climbing plants in general are no more susceptible to pest and disease attack than other plants, again, their habit tends to magnify the problems. The environment close to a wall or other support is not only drier than that in the open, it also tends to be warmer, and while it offers shelter to plants it encourages problems too. Aphids, red spider mite and other pests are often more prevalent, or at least appear rather earlier in the season, in such situations than in the open garden.

Among diseases, powdery mildew is the most common since it is one of the relatively few that require dry, hot conditions for maximum proliferation. As with pests, it tends to be seen on climbers before it appears on plants in more exposed positions, and it may well be that climbers provide a sheltered habitat for mildew and other garden pests and diseases which allows them to survive the winter. The dense foliage of some evergreen climbers, for example, can harbour colonies of snails. On the other hand, because the soil in which climbing plants grow is usually much drier than elsewhere, those root-decaying fungi that thrive in stagnant, waterlogged conditions tend to be less prevalent.

With any climbing or wall-trained plant, it is vital to pay careful and regular attention to ties, not only because of the straightforward injury they may inflict on the plant if they are allowed to get too tight, but also because abrasion of the bark may admit decay or canker-causing fungi that will then spread into healthy tissues.

Actinidia

A genus with two popular and fairly hardy deciduous species, grown for rather different purposes. *A. kolomikta* is an ornamental with appealingly variegated foliage; *A. chinensis* (now sometimes called *A. deliciosa*) is the Chinese gooseberry or kiwi fruit. You will need both male and female plants to effect pollination and fruit production. Although there is now a hermaphrodite form, it has not been available long enough to be assessed properly.

SOIL Moist, fairly rich, intolerant of very dry conditions.

SITUATION South- or south-west-facing wall. The variegation of *A. kolomikta* is not usually apparent on plants under four to five years old, and is best in the early part of the season.

WATERING AND FEEDING Mulch in autumn and spring. Feed with a balanced rose or similar potash-rich fertilizer in mid-spring, and again around midsummer.

PRUNING AND SUPPORT For *A. kolomikta*, no pruning is necessary; train and prune *A. chinensis* as a grapevine. Support by tying to horizontal wires pegged to a wall.

COMMON PROBLEMS None.

PROPAGATION Semi-ripe cuttings in summer.

TROUBLESHOOTING Overgrown and neglected plants will usually regenerate satisfactorily if cut back very hard in spring.

SIZE The species *A. kolomikta* reaches about 1.5 × 1.5m/5 × 5ft after five years, and then rather slowly will ultimately reach about 6 × 6m/20 × 20ft. *A. chinensis* is very vigorous and can reach 15 × 12m/50 × 40ft eventually, although it should never be allowed to attain anything like this potential if pruned annually.

Actinidia kolomikta

Ampelopsis brevipedunculata

Ampelopsis

Some species of *Parthenocissus* are sometimes called *Ampelopsis* but I am restricting this account to *A. brevipedunculata*, a hardy deciduous twining tendril climber, usually with good autumn leaf colour and suitable for sites where its vigour can be allowed free rein.

SOIL Most, provided neither very wet nor very dry.

Ampelopsis – Clematis

SITUATION Best in very light shade; the most widely grown form, the variegated 'Elegans', requires some shelter.

WATERING AND FEEDING Mulch in autumn and spring. Feed with a balanced general fertilizer in mid-spring.

PRUNING AND SUPPORT No pruning is necessary with the green-leaved species, although it can be cut back as necessary in spring to maintain it within bounds. The variegated 'Elegans' performs best when a proportion of the previous season's lateral shoots is cut back each spring, to within two buds of the base. This will produce plenty of young shoots with good leaf variegation. The best support is provided by horizontal wires pegged to a wall, pergola or fence.

COMMON PROBLEMS None.

PROPAGATION Semi-ripe cuttings in summer.

TROUBLESHOOTING Over-vigorous plants will usually regenerate satisfactorily if cut back hard in spring.

SIZE About 1.5 × 1.5m/5 × 5ft after five years, the variegated form eventually attaining about 4 × 4m/13 × 13ft after eighteen or twenty years, and the green-leaved species perhaps twice as much.

Clematis

A genus of twining, deciduous or evergreen plants which comprises the largest and most popular group of flowering climbers, with a very wide range in flower type and considerable variation in vigour. While the soil requirements are fairly constant, some varieties must have shelter. Pruning methods vary but are in essence perfectly logical.

SOIL Tolerates most, but always best in moderately alkaline, rich, deep loam; much less satisfactory in acid or poor soils.

SITUATION Varies; none except the very vigorous forms, such as the varieties derived from *C. montana* or *C. tangutica*, are very wind tolerant; they are easily torn from their supports in windy conditions. The evergreen forms are mostly tender, with the significant exception of the vigorous *C. armandii*, although even this will be ragged without the shelter of a warm wall. Most of the early-flowering, deciduous species also require a warm south- or south-west-facing wall. Many large, single-flowered hybrids give their best flower colour when the head of the plant is in the shade. For this reason, they thrive well on a north-facing wall; as also do the bell-flowered varieties of *C. alpina*. Double- and semi-double-flowered hybrids should have a south- or south-west-facing position. All clematis benefit from having the roots and lower part of the stem shaded.

The vigorous varieties and species are best grown through or over some other vegetation, such as a large old tree or hedge. Only the less vigorous types, including most of the large-flowered hybrids, are really satisfactory trained against a wall. On a wall, trellis raised on battens gives the most effective support.

WATERING AND FEEDING Mulch in autumn and spring. Feed with a balanced rose or other potash-rich fertilizer in mid-spring, and either the same again after midsummer, or give a potash-rich liquid feed every three weeks during the summer.

Planting clematis

PLANT DEEPLY To help clematis establish well, dig a hole much deeper than usual and bury the bottom 15cm/6in of stem below the soil surface. This helps minimize the likelihood of clematis wilt.

Clematis 'Etoile Violette'

PRUNING Clematis are divided into three main groups for pruning purposes, each method of pruning depending entirely on the time of flowering and vigour of the variety.

GROUP 1 These are the evergreen forms and the varieties derived from *C. alpina*, *C. macropetala* and *C. montana*. They all flower early in the year, on the previous year's wood, and pruning comprises the cutting back immediately after flowering of all weak and dead stems to just above a bud. Large, well-established plants growing where they may be allowed free rein (which certainly should mean most specimens of the very vigorous *C. montana* type) need not be pruned.

Pruning clematis, group 1

PRUNE AFTER FLOWERING

The flowers of clematis in this group will all have been borne on growth made in the previous season, so the plant may need a tidy up after flowering to help it to produce plenty of healthy new wood to flower the following year. Therefore where practical, cut back some of the flowered stems to just above a bud. These varieties can be left completely unpruned if space allows.

Old flowered shoots can be left or cut back to a bud

The plant will quickly produce a tangled mass of stems that can be difficult to prune

Clematis

Pruning clematis, group 2

▶ **EARLY SPRING** Clematis in this group produce their flowers on wood made the previous season, but they need to be pruned early in the year, before they flower, to keep them tidy and to encourage new growth. Cut out completely any dead or weak stems. Cut back remaining stems by about 25–30cm/ 10in–1ft, to a strong pair of buds. Although a few buds will be removed by pruning in this way, there will be plenty left to produce flowers.

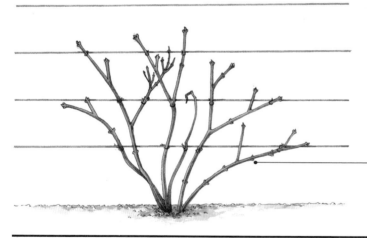

◀ **AFTER PRUNING** The plant will not be significantly reduced in size, but buds all along the stems will now break and flower. New growth should now be produced from the base of the plant.

The buds along the stems should now break

GROUP 2 These also produce their flowers on the previous season's wood, and comprise the early and mid-season single-flowered hybrids, and the double- and semi-double-flowered hybrids. These should be pruned in early spring by cutting out any dead or weak stems and cutting back the remainder by about 25–30cm/10in–1ft, to just above a strong pair of buds. Any remaining dead leaf stalks should be cut away and the stems retied to their supports, allowing plenty of space between each.

GROUP 3 These plants are the varieties of the C. × *jackmanii* type, the late large-flowered hybrids, the varieties derived from C. *viticella* and C. *texensis*, the late-flowering species such as C. *tangutica*, and the so-called herbaceous types. They all flower late in the season on the current year's wood, and their top growth dies back during the winter. Pruning comprises cutting back all of the previous season's growth, in early spring, to just above a pair of strong buds about 75cm/2½ft above soil level.

Pruning clematis, group 3

▲ **EARLY SPRING** The clematis in this group are the most vigorous forms, and require the most drastic pruning. By late winter or early spring, all the top growth will have died off but green buds will be appearing along the stems. Cut the plant back to the lowest strong pair of buds, ideally about 75cm/2½ft above soil level. If left unpruned, group 3 clematis become very untidy indeed, with new growth always at the top of the plant and tangled up with dead stems.

▶ **AFTER PRUNING** The plant will look very insubstantial, but will quickly put on a great deal of top growth again, and will throw up new stems from the base of the plant. If slugs and snails are a problem in your garden, ensure adequate protection while the shoots are developing low down on the stems.

COMMON PROBLEMS Mildew; clematis wilt – plants suddenly die back without warning. If this occurs, immediately cut back to sound wood close to soil level and drench the area with a systemic fungicide. Plants generally recover, but if the effects are repeated, uproot and destroy the plant and before replanting with fresh stock, dig a hole of 30cm/1ft all round and replace the soil with fresh from elsewhere in the garden. Always plant clematis with the bottom 15cm/6in of the stem buried below soil level, to aid new root development (see page 86).

PROPAGATION Softwood cuttings in early summer, cut inter-nodally, is the best method although it is less successful with large-flowered hybrids; layering is also generally satisfactory.

TROUBLESHOOTING Old and overgrown plants can almost always be rejuvenated by cutting them back as hard as desired in early spring. One season's flowers may be lost but there will be ample opportunity to re-establish the correct pruning regime.

Clematis – Lonicera

Hedera colchica 'Sulphur Heart'

SIZE Varies greatly, depending on variety and how assiduously it is pruned. Pruned as I have suggested, and provided that the very vigorous types are not planted against a wall, it should be possible to restrict most varieties to a wall space of between $2 \times 1m/6\frac{1}{2} \times 3ft$ and about $4 \times 4m/13 \times 13ft$. Left to their own devices, the most vigorous forms such as *C. tangutica*, or the varieties of *C. montana*, will cover an old tree of $5 \times 5m/16 \times 16ft$ in about seven years.

Hedera IVY

The ivies, as a group, include some of the best, most reliable and attractive of evergreen climbers; certainly of the evergreen self-clinging climbers. They are grown almost entirely for their foliage appeal and there are now varieties suitable for many different garden purposes.

SOIL Any, although some varieties are difficult to establish and are least successful in very dry soils.

SITUATION Full sun to light or deep shade, depending on variety; the larger-leaved and variegated forms are generally better in full sun. Liable to be browned if exposed to cold winds. In the wild, ivies grow on trees but this is not a practice to be encouraged in gardens. Young trees are likely to suffer adversely from the competition, while older ones may become unstable.

WATERING AND FEEDING Until the plant is well established mulch in autumn and spring, and feed with a balanced general fertilizer in mid-spring.

PRUNING AND SUPPORT No pruning is necessary but ivies may be pruned in spring to maintain a neat appearance. The small-leaved varieties may be trimmed with shears but secateurs should be used on large-leaved forms. Ivies are firmly self-clinging once established, so are best not grown over wooden or other structures of limited durability. They will damage old and crumbly bricks and mortar but are perfectly safe on sound brickwork. When first planted, some ivies fail to climb and no amount of tying up will induce them to do so. After a year or two, however, during which time they form a mound of growth, they begin to climb of their own accord.

COMMON PROBLEMS None.

PROPAGATION Semi-ripe cuttings in summer or from naturally formed layers.

TROUBLESHOOTING Overgrown and neglected plants will usually regenerate satisfactorily if cut back very hard in spring.

SIZE Varies greatly, depending on variety, so check label information carefully. Without pruning, most varieties, certainly most forms of *H. helix*, will reach about $2 \times 2m/6\frac{1}{2} \times 6\frac{1}{2}ft$ after five years, $3–4 \times 3–4m/10–13 \times 10–13ft$ after ten years, and perhaps $8 \times 8m/26 \times 26ft$ after twenty, although the popular 'Goldheart' is rather more vigorous and more upright in habit. The most vigorous ivy that I have grown is the large-leaved *H. canariensis* 'Gloire de Marengo', which reached $6 \times 6m/20 \times 20ft$ after ten years and showed no signs of abating. At the other extreme some of the small-leaved varieties, such as 'Crippsii', will barely reach $2 \times 2m/6\frac{1}{2} \times 6\frac{1}{2}ft$ after fifteen years.

Hydrangea

Although most of the familiar hydrangeas are shrubs, there is one useful self-clinging deciduous climber, *H. petiolaris*, and a few similar plants in the closely related genus *Schizophragma*.

SOIL Rich and moist, at least until plants are well established, but not prone to waterlogging; tolerant of acidity and alkalinity.

SITUATION Full sun to moderate shade; this plant grows very well against a north-facing wall.

WATERING AND FEEDING Mulch in autumn and spring. Feed with a balanced rose or similar potash-rich fertilizer in mid-spring, and again around midsummer.

PRUNING None necessary but prune as hard as desired in spring.

COMMON PROBLEMS None.

PROPAGATION By layering.

TROUBLESHOOTING Old, woody or winter-damaged plants of most varieties will regenerate if cut back hard in spring.

SIZE About 2×2m/$6\frac{1}{2} \times 6\frac{1}{2}$ft after five years, 7×7m/23×23ft after ten years, and maybe $12–14 \times 12–14$m/$40–46 \times 40–46$ft ultimately.

Hydrangea petiolaris

Lonicera HONEYSUCKLE

Although there are some fine shrubby and evergreen species, it is as deciduous or semi-evergreen climbers that the honeysuckles are best known. They have some great merits, most importantly the fine perfume that most possess. Against this must be set the fact that they are rather unkempt plants and never at their best when forced to grow up a trellis on a wall, in limited space.

SOIL Always best in a moist, organic loam and rarely successful in very dry or very wet conditions.

SITUATION Full sun to moderate shade; most climbing honeysuckles are naturally woodland plants.

WATERING AND FEEDING Mulch in autumn and spring. Feed with a balanced rose or similar potash-rich fertilizer in mid-spring, and again around midsummer.

PRUNING AND SUPPORT The best support is provided by an old tree, a large hedge or a large and substantial fence, preferably in wilder, less tidy parts of the garden. Although honeysuckles will thrive and flower without pruning, the vigour of an established plant and its overall appearance will be improved if the oldest one third of the shoots is cut back to soil level every spring.

COMMON PROBLEMS Mildew; aphids.

PROPAGATION Semi-ripe cuttings in summer, but some varieties are notoriously difficult to strike. Layering may be successful.

TROUBLESHOOTING Fairly old and overgrown plants can usually be rejuvenated by cutting them back to soil level in spring, spreading the work over two consecutive springs. Very old plants with a really stout, woody trunk are best replaced.

SIZE Varies considerably, depending on variety. As a guide, forms of the common *L. periclymenum* will reach about 2×2m/$6\frac{1}{2} \times 6\frac{1}{2}$ft after five years, 4×4m/13×13ft after ten years and perhaps 6×6m/20×20ft eventually. Most other species are rather less vigorous, although *L. tragophylla* may reach twice this size.

Lonicera periclymenum

Parthenocissus – Rosa

Parthenocissus tricuspidata

Parthenocissus VIRGINIA CREEPER

This group of invaluable deciduous climbers has suffered a fair number of name changes over the years, some species being assigned to *Vitis* and others to *Ampelopsis*. But most are known collectively by the common name of Virginia creeper.

SOIL Most, but least successful where very dry.

SITUATION Full sun to light shade.

WATERING AND FEEDING Mulch in autumn and spring. Apply a balanced general fertilizer in mid-spring and in midsummer.

PRUNING AND SUPPORT The most popular species, *P. tricuspidata*, is self-clinging but, like ivies, should not be planted against unsound brickwork. *P. henryana* and *P. quinquefolia* require support on wires at least when young, while *P. inserta* will require wire support permanently. No pruning is necessary but all species may be clipped in spring or summer to keep them within bounds.

COMMON PROBLEMS None.

PROPAGATION Semi-ripe cuttings in summer or by layering.

TROUBLESHOOTING Plants that have outgrown their allotted space may be cut back hard and will rejuvenate satisfactorily. If necessary, plants may also be cut back to soil level in spring and will regrow, although the work is best spread over two years.

SIZE Early establishment may be slow but all forms should reach $2 \times 2m/6\frac{1}{2} \times 6\frac{1}{2}ft$ after five years, $5 \times 5m/16 \times 16ft$ after ten years and $10 \times 10m/33 \times 33ft$ after twenty years.

Passiflora PASSION FLOWER

There can be few plants as compelling in bloom as the exotic and bizarre passion flower. Its hardiness is reliable only in milder areas or sheltered corners, however.

SOIL Most, but least successful where very dry or very alkaline.

SITUATION Full sun to light shade; in cold and frost-prone areas, it must be grown against a warm south- or south-west-facing wall. Passion flowers usually flower best when their roots are confined to an area of about $45 \times 45cm/1\frac{1}{2} \times 1\frac{1}{2}ft$ by paving slabs sunk vertically in the soil to create a bottomless pit.

WATERING AND FEEDING Mulch in autumn and spring. Feed with a balanced rose or similar potash-rich fertilizer in mid-spring, and again around midsummer.

PRUNING AND SUPPORT Best trained loosely against horizontal wires. No pruning is necessary to encourage flowering but there will almost inevitably be some shoot death from frost damage; such dead or damaged growth should be cut back to within 60cm/2ft of soil level in spring.

COMMON PROBLEMS Apart from frost, virus often causes leaf crumpling; various insects may tatter the leaves.

PROPAGATION Semi-ripe cuttings in summer.

TROUBLESHOOTING Plants that have outgrown their allotted space may be cut back hard to soil level and will usually rejuvenate.

SIZE Up to $2-3 \times 2-3m/6\frac{1}{2}-10 \times 6\frac{1}{2}-10ft$ after five years and $6-7 \times 6-7m/20-23 \times 20-23ft$ in mild areas after fifteen or eighteen years.

Passiflora caerulea

Rosa ROSE

There are climbing forms of most of the roses also grown as bushes, and they have much of their cultivation in common. Additionally, there are a few roses derived from species that exist only in a climbing or scrambling form.

SOIL Although tolerant of a wide range of soil types, climbing roses – like bush roses – will always be most successful in a rich, moisture-retentive soil, but this could range from an organic loam to a heavy clay. Light soils will produce good roses provided large quantities of organic matter are incorporated; this is especially important for climbing roses, which tend to be grown in places that are inherently very dry, such as close to walls or other supports. Roses are least successful on very acidic soils, while in very alkaline conditions they may suffer from severe leaf chlorosis.

SITUATION Full sun or light shade. Some varieties in almost all groups of climbing roses are successful in deeper shade, while some, most notably the tea roses and some of the less common species, are more tender and require shelter from cold winds.

WATERING AND FEEDING Mulch in autumn and spring; mulching and watering is especially important for climbing roses. Feed with a balanced rose or similar potash-rich fertilizer in mid-spring, and again after midsummer.

PRUNING CLIMBERS These require much less pruning than their bush counterparts and, in general, pruning in autumn should comprise the shortening of any very long and whippy shoots followed, in spring, by the cutting out of dead or diseased stems and light cutting back of the tips of old flowered shoots. Pruning of the very vigorous near-species, such as *R. filipes* 'Kiftsgate', will quickly become impractical.

Some varieties of climbing rose, especially certain climbing hybrid teas, develop a permanent framework of stems that produces each year a regular pattern of side-shoots on which the flowers are borne. These side-shoots, once flowered, should be cut back in the spring of the following year to within 5cm/2in of their junction with the main stems.

RAMBLERS True rambling roses are pruned differently for, instead of bearing their flowers on side-shoots from a permanent framework, most produce long new shoots each year on which the flowers are borne, and once those flowers have faded, these shoots will not flower again and are of no further use. The precise method of pruning varies between varieties, but as so few different types of rambler are now grown (they are very prone to mildew and flower once only in early summer), I will restrict this description to the commonest of those still found. On large old plants of 'Dorothy Perkins' or 'American Pillar', cut all flowered stems back to soil level after flowering. On younger plants, cut back flowered side-shoots to within about 10cm/4in of their junction with main stems. On 'Albertine', 'Albéric Barbier', 'Pink Perpétué' and 'New Dawn', cut back up to one third of the old flowered stems to soil level after flowering, and cut back the flowered side-shoots on the remainder to within about 10cm/4in of their junction with the main stems.

Rosa – Solanum

Pruning climbing roses

▶ **SPRING** Identify the permanent framework of stems which each year produce side-shoots on which flowers are borne. The permanent stems should be tied down horizontally, with all the flowering side-shoots growing vertically. Each spring, any weak or diseased main stems should be cut out but on a healthy, established rose, no main stems at all need be cut. Then cut back all the side-shoots hard, to a bud within 5cm/2in of the junction with the main stems.

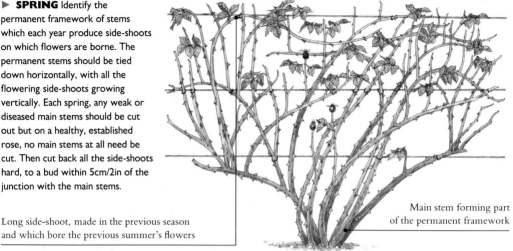

Long side-shoot, made in the previous season and which bore the previous summer's flowers

Main stem forming part of the permanent framework

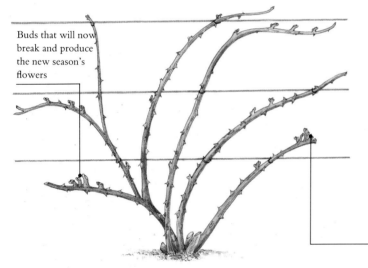

Buds that will now break and produce the new season's flowers

◀ **AFTER PRUNING** Re-tie all the main stems that remain, pulling them down to the horizontal and ensuring that the ties are quite loose and will not chafe the stems. New side-shoots will now develop from this permanent framework, to flower later in the year. In the autumn, tip back any excessively long side-shoots to avoid wind damage during the winter.

Stubs of previous year's side-shoots

COMMON PROBLEMS Aphids; mildew (especially important on climbers and ramblers); black spot; rust.

PROPAGATION Hardwood cuttings in early winter, although these are often very difficult to strike from climbing hybrid teas and floribundas.

TROUBLESHOOTING Old and overgrown plants can often be rejuvenated by cutting back the shoots to just above soil level in spring, spreading the work over three years so that no more than one third of the shoots is cut out at any one time. Although there are some notable and fine very old rose specimens, generally they have been tended throughout their lives, and my feeling is that a neglected rose more than eight or ten years old is best replaced.

The commonest problem with climbing roses is that all of the flowers are borne at the top of the plant. This is remedied very easily by pulling down the vertical shoots and tying them horizontally to cover the wall or other support. Buds will then break along the whole length of the stem. As with bush forms, most climbing roses are grafted on to rootstocks of different varieties, chosen for their rooting rather than their flowering attributes. Suckers may arise and must be pulled away promptly.

SIZE Enormously variable so it is important to check label descriptions. The shortest-growing climbers, commonly called pillar roses, will not attain a height of much more than 2m/6½ft. The majority of modern climbers will reach about 5m/16ft but some of the older varieties and some of the species are very much more vigorous and can attain as much as 15m/50ft.

Solanum

The climbing solanums are deciduous or semi-evergreen relatives of the potato, and immediately recognizable as such from the form of their flowers. They are vigorous, but reliably hardy only in milder areas. *S. crispum*, the so-called climbing potato, tends to grow more in the form of a lax shrub but I find it is better treated as a climber.

Solanum crispum 'Glasnevin'

SOIL Most, but least successful where very dry.

SITUATION Full sun to light shade, and always best against a warm south- or south-west-facing wall.

WATERING AND FEEDING Mulch in autumn and spring. Feed with a balanced rose or similar potash-rich fertilizer in mid-spring, and again around midsummer.

Solanum – Vitis

Tropaeolum speciosum

PRUNING AND SUPPORT Best trained loosely against horizontal wires. Solanum is very free-flowering but rather ungainly in its growth habit, so annual pruning is necessary each spring to keep it compact and tidy. Cut out completely one or two of the oldest stems, to a vigorous young shoot. Cut back very straggly or overlong stems, and stems growing forwards away from the wall, to a junction with strong young growth. Tie in all new shoots.

COMMON PROBLEMS None.

PROPAGATION Semi-ripe cuttings in early summer.

TROUBLESHOOTING Plants that have outgrown their allotted space may be cut back hard, and will usually rejuvenate.

SIZE Varies slightly between species, the more shrubby *S. crispum* generally being rather less vigorous than *S. jasminoides*, which will reach $2 \times 2m/6\frac{1}{2} \times 6\frac{1}{2}ft$ after five years, and perhaps $5 \times 5m/16 \times 16ft$ after twenty years.

Tropaeolum

Perhaps best known in the form of the species grown as annuals – the nasturtium and the canary creeper. But there are related and valuable perennial climbing species too, most notably the orange-yellow *T. tuberosum* and the more hardy, scarlet-flowered *T. speciosum*, the Scots or Chilean flame flower. The latter's common names betray its fondness for a mild, moist climate.

SOIL Tolerates a wide range but must be free-draining yet moist and preferably organic; intolerant of alkalinity.

SITUATION Full sun to light shade with shelter from cold winds; preferably sited so that its roots are in shade.

WATERING AND FEEDING Mulch in autumn and spring. Feed with a balanced rose or similar potash-rich fertilizer in mid-spring, and again around midsummer.

PRUNING AND SUPPORT No pruning is needed as the growth above ground dies down in the winter. They are best allowed free rein over some natural support such as a large evergreen hedge or coniferous tree.

COMMON PROBLEMS None.

PROPAGATION Basal cuttings in spring: take a non-flowering shoot from the base of the plant, or even just below ground level.

TROUBLESHOOTING Unlikely to be necessary.

SIZE Will attain an annual height of about 3m/10ft after four or five years, and a similar spread depending on the support.

Vitis VINE

The best known and most important species of *Vitis* is the grape-vine, although there are one or two ornamental species also, most notably the large-leaved *V. coignetiae*.

SOIL Most, but least successful where very dry or waterlogged.

SITUATION Full sun to light shade, but in northern areas it always grows best, and grape production is always better, against a warm south- or south-west-facing wall.

WATERING AND FEEDING Mulch in autumn and spring. Feed with a balanced rose or similar potash-rich fertilizer in mid-spring,

Regular annual pruning of outdoor vines

▶ **WINTER** Once the basic fan framework of the vine is established (see page 98), prune in winter to remove all of the previous season's growth: cut back all the extension growth on the main stems or rods to a strong pair of buds; and cut back the strongest side-shoots to two buds from their junction with the main rod.

Last season's extension growth, to be cut back completely

Main stem or rod

Side-shoot, to be removed

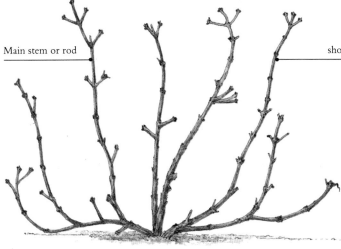

Main stem or rod

Buds will break to become side-shoots: these should be thinned out in spring

◀ **AFTER PRUNING** The basic framework of stems or rods will now be clear. Further pruning is required in spring: thin out the side-shoots as they elongate to leave one for every 45cm/1½ft of rod length. Tie the side-shoots to the wires.

and again around midsummer. Fruiting vines benefit from considerable additional watering when in fruit.

PRUNING AND SUPPORT Although fruit of sorts will be produced with little or no pruning, the fruiting varieties soon become an unkempt mess and both for the best appearance and best crop, it is worth taking a little care to train and prune vines correctly. In northern climates it isn't really worthwhile taking the pruning to the lengths adopted for a greenhouse vine, as the outdoor crop will always be a poor relation of that under glass. This is one pruning regime among many based on the principle of encouraging fruit-bearing wood to grow on stems one year old; sometimes those stems may be reduced to a spur.

Vitis – Wisteria

Vitis coignetiae

In the first season after planting, loosely tie in all shoots to a system of horizontal support wires. In the following winter, select the strongest two or three of these shoots, cut them back by about half, spread them so they are spaced more or less equidistantly, and tie them to the support wires in a fan pattern. These will form the main stems or rods of the vine and each season's extension growth on them should be cut back by about half each winter until they are as long as space allows. Thereafter all the extension growth should be cut back each time.

Also each winter, cut back side-shoots to two buds from their bases. In the spring, after the side-shoots have begun to elongate, prune to leave one side-shoot for every 45cm/1½ft of rod length, tie them to the support wires and pinch out the tips when they have reached their allotted length. Thereafter, every winter, cut back these side-shoots to two buds from the base, and every spring thin out the side-shoots as before.

The ornamental fruiting vine, *V.* 'Brant', should be treated in exactly the same way.

The foliage ornamental *V. coignetiae* may also be pruned in this way for the neatest effect, but it may equally be allowed to ramble, unpruned, over an archway, pergola or similar support, if space permits.

COMMON PROBLEMS Mildew; grey mould on fruit.

PROPAGATION Semi-ripe cuttings in early summer; the best results are usually obtained from 'eyes', 2.5–4cm/1–1½in-long cuttings taken to include a node with buds.

TROUBLESHOOTING Provided they are not very old and woody, plants that have outgrown their allotted space may be cut back hard to soil level and will usually rejuvenate satisfactorily.

SIZE Vines really should be pruned to keep them within an allotted space, and a wall area of about 3–4 × 2–3m/10–13 × 6½–10ft should be manageable. Unpruned, a grapevine will reach about 3 × 3m/10 × 10ft in five years, 6 × 6m/20 × 20ft after ten years, and perhaps 10 × 10m/33 × 33ft ultimately. The ornamental *V. coignetiae* will grow faster and larger than a fruiting vine, probably by about half as much again.

Wisteria

Sometimes called the queen of climbers, the deciduous wisteria is a fine and very hardy flowering plant, but it is also a vigorous one and must be allowed space to grow. It is usually grown against a wall, but can be trained as a standard around a central support.

SOIL Most, provided there is adequate rooting depth; dryness is tolerated once the roots are well established.

SITUATION Full sun to moderate shade; although flowering is undoubtedly best on a south- or south-west-facing wall, I have a very successful and free-flowering old plant facing north-east.

WATERING AND FEEDING Until well established and preferably permanently. Mulch in autumn and spring. Feed with a balanced rose or similar potash-rich fertilizer in mid-spring, and again around midsummer. Contrary to some advice, wisteria will not flower better if starved.

Regular annual pruning of established wisteria

AFTER PRUNING, WINTER
Wisterias are vigorous and should be pruned hard in winter. Identify the stems which make up the permanent framework, and the side-shoots that flowered the previous season. Cut back all these side-shoots to three buds from their junction with the main stems (see inset, above). The plant will be much reduced in bulk, but will produce plenty of shoot growth for pruning in the summer (see text).

PRUNING AND SUPPORT A very stout system of support wires will be required initially. Thereafter, mature wisteria stems are best supported by being tied carefully and individually to stout vine-eyes or similar supports pegged to the wall. In the first season after planting, loosely tie in all shoots to the support wires. In the following winter, select three to five shoots to form the main framework of the plant (depending on space available), cut them back by about half, spread them so they are spaced more or less equidistantly, and tie them to the support wires. Thereafter, each summer cut back all long, whippy side-shoots to about 25cm/10in in length, except for any that you require to fill in gaps in the main framework. In the following winter, cut these shortened shoots back further to three buds from the base. But no matter how careful your pruning, a wisteria is unlikely to flower in under five to seven years.

COMMON PROBLEMS None.

PROPAGATION By layering or by semi-ripe cuttings taken in late summer.

TROUBLESHOOTING Should not be necessary but established wisterias are all but indestructible, and damaged or overgrown plants may be cut back very hard into old wood, in spring, and will regenerate.

SIZE Without pruning, will reach about 5 × 5m/16 × 16ft after five years, 10–12 × 10–12m/33–40 × 33–40ft after ten years, and up to 20 × 20m/65 × 65ft ultimately.

PERENNIALS

Acanthus	Kniphofia
Achillea	Lamium
Aconitum	Ligularia
Alcea	Limonium
Alchemilla	Lobelia
Anemone	Lupinus
Anthemis	Lychnis
Aquilegia	Meconopsis
Artemisia	Mentha
Aster	Nepeta
Astilbe	Oenothera
Astrantia	Omphalodes
Bellis	Paeonia
Bergenia	Papaver
Campanula	Penstemon
Centranthus	Perovskia
Chrysanthemum	Phlox
Coreopsis	Phormium
Delphinium	Platycodon
Dicentra	Polygonatum
Digitalis	Polygonum
Doronicum	Pulmonaria
Echinacea	Ranunculus
Echinops	Romneya
Epimedium	Rudbeckia
Eryngium	Ruta
Erysimum	Salvia
Euphorbia	Sanguinaria
Geranium	Stachys
Geum	Thalictrum
Gypsophila	Verbascum
Helenium	Veronica
Helleborus	Yucca
Hemerocallis	Ferns
Heuchera	Grasses
Hosta	Sedges and rushes

Principles of care

Herbaceous perennials are ornamental plants that have no above-ground woody framework and, with a few exceptions, die down at the end of the growing season to survive as an underground rootstock; they are generally differentiated from so-called bulbous plants (see pages 142–65) by the absence of any swollen, food storage structure. They were once grown exclusively in herbaceous borders but are now more commonly used in combination with shrubs in mixed plantings, the shrubs providing a permanent framework after the perennials have died down; or occasionally the more 'architectural' species might be grown as isolated specimens. Most herbaceous perennials (and certainly the taller types) are unsuitable subjects for growing in containers.

SOIL AND SITE REQUIREMENTS

There are species and varieties suitable for all types of soil and the commonest causes of failure are inappropriate soil or site conditions. Few herbaceous perennials will tolerate more than light shade, and among those few it is important to distinguish between the species that are tolerant of dry shade and those that must have moisture.

FEEDING AND WATERING

Herbaceous perennials need to be fed, certainly once and preferably twice each year, with a balanced general purpose fertilizer if they are to give of their best. Very vigorous or fast-growing types will also benefit from a foliar application of liquid fertilizer during the summer months, although I don't consider this essential and have not included it in my advice on individual species. Few types are well adapted to

Providing wrap-around support

▲ **SPRING** As growth appears, push three to five canes into the ground around the plant and tie string loosely around, keeping the top string below the top of the leaves. Ideally, start with short canes, and exchange them for progressively longer ones as the plant grows up.

▶ **2. SUMMER** Add more string to keep the plant well supported; its leaves will soon conceal the string and canes.

very dry soils and almost all will therefore benefit from the application of a moisture-retaining mulch in spring. If organic mulching material is in short supply it may be confined to the area around the root crown of each plant but, ideally, the soil surface over the entire bed should be mulched to improve root growth and limit water loss by evaporation.

In very dry seasons it may be necessary to use hoses or sprinklers (if permitted), but if the plants need regular watering even in the course of a normal summer it generally means that they have not been chosen correctly for the soil conditions, or perhaps have been inadequately mulched in advance.

GENERAL MANAGEMENT

Most perennials require cutting down to soil level at the end of the growing season, but for all but the very hardiest varieties this operation is better left until the spring in areas subject to cold winters. The dead shoot growth will provide some protection against penetrating frost, and any seed-heads will offer food for birds. Additional protection can be provided by an autumn organic mulch mounded around the root crowns. In the case of the relatively small number of evergreen perennials, dead leaves should be cut away but under no circumstances should the plant be cut back to ground level.

The majority of perennials require staking, although the trend in recent years has been towards lower-growing varieties with stiffer, more self-supporting stems. Staking can be by means of individual (and preferably unobtrusive) canes, or by a wrap-around support in which the entire clump is more loosely confined: canes and string are the cheapest but most fiddly method, interlocking metal stakes the most elegant.

PROPAGATION

Almost all types of perennial benefit from being lifted and divided every few years, the frequency of this operation varying with the vigour of the variety and, to a lesser extent, the growing conditions. Division is also the most reliable method of propagation, although a considerable number of perennials (especially the true species) can be propagated from seed; for others softwood cuttings are the best method. The many varieties with fully double flowers produce no seed and can only, therefore, be multiplied by division.

Acanthus BEAR'S BREECHES

A small genus of large, rather glossy and prickly-leaved, semi-evergreen plants with tall spikes of white, pinkish or mauve flowers. *A. mollis* is the commonest species, but *A. spinosus* is more stately. Bear's breeches are usually grown at the back of borders large enough to accommodate their rather gaunt appearance, and although they are hardly graceful plants, they are usefully large, easy to grow and invariably cause comment.

SOIL Deep, rich, preferably well drained.

SITUATION Always performs best in full sun, although will also tolerate light shade.

WATERING AND FEEDING Mulch in autumn and spring. Feed with a balanced general purpose fertilizer in mid-spring and again around midsummer.

MANAGEMENT Cut back dead flower spikes after flowering. In winter in colder areas, the crowns may need mulch protection. Little staking is necessary.

COMMON PROBLEMS None.

PROPAGATION Division in autumn or spring but root cuttings in winter are better; can be grown from seed.

TROUBLESHOOTING None necessary.

SIZE Reaches 1–1.5m × 50cm/3–5 × 1½ft in three years.

Acanthus mollis

Achillea – Alchemilla

Achillea filipendulina

Achillea YARROW

A rather large genus of semi-evergreen, rather stiff-stemmed hardy perennials. Perhaps the most familiar and most invasive is *A. millefolium*, the weed yarrow, but there are several useful and versatile, if unexciting, medium-sized border perennials, such as *A. filipendulina*, with white, yellow or pinkish flower heads.

SOIL Light, preferably fertile soil, but tolerant of fairly thin, poor and alkaline conditions.

SITUATION Always performs best in full sun, although will also tolerate light shade.

WATERING AND FEEDING Mulch in autumn and spring. Feed with a balanced general purpose fertilizer in mid-spring and again around midsummer.

MANAGEMENT Cut back dead flower spikes after flowering; only taller forms require staking.

COMMON PROBLEMS None.

PROPAGATION Basal cuttings in spring or early summer, or division in autumn or spring.

TROUBLESHOOTING None necessary.

SIZE Varies with variety; taller forms such as *A. filipendulina* 'Gold Plate' reaches 1.5m × 50cm/5 × 1½ft in three years, but many others, such as the newer German hybrids, will not exceed 60 × 30cm/2 × 1ft.

Aconitum MONKSHOOD

Deciduous perennials with characteristically hooded flowers in shades of blue or white. The roots are poisonous and the plants rather sinister in appearance, but because they are easy to grow and relatively trouble free – qualities that are ever more valuable in the modern garden – I am convinced that this is one of the herbaceous genera most likely to stage a comeback.

SOIL Moist, well drained, rich, organic, intolerant of light or poor soils or of waterlogging.

SITUATION Full sun or light shade.

WATERING AND FEEDING Mulch in autumn and spring. Feed with a balanced general purpose fertilizer in mid-spring and again around midsummer. It is very important not to allow the soil to dry out in summer.

MANAGEMENT Thin out the flower spikes in spring to leave five or six per mature plant, then cut back dead flower spikes after flowering; only taller forms require staking. *A. volubile* (now *A. hemsleyanum*) is a scrambling plant, best grown in wilder parts of the garden and allowed to grow over and through shrubs.

COMMON PROBLEMS None.

PROPAGATION Division in spring, some forms from seed.

TROUBLESHOOTING None necessary.

SIZE Varies considerably between species and varieties. Among the commoner forms, the scrambling *A. volubile* will attain 2.5 × 1.5m/8 × 5ft after about four years; most others, including *A.* 'Ivorine' and *A. carmichaelii* 'Arendsii', will reach about 1.5m × 50cm/5 × 1½ft, but there are also dwarf rock garden forms.

Aconitum napellus

Alcea HOLLYHOCK

Familiar garden plants for many years, hollyhocks have come to be identified with the cottage style of garden. Most are actually biennial, although some are short-lived perennials; but all grow so large that they are more conveniently considered with other herbaceous perennials. Rust disease can be a very serious problem on hollyhocks in many gardens.

SOIL Well drained, fairly rich; hollyhocks are tolerant of some dryness and are successful when grown close to walls, but they are intolerant of wet, heavy soils.

SITUATION Full sun or very light shade.

WATERING AND FEEDING Mulch in autumn and spring. Feed with a balanced general purpose fertilizer in mid-spring, and again around midsummer, or apply a liquid fertilizer high in potash at three-week intervals during rapid growth in summer.

MANAGEMENT Cut off dead flower spikes after flowering; pull away lower leaves if they show signs of rust early in the season, as it is from these that the disease spreads up the plant. Collect and destroy old foliage in autumn to lessen the amount of disease surviving the winter.

COMMON PROBLEMS Rust; whitefly.

PROPAGATION Only possible from seed.

TROUBLESHOOTING If individual plants become severely affected by rust, destroy them before the disease spreads to others.

SIZE The best and most common forms, including the popular biennial *A. rosea* 'Chater's Double', will reach about 2–2.5m × 60cm/6½–8 × 2ft by flowering time in the second year.

Alcea rosea

Alchemilla LADY'S MANTLE

Deciduous but nonetheless one of the most useful and pretty of all ground-cover plants, extremely easy to grow and tolerant of a wide range of conditions. The lady's mantles self-seed freely, and seedlings may need to be removed where not wanted.

SOIL Most, but least successful in very dry or very wet conditions, and best in deep rich loams.

SITUATION Full sun to moderate shade.

WATERING AND FEEDING Mulch in spring before the foliage emerges (mulching in autumn is not really practical because of the ground-covering leaves). Feed with a balanced general purpose fertilizer in mid-spring. Where space is not restricted and growth need not be curtailed, a second feed after midsummer can usefully be applied.

MANAGEMENT In late autumn or early winter cut back foliage with shears once it has died down and browned.

COMMON PROBLEMS None.

PROPAGATION Division in spring or autumn, or by the many self-sown seedlings.

TROUBLESHOOTING Not likely to be necessary.

SIZE The common form, *A. mollis*, will attain 50 × 50cm/1½ × 1½ft after two years; the less vigorous *A. alpina* will spread to a similar size, but only attain half the height.

Alchemilla mollis

Anemone

Anemone × hybrida

There are several quite distinct sub-groups in the genus *Anemone* (see also page 147) and the most useful border plant is that generally known as the Japanese anemone, *A. × hybrida*. Its white or pink flowers are among the delights of the garden in late summer but the plant is almost too easy to grow and its invasive nature requires watching.

SOIL Almost any, tolerant of fairly wet and fairly dry conditions and also of moderate acidity and alkalinity.

SITUATION Full sun to light shade.

WATERING AND FEEDING Mulch in autumn and spring. Feed with a balanced general purpose fertilizer in mid-spring and again around midsummer.

MANAGEMENT Cut back dead flower stems after flowering and cut foliage back to soil level as soon as it browns with frost. In mild winters, the foliage will persist for several months. The plants do not require staking. Where Japanese anemones threaten to become invasive they are best divided every three years; but on the whole they dislike disturbance, and in a semi-wild situation can be allowed free rein.

COMMON PROBLEMS None.

PROPAGATION Division in autumn or spring.

TROUBLESHOOTING None necessary.

SIZE Will reach 1–1.5m × 50–60cm/3–5 × 1½–2ft in three years, depending on the growing conditions.

Anthemis

This is a genus of feathery-foliaged, evergreen, ground-covering plants, of which the most common and important is the herb camomile (now known as *Chamaemelum*): in its flowering forms it is sometimes grown for culinary use or at the front of the border, but in its non-flowering form, *C. nobile* 'Treneague', is used for small, ornamental lawns.

SOIL Free-draining, fairly rich, light; will fail miserably on cold or wet soils.

SITUATION Full sun to very light shade; camomile lawns will succeed only in full sun and with shelter from cold winds.

WATERING AND FEEDING Mulching is seldom practicable (and certainly not on ornamental lawns) because of the close mat of foliage, so assiduous watering is essential, especially during dry spells in spring. Feed with a balanced general purpose fertilizer in mid-spring and apply liquid feed during the summer.

MANAGEMENT Little attention is needed on flowering forms other than lightly trimming the plants back in spring. Camomile lawns should be trimmed very lightly in summer with shears or with a rotary lawn mower with the blades set high. Weed control (including the control of grasses) is important, but must be done by hand.

COMMON PROBLEMS None.

PROPAGATION Basal cuttings in early summer, or some forms from seed.

Chamaemelum nobile 'Flore Pleno'

TROUBLESHOOTING Not likely to be necessary; camomile will suffer if the growing conditions are unsuitable, and in such circumstances there is no point in persevering. Camomile lawns will not take heavy wear.

SIZE Individual plants will attain 10 × 45cm/4 × 18in in two years; for lawns, they should be spaced 20cm/8in apart.

Aquilegia COLUMBINE

Hardy, deciduous, spring-flowering border plants, among my personal favourites for their easy maintenance. The older forms are indispensable cottage garden plants, and although they tend to be short-lived, they easily self-seed and spread.

SOIL Most, equally successful on light and heavy soil provided it is not seriously waterlogged.

SITUATION Full sun to moderate shade; I grow the old 'granny's bonnet' varieties (*A. vulgaris*) very successfully under trees.

WATERING AND FEEDING Mulch in autumn and spring. Feed with a balanced general purpose fertilizer in mid-spring and again after midsummer.

MANAGEMENT Cut back dead flower heads after flowering and before the seed is shed; divide every three years or, if mixed colour varieties are being grown, simply discard old plants and make use of self-sown seedlings. If rain or wind make the taller forms flop, light staking will keep them tidy.

COMMON PROBLEMS Aphids; mildew.

PROPAGATION See above. Can be grown from seed.

TROUBLESHOOTING Not likely to be necessary.

SIZE Most of the commoner border varieties, including *A. vulgaris*, will attain 1m × 50cm/3 × 1½ft after two years.

Aquilegia vulgaris

Artemisia 'Powis Castle'

Artemisia

More or less hardy clump-forming plants, most with greyish or silvery evergreen foliage and usually grown to provide contrast with other, grander plants. Like so many silver-leaved species, they are only really successful when conditions are similar to those in Mediterranean gardens. Although this is a fairly large genus, with some dwarf alpine species, most of the common border types can be divided into the more herbaceous, clump-forming varieties, and the larger, more woody, semi-shrub forms.

SOIL Light, free-draining, successful in alkaline conditions.

SITUATION Full sun to very light shade.

WATERING AND FEEDING Mulch in autumn and spring. Feed with a balanced general purpose fertilizer in mid-spring and again after midsummer.

MANAGEMENT Trim lightly in spring; divide every three or four years in spring.

COMMON PROBLEMS None.

PROPAGATION Basal cuttings in early summer, or by division of fairly young plants in spring. Old plants develop very woody, hard clumps that are difficult to divide.

TROUBLESHOOTING Not likely to be necessary; old and woody plants can be cut hard back to soil level in spring and will often rejuvenate, but they are best discarded and replaced.

SIZE Most of the commoner border varieties, including the popular *A. absinthium* 'Lambrook Silver', will reach about 80 × 50cm/ 2½ × 1½ft in three years; the more shrubby forms, including *A.* 'Powis Castle', will reach about 1 × 1m/3 × 3ft in the same time.

Aster MICHAELMAS DAISY

Not to be confused with the annual bedding asters in the genus *Callistephus*, this is the genus of Michaelmas daisies, among the most dependable of border perennials for the autumn. Select varieties that have some resistance to mildew.

SOIL Almost any, provided it is not very heavy or waterlogged.

SITUATION Full sun to light or partial shade.

WATERING AND FEEDING Mulch in autumn and spring. Feed with a balanced general purpose fertilizer in mid-spring and again after midsummer.

MANAGEMENT Cut back to soil level after flowering. Taller varieties will need some wrap-around support. Divide every four or five years.

COMMON PROBLEMS Mildew, best avoided by not growing the *A. novi-belgii* varieties.

PROPAGATION Division in spring or autumn, or from basal cuttings in spring.

TROUBLESHOOTING Not likely to be necessary; old and very woody plants are best discarded.

SIZE The taller-growing forms of *A. novae-angliae* will reach about 75–90 × 60cm/2½–3 × 2ft in two or three years. The dwarf *A.* × *thompsonii* 'Nanus' will only reach about 50 × 50cm/1½ × 1½ft in the same time.

Aster novae-angliae

Astilbe

The feathery-flowered hardy astilbes are among the more instantly recognizable herbaceous perennials. They are colourful, sometimes too colourful, and very easy to grow – provided you appreciate that they are demanding in their site requirements.

SOIL Moist and rich; these are really plants for the water garden, and whilst they will succeed in a normal border, they must be grown in rich soil that is never allowed to dry out.

SITUATION Will tolerate full sun and also moderate shade but I find them best in light shade.

WATERING AND FEEDING Mulch in autumn and spring. Feed with a balanced general purpose fertilizer in mid-spring and again after midsummer. If grown as a border plant, water in dry spells.

MANAGEMENT Leave dead flower spikes to provide interest during the winter and then cut back in spring. Disturb and divide as infrequently as possible – they can be difficult to re-establish.

COMMON PROBLEMS None.

PROPAGATION Division in autumn or spring; the species may be grown from seed.

TROUBLESHOOTING Not likely to be necessary.

SIZE Apart from a few, less common, dwarf forms, will reach about 1 × 1m/3 × 3ft in three years.

Astilbe × arendsii

Astrantia MASTERWORT

Never distinguished but always interesting, always easy and, I think, among the prettiest of hardy deciduous perennials.

SOIL Tolerates most, provided not subject to waterlogging; successful in relatively poor soils, although they will require some additional feeding.

SITUATION Tolerates full sun but performs best in light to moderate shade.

WATERING AND FEEDING Mulch in autumn and spring. Feed with a balanced general purpose fertilizer in mid-spring and again after midsummer.

MANAGEMENT Leave dead flower spikes until well into the autumn to provide interest and then cut back to soil level. Divide in spring every four or five years.

COMMON PROBLEMS None.

PROPAGATION Division in autumn or spring, or from seed.

TROUBLESHOOTING Not likely to be necessary.

SIZE Reaches 75 × 45cm/2½ × 1½ft in three years.

Bellis DAISY

For many gardeners, the genus *Bellis* is the daisy that they eradicate from their lawns, but it has attractive relatives that make cheerful clump-forming, extremely hardy perennials – some commonly grown as biennials.

SOIL Any, but least successful in highly acid soils.

SITUATION Full sun to moderate shade; fully hardy and tolerant of cold winds.

Astrantia major

Bellis – Centranthus

Bellis perennis

WATERING AND FEEDING Mulch in autumn and spring. Feed with a balanced general purpose fertilizer in mid-spring and again after midsummer.

MANAGEMENT Deadhead regularly during the summer; divide every four or five years.

COMMON PROBLEMS None.

PROPAGATION Division in autumn or spring, or from seed.

TROUBLESHOOTING Not likely to be necessary.

SIZE Reaches 20 × 20cm/8 × 8in in two years, and if grown as perennials will slowly spread by about 10cm/4in per year.

Bergenia

If your requirement is for a hardy, evergreen, ground-cover perennial with large leaves and good, if not spectacular, flowers, then bergenias are for you. And especially so if you require plants that are happy in shade.

SOIL Any, including heavy clay; the attractive leaf colours seem to develop best in poorer soils.

SITUATION Full sun to moderate shade; although leaf colour is probably best in full sun, I have obtained good results in shade from such purple-foliaged forms as *B.* 'Bressingham Ruby'. The large leaves can be damaged and tattered in strong or cold winds so bergenias are best in a spot with some shelter.

WATERING AND FEEDING Mulch in autumn and spring. Feed with a balanced general purpose fertilizer in mid-spring and again after midsummer.

MANAGEMENT Deadhead after flowering; divide every four or five years.

COMMON PROBLEMS None.

Bergenia 'Ballawley'

PROPAGATION Division in autumn or spring.
TROUBLESHOOTING Not likely to be necessary.
SIZE Most varieties will attain about 30–45 × 30–45cm/1–1½ × 1–1½ft in three years.

Campanula BELLFLOWER

The genus *Campanula* is a large one and includes a number of popular, hardy varieties for the border, all fairly adaptable; other members are discussed with rock garden plants (see page 170).
SOIL Tolerates most, but unsatisfactory in very wet or very acid conditions; usefully tolerant of high alkalinity.
SITUATION Full sun to moderate shade, preferably with some shelter from strong winds.
WATERING AND FEEDING Mulch in autumn and spring, feed with a balanced general purpose fertilizer in mid-spring and again after midsummer.
MANAGEMENT Cut back old flowered stems to soil level after flowering. Divide every four or five years. In my experience campanulas are extremely difficult to stake, as their flowering stems are pliable and bend as soon as they begin to grow. Wrap-around support is not effective and the only real solution, if you want to stake the plant, is to use several tiers of the criss-cross, trivet-style supports, placed one above the other as the stems elongate. Some campanulas can be grown without any staking, and for *C. persicifolia* in particular it is rarely necessary.
COMMON PROBLEMS Mildew; slugs.
PROPAGATION Division in autumn or spring; some varieties from seed.
TROUBLESHOOTING Not likely to be necessary.
SIZE The common border perennials are varieties of *C. latifolia*, *C. lactiflora* and *C. persicifolia*, which will attain a height of 1.2m/4ft and a spread of 60cm/2ft within two or three years.

Centranthus VALERIAN

Among the most delightful sights on old or ruined buildings are the clumps of red and white valerian growing from gaps in the stonework and mortar. Where similar conditions can be met in the garden they will thrive – and also self-seed rather aggressively.
SOIL Light, free-draining, alkaline, preferably rather poor.
SITUATION Full sun to very light shade.
WATERING AND FEEDING Mulch in autumn and spring. Feed with a balanced general purpose fertilizer in mid-spring and again after midsummer.
MANAGEMENT Cut down to soil level in autumn. The flower stems tend to flop outwards towards the end of the flowering period and are best supported with wrap-around support. Divide every three years.
COMMON PROBLEMS None.
PROPAGATION Division in autumn or spring, or from seed.
TROUBLESHOOTING None normally necessary.
SIZE Will reach 1m × 70cm/3 × 2½ft after two years.

Campanula latifolia

Centranthus ruber

Chrysanthemum

Florists' chrysanthemum

Chrysanthemum

Although botanists have now split up the old genus *Chrysanthemum* into smaller groups, I am retaining it here to cover the plants that might be used in a mixed border – *C. rubellum*; the hardy shasta daisy varieties derived from *C. × superbum* (*C. maximum*); the less than hardy marguerites (*C. frutescens*); and the early-flowering florists' or 'border' chrysanthemums, in a wide range of flower size and form. I am excluding the late-flowering florists' chrysanthemums which are raised in pots for blooming in a cool greenhouse, as these tend to be a specialist's plant.

SOIL Widely tolerant of soil types, provided it is well drained, fairly rich and neither highly acidic nor alkaline.

SITUATION Full sun to light shade, preferably with some shelter from cold winds.

WATERING AND FEEDING *C. RUBELLUM* AND SHASTA DAISIES Mulch in autumn and spring. Feed with a balanced general purpose fertilizer in mid-spring and again after midsummer.

MARGUERITES When in open ground, mulch in autumn and spring. Feed with a balanced general fertilizer in spring and again after midsummer. When grown in pots, use John Innes No. 2 potting compost, mulch the pot, and liquid feed weekly during summer.

FLORISTS' CHRYSANTHEMUMS Fork in a balanced general fertilizer one to two weeks before planting out the young or overwintered plants, and apply the same again as a top dressing about one month later. Do not mulch immediately after planting as newly planted border or florists' chrysanthemums are prone to damage from overwatering, but mulch in the usual way after about three weeks when the plants are well established.

MANAGEMENT *C. RUBELLUM* AND SHASTA DAISIES Cut back old flowered stems to soil level after flowering. Divide shasta daisies every two or three years (this is most important to maintain vigour), and *C. rubellum* every three or four years. The stems of shasta daisies easily kink and the entire plant can look open and unkempt, so stake them early in the season by placing several tiers of the criss-cross, trivet-style supports one above the other as the plant grows up.

MARGUERITES These are only hardy outdoors in very mild areas and are best grown in pots and taken into a cool greenhouse in late autumn. They are most attractive when grown as standards by staking the strongest stem and pinching out any side-shoots that emerge low down.

FLORISTS' CHRYSANTHEMUMS Plant out hardened-off plants in late spring each year – up to three weeks before the last frost is likely in your area. Insert a bamboo stake for each plant at planting time.

This type of chrysanthemum requires 'stopping', that is, the growing tip of the main stem is removed as far as the uppermost fully developed leaves. The reasons for this are to encourage the development of side-shoots and so make the plant bushier, to concentrate its energies into producing better blooms, and to bring the flowering season forward, so that there is less danger of the plant producing its best flowers just as the first frosts of autumn begin.

Chrysanthemum

Most gardeners in Britain would be safe stopping their chrysan-themums before the end of May, but for those growing plants to show, the time for stopping is rather critical, as it chiefly governs when the plants will flower. (On chrysanthemums, flowering is also related to temperature and day length: the longer the day, the later the plants will flower.) Each gardener will have to make his own decision about when to stop, for it will be different according to the variety, the age of the plants and the soil conditions. In Britain, gardeners in the north of the country find the second week of May best, while those in the south of the country, with sunnier, longer days, find one week later more suitable.

Once the plant has been stopped, side-shoots will develop. Some of these should also be removed for best results, so pinch them out one at a time as they emerge, until between six and eight remain. In due course the side-shoots produce their own side-shoots, and these should all be pinched out. As summer reaches its peak each side-shoot will be bearing a flower bud at its tip, with others surrounding it. On large-flowered varieties these extra buds should be pinched out to leave just the terminal bud, which will produce good-sized blooms. On spray varieties, between five and seven buds should be left on each shoot to flower. Until the plants have flowered, shoots arising from the base of the plants should be pulled off; after the main flowering they can be allowed to develop to produce sprays of additional small blooms.

In late autumn the plants should be lifted. Cut off any basal shoots, but leave about 60cm/2ft of the main stem: this will produce shoots for cuttings in the spring. Shake off excess soil and plant the rootstocks (called stools) very shallowly in boxes of John Innes No. 1 potting compost, old coir compost or a mixture of slightly damp peat and sand. Water to make the compost damp; but do not overwater. Store the stools in a well-ventilated cold frame, protected from more than one or two degrees of frost. Soon after midwinter the boxes should ideally be moved into a cool greenhouse offering a temperature of about 7°C/45°F, and given a little water; they can be left in the cold frame, but will start much later into growth in the next season, and will not really catch up with those kept in warmer conditions.

The overwintered stools should be hardened off over about a week before planting out in the border. They can be left entire, or divided first, but after a few years flower quality will deteriorate. The best course is to renew the stock from cuttings at least every two years.

COMMON PROBLEMS *C. RUBELLUM*, SHASTA DAISIES AND MAR-GUERITES Normally none.

FLORISTS' CHRYSANTHEMUMS Mildew; rust; grey mould; virus; leaf miners; aphids; slugs; eelworm.

PROPAGATION *C. RUBELLUM* AND SHASTA DAISIES Division in spring (important to maintain vigour anyway).

MARGUERITES Semi-ripe cuttings in autumn or softwood cuttings in spring.

FLORISTS' CHRYSANTHEMUMS Division in spring or basal cuttings in spring. If few or no basal cuttings form, shoots arising from the old main stem may be used instead. Root the cuttings in trays of

Chrysanthemum – Digitalis

Coreopsis verticillata

Delphinium 'Pacific Giant'

John Innes seedling compost, then move them on to individual 9cm/3½in diameter pots filled with John Innes No. 1 potting compost, subsequently hardening off the plants.

TROUBLESHOOTING Not likely to be necessary if plants are renewed as described. Any florists' chrysanthemums showing abnormal flower or leaf development are probably affected with virus and should be destroyed.

SIZE Shasta daisy 1m × 60cm/3 × 2ft after three years. *C. rubellum* 80 × 50cm/2½ × 1½ft in two years. Marguerite 1–1.2 × 1m/3–4 × 3ft within a year. Most varieties of florists' chrysanthemum will attain about 1–1.5m × 60–90cm/3–5 × 2–3ft within a year.

Coreopsis

An attractive group of yellow, daisy-flowered perennials, with most forms being lower growing and more compact than many other similar flowers. They are hardy but benefit from some extra winter protection in all except the mildest areas.

SOIL Free-draining, moist, rich.

SITUATION Full sun.

WATERING AND FEEDING Mulch in autumn (which will give that important winter protection), and again in spring. Feed with a balanced general purpose fertilizer in mid-spring and again after midsummer.

MANAGEMENT Cut back all growth above ground to soil level in autumn. No staking is needed. Divide every three years in spring.

COMMON PROBLEMS None.

PROPAGATION By division (all varieties); some forms will strike from cuttings.

TROUBLESHOOTING None should be necessary but the plants tend to be short-lived and may decline after five or six years, especially if not divided regularly.

SIZE Most varieties will reach about 45–60 × 20–45cm/1½–2ft × 8in–1½ft in two years.

Delphinium

These are among the classic border perennials, and some varieties are probably the tallest, but they are not the easiest to grow. Care must be taken in siting them and they require more than the average amount of attention if they are to be successful.

SOIL Rich, well-drained organic loams are ideal. They will not succeed in heavy cold clays or in very dry or poor soils, but are tolerant of alkalinity.

SITUATION Full sun to light shade; shelter from strong winds is essential for the taller varieties – while there are so-called dwarf delphiniums, they have nothing of the stateliness of the classic, tall delphinium and even they require some wind protection.

WATERING AND FEEDING Mulch in autumn and spring. Feed with a balanced general purpose fertilizer in mid-spring and again after midsummer.

MANAGEMENT Staking is most important and should be done early. To avoid having the border decorated with 3m/10ft tall canes from the beginning of the season, when the vegetation around them is only knee high, I prefer to do a little extra work and replace short with medium length and then, finally, long supports as the plants grow. Although it is not essential, the best results will be obtained if the flowering stems are thinned out as they emerge, to leave no more than the five or six strongest, well spaced. Cut down old flowering spikes promptly after the flowers fade. Divide every four or five years in spring.

COMMON PROBLEMS Slugs; mildew.

PROPAGATION From basal cuttings, by division in spring, or a few varieties from seed.

TROUBLESHOOTING Not likely to be necessary.

SIZE The taller varieties will attain $3m \times 75cm/10 \times 2\frac{1}{2}ft$ in a season, the dwarf types no more than a third of this.

Dicentra BLEEDING HEART

These are relatives of the poppies but are quite unlike them, having long stems of pendant, almost bell-like flowers. They are not easy plants to position for the best visual effect and are also rather demanding in their site requirements.

SOIL Rich and organic, moist but well drained.

SITUATION Always best in cool positions in light shade.

WATERING AND FEEDING Mulch in autumn and spring. Feed with a balanced general purpose fertilizer in mid-spring and again after midsummer. Most intolerant of drying out which induces very rapid wilting.

MANAGEMENT Difficult to stake and should really be planted where their somewhat spreading habit can be allowed full rein. Divide every three or four years in spring, but do so carefully for the fleshy roots are very brittle and easily damaged.

COMMON PROBLEMS Slugs.

PROPAGATION Root cuttings in winter, division in spring, or the species from seed.

TROUBLESHOOTING Not likely to be necessary.

SIZE Up to $1m \times 50cm/3 \times 1\frac{1}{2}ft$ within two years.

Dicentra spectabilis

Digitalis FOXGLOVE

The pink or white, fully hardy foxglove (*D. purpurea*) is known to every gardener. It may not be reliably perennial in most gardens, but this is not true of some of its less well-known relatives, which come in a range of colours and are equally easy to grow.

SOIL Tolerates most, but best in moist, organic soil with no tendency to waterlogging.

SITUATION Foxgloves are always best in cool positions, in light to moderate shade.

WATERING AND FEEDING Mulch in autumn and spring. Feed with a balanced general purpose fertilizer in mid-spring and again after midsummer.

MANAGEMENT Staking is barely necessary for *D. purpurea* but related species may need light support. *D. purpurea* tends to be biennial so maintain a few self-sown seedlings (of which there will

Digitalis ambigua

Doronicum 'Spring Beauty'

Echinacea purpurea

be plenty). To be certain that a population of white-flowered plants remains white, pull out any seedlings in the vicinity whose flowers show any pink in the buds; if such plants are allowed to remain until the flowers are fully open, pollen will be transferred and the offspring will also be pink. Truly perennial species should be divided every four or five years in autumn or spring.

COMMON PROBLEMS None.

PROPAGATION It may be possible to take offsets or basal cuttings in spring but from seed is the more reliable method.

TROUBLESHOOTING Not likely to be necessary.

SIZE Varies with species from about 75 × 30cm to 1.5m × 50cm/ 2½ × 1ft to 5 × 1½ft in two years.

Doronicum   LEOPARD'S BANE

These early-flowering, hardy yellow border daisies are useful and easy fillers, but will never win prizes.

SOIL Tolerates most, but tends to suffer even worse than other daisy-like plants from mildew in dry sites.

SITUATION Full sun to light shade.

WATERING AND FEEDING Mulch in autumn and spring. Feed with a balanced general purpose fertilizer in mid-spring and again after midsummer.

MANAGEMENT Staking is barely necessary other than in windy sites, as the stems are relatively stiff. Cut down dead flower stems immediately after the blooms have faded and cut down the foliage as soon as it yellows with mildew. Divide every four or five years in autumn or spring.

COMMON PROBLEMS Mildew.

PROPAGATION Division in autumn or spring.

TROUBLESHOOTING Not likely to be necessary; even plants severely affected with mildew will regrow in the following year.

SIZE The common varieties will attain about 1m × 40cm/3ft × 16in after two or three years.

Echinacea   PURPLE CONE FLOWER

Another genus in that large and valuable group of perennial daisies that have a prominent raised centre to the flowers, but these are unusual in having pink, red or white colours.

SOIL Tolerates most but best in free-draining, moist, rich soils.

SITUATION Full sun.

WATERING AND FEEDING Mulch in autumn and spring. Feed with a balanced general purpose fertilizer in mid-spring and again after midsummer.

MANAGEMENT Cut back all growth above ground to soil level in autumn. Many of the common varieties of *E. purpurea* are tall and will require individual canes or wrap-around staking. Divide every three or four years in spring.

COMMON PROBLEMS None.

PROPAGATION Division in autumn or spring.

TROUBLESHOOTING None normally necessary.

SIZE *E. purpurea* will reach 1m × 50cm/3 × 1½ft after three years.

Echinops   GLOBE THISTLE

As part of a mixed planting the characteristic spikes of the echinops thistles are most effective. They are fully hardy but a little difficult to grow to their best because most gardens have border soil that is too good for them.

SOIL Most, but produce their most lush foliage and flowers in rather poor conditions.

SITUATION Full sun to very light shade.

WATERING AND FEEDING Mulch in autumn and spring. Feed with a very light dressing of balanced general purpose fertilizer in mid-spring and again after midsummer.

MANAGEMENT Staking is barely necessary but the heavy stems tend to spread if they are not at least loosely tied. Cut down dead flower stems as soon as the flowers have faded and cut back the foliage as it browns and shrivels with mildew. Divide every four years in spring.

COMMON PROBLEMS Mildew and general leaf discolouration.

PROPAGATION Division in autumn or spring, root cuttings in winter, or from seed.

TROUBLESHOOTING Not likely to be necessary.

SIZE The commonest form is *E. ritro*, which will reach 1.5 × 1m/ 5 × 3ft in three years, although there are other, smaller varieties.

Echinops ritro

Epimedium

Epimediums are fairly low-growing, clump-forming and more or less evergreen plants that have a special merit in their tolerance of shady, difficult conditions in which many other plants fail. I find they make excellent companions to *Omphalodes*.

SOIL Tolerates most, including dry soils where the plants will perform adequately; but they produce their most luxuriant and attractive foliage in moist, rich conditions.

SITUATION Light to moderate or even deep shade.

WATERING AND FEEDING Mulch in autumn and spring. Feed with a balanced general purpose fertilizer in mid-spring and again after midsummer.

MANAGEMENT Trim back browned or dead leaves as appropriate but do not cut them back to soil level unless they are completely browned by cold weather. The plants may be left undisturbed as ground cover or divided every four or five years.

COMMON PROBLEMS None.

PROPAGATION Division in autumn or spring.

TROUBLESHOOTING None normally necessary.

SIZE Most forms will reach about 30–45 × 30–45cm/1½ × 1–1½ft after three or four years, depending on the soil conditions.

Eryngium   SEA HOLLY

The spiky sea holly often looks best grown as an individual specimen, with its glaucous foliage contributing to its overall appeal. Coastal gardens generally offer the best conditions.

SOIL Light, free-draining, but fertile.

Epimedium × rubrum

Eryngium – Geranium

Eryngium alpinum

SITUATION Full sun to very light shade. Sea holly is intolerant of cold wind but is very reliable in coastal gardens as it is unaffected by salt spray.

WATERING AND FEEDING Mulch in autumn and spring. Feed with a balanced general purpose fertilizer in mid-spring and again after midsummer.

MANAGEMENT Should not need staking and apart from taking off dead flower heads, little attention is needed. Divide every four or five years in spring. *E. giganteum* is grown as a biennial.

COMMON PROBLEMS None.

PROPAGATION Division in spring, root cuttings in winter, the species from seed.

TROUBLESHOOTING Not likely to be necessary.

SIZE One of the most popular varieties is also the largest, *E. giganteum*, which will attain 1.2–1.5m × 75cm/4–5 × 2½ft in two years. *E. bourgatii* is longer-lived and will reach 60 × 20cm/2 × 1ft.

Erysimum

Popularly called perennial wallflowers, the low-growing erysimums have returned to favour in recent years. They are easy and undemanding but neglect will allow them to become straggly.

SOIL Most, provided it is well drained and fairly fertile; erysimum will not succeed in clay.

SITUATION Full sun to light shade.

WATERING AND FEEDING Mulch in autumn and spring. Feed with a balanced general purpose fertilizer in mid-spring and again after midsummer.

MANAGEMENT Divide every two or three years in spring or, better, renew plants from cuttings after a similar time.

COMMON PROBLEMS None.

PROPAGATION Semi-ripe cuttings in early summer, or seed.

TROUBLESHOOTING Not likely to be necessary.

SIZE Will spread to about 30 × 45cm/1 × 1½ft in three years.

Euphorbia

One of the most versatile genera of garden plants with deciduous and evergreen, winter- and summer-flowering species, and varieties suitable for most situations. Their usually greenish bracts and overall form are highly distinctive.

SOIL Varies with species; most of the large summer-flowering species will succeed best in fertile but light free-draining soils; the winter-flowering and shade-tolerant species require slightly wetter and heavier conditions.

SITUATION Full sun (most large, summer-flowering types) to light shade (most winter-flowering forms), or moderate to deep shade (*E. robbiae*).

WATERING AND FEEDING Mulch in autumn and spring. Feed with a balanced general purpose fertilizer in mid-spring and again after midsummer.

MANAGEMENT The very large-headed, summer-flowering euphorbias may require light wrap-around staking to prevent

Erysimum 'Bowles' Mauve'

them from flopping; other varieties should need none, and require little other attention. Most types do not divide very successfully.

COMMON PROBLEMS None.

PROPAGATION Tip or basal cuttings in spring, semi-ripe cuttings in late summer, or from seed.

TROUBLESHOOTING Not likely to be necessary.

SIZE Varies considerably between species, so read label information. There are a few dwarf forms suitable for the rock garden, such as E. *myrsinites* with a height and spread of 5–10 × 15–20cm/ 2–4 × 6–8in over three years. Most of the medium-sized herbaceous species will reach about 75cm–1m × 50cm/2½–3 × 1½ft after two or three years, and some of the larger, summer-flowering types, such as E. *characias wulfenii*, will be half as large again.

Euphorbia characias wulfenii

Geranium

Probably the easiest and, overall, most useful of all genera of herbaceous perennials. Given the wide range of species and varieties, and allowing only for their slightly limited colour range, there must be a geranium to suit almost every garden.

SOIL Almost any, provided it is not very heavy or waterlogged. The shade-loving species are mostly tolerant of drier conditions too. All the geraniums are tolerant of moderate acidity and, in some cases, high alkalinity.

SITUATION Varies with species. Most are best in full sun to light shade, although there is a small group of species, ranging from the fairly tall G. *phaeum* to the ground-covering G. *macrorrhizum*, that is tolerant of deep shade.

WATERING AND FEEDING Mulch in autumn and spring. Feed with a balanced general purpose fertilizer in mid-spring and again after midsummer.

MANAGEMENT The lower-growing geraniums require no staking. The taller-growing forms, such as G. 'Johnson's Blue', G. *wallichianum* ('Buxton's Blue'), G. *ibericum* or G. *pratense*, may be staked, although their stems and leaf stalks are so soft and pliable, and also so numerous, that this cannot be done on an individual basis; the best plan is to use metal stakes or thin canes and carefully provide support around the whole of each clump. A few forms (the variety G. × *oxonianum* 'Claridge Druce' most notably) self-seed very freely and unless they are required as ground cover, these seedlings must be assiduously pulled out. Divide the more vigorous forms every two years in autumn or spring; the remainder, every four or five years.

COMMON PROBLEMS None.

PROPAGATION Division in autumn or spring, or from seed.

TROUBLESHOOTING Not likely to be necessary.

SIZE Varies between species and varieties. As a guide, the smallest, such as G. *cinereum*, are really little more than rock garden plants, reaching perhaps 10 × 20cm/4 × 8in in two years; the ground-covering G. *macrorrhizum* will reach 35 × 60cm/1 × 2ft in two years; the upright forms such as G. 'Johnson's Blue' 30 × 60cm/1 × 2ft in two years; and the more vigorous G. × *oxonianum* 'Claridge Druce' 75 × 75cm/2½ × 2½ft in two years.

Geranium endressii 'Wargrave Pink'

Geum 'Borisii'

Geum

Undistinguished but useful, easy and hardy plants to add to the overall impact of a large border.

SOIL Almost any, provided it is not very heavy or waterlogged.

SITUATION Full sun to light shade.

WATERING AND FEEDING Mulch in autumn and spring. Feed with a balanced general purpose fertilizer in mid-spring and again after midsummer.

MANAGEMENT I find it unnecessary to stake geums, although the taller varieties such as *G. chiloense* 'Mrs Bradshaw' may require some support if growing in an exposed situation. Divide every four or five years in autumn or spring.

COMMON PROBLEMS None.

PROPAGATION Division in autumn or spring, or from seed.

TROUBLESHOOTING Not likely to be necessary.

SIZE Most varieties will attain about 30×30cm/1×1ft in two years; *G. chiloense* 'Mrs Bradshaw' and *G.* 'Lady Stratheden' will reach about $60–80 \times 45$cm/$2–2\frac{1}{2} \times 1\frac{1}{2}$ft in the same time.

Gypsophila   BABY'S BREATH

There are two common garden gypsophilas of similar form: the annual varieties derived from *G. elegans*, and the short-lived perennial *G. paniculata*. The perennials are pretty but often disappointing plants, with rather strict site and cultivation requirements.

SOIL Moist, rich, free-draining soils give the best results, although the plants are tolerant of drier conditions. They are quite intolerant of heavy, clayey or cold soils.

SITUATION Full sun, preferably with shelter from cold wind.

WATERING AND FEEDING Mulch in autumn and spring. Feed with a balanced general purpose fertilizer in mid-spring and again after midsummer.

MANAGEMENT The plants greatly resent any disturbance, and attempts at moving or dividing gypsophilas almost always end unsuccessfully.

COMMON PROBLEMS None.

PROPAGATION Not reliable enough to be practical.

TROUBLESHOOTING When the plants begin to decline (they may rather suddenly wilt during the summer), it is not practical to rejuvenate them; these are fairly short-lived plants that will need replacing after five or six years.

SIZE The commonest and most popular variety, *G. paniculata* 'Bristol Fairy', should attain 80×80cm/$2\frac{1}{2} \times 2\frac{1}{2}$ft in three years.

Gypsophila paniculata 'Bristol Fairy'

Helenium   SNEEZEWEED

Among the easiest and most reliable of autumn border perennials, heleniums belong to a large group of daisy-like plants distinguished by pronounced button-like centres to the flowers, rich red, gold and yellow colours, and a rather appealing, spicy smell.

SOIL Tolerates most, but best in rather moist, rich and free-draining soils.

SITUATION Full sun.

WATERING AND FEEDING Mulch in autumn and spring. Feed with a balanced general purpose fertilizer in mid-spring and again after midsummer.

MANAGEMENT Stake early to prevent the rather weak flower stems from flopping. Divide every four or five years.

COMMON PROBLEMS None.

PROPAGATION Division in autumn or spring.

TROUBLESHOOTING Not normally necessary.

SIZE Will reach 1–1.2m × 60–75cm/3–4 × 2–2½ft after three years.

Helleborus

Although the range of species is small, hellebores are among the most useful of ornamental herbaceous perennials. They are shade-tolerant, provide foliage interest through the winter, and have a considerable variation in flower colour and form.

SOIL Tolerates most, but will generally give best results in moist, organic loams that are neither strongly acid nor alkaline.

SITUATION Light to moderate shade, with some shelter; ideally placed in woodland conditions or in the partial shade beneath isolated trees.

WATERING AND FEEDING Mulch in autumn and spring. Feed with a balanced general purpose fertilizer in mid-spring and again after midsummer.

MANAGEMENT Dead or tattered leaves should be cut off at soil level in spring, allowing the emerging flowers to be seen to best advantage. The faded flowers should be left until they set seeds, partly because they remain attractive but also because self-sown seedlings often produce interesting and attractive variations. The early-flowering species, especially *H. niger*, the so-called Christmas rose, will give better blooms if protected from rain and soil splash: place cloches over them in late autumn as the flower buds swell, and leave them on until the flowers open. In borders, hellebores are best divided every four or five years; in woodland positions, they may be left undisturbed.

COMMON PROBLEMS Leaf spotting occurs on most hellebores but is rarely serious. A basal stem rot may be troublesome on *H. niger* and can be minimized by using cloches.

PROPAGATION Division in spring (some species); basal, preferably rooted cuttings in spring; or the species from seed.

TROUBLESHOOTING Unlikely to be necessary.

SIZE Varies slightly between species but is usually around 30–60 × 30–45cm/1–2 × 1–1½ft in three years.

Hemerocallis DAY LILY

The day lilies have come into prominence over the past few years with a great increase in the range of varieties available; many are much less invasive than some of the older forms. They are easy and useful hardy plants for the mixed border.

SOIL Tolerates many but generally best in free-draining, rich, moist conditions.

Helenium 'Moerheim Beauty'
Helleborus orientalis
Hemerocallis hybrid

Hemerocallis – Lamium

Heuchera micrantha 'Palace Purple'

SITUATION Full sun to light shade.

WATERING AND FEEDING Mulch in spring and early autumn. Feed by top dressing with bonemeal or a proprietary bulb fertilizer in early spring; and, if possible, giving a liquid feed every fortnight during the summer.

MANAGEMENT Cut down the flower stems as the flowers fade and cut all growth above ground to soil level in winter. Divide every three years.

COMMON PROBLEMS None.

PROPAGATION Division in autumn or spring.

TROUBLESHOOTING Unlikely to be necessary.

SIZE Most varieties will reach a height of about 1m/3ft and will spread to about 50–60cm/2ft within two or three years.

Heuchera CORAL FLOWER

Heucheras have always had a following, and they are certainly undemanding and useful for colourful and evergreen foliage in rather difficult situations.

SOIL Tolerates most soil types, although is less reliable in very heavy or wet soils.

SITUATION Light to moderate or even deep shade.

WATERING AND FEEDING Mulch in autumn and spring. Feed with a balanced general purpose fertilizer in mid-spring and again after midsummer.

MANAGEMENT Cut away dead or ragged foliage in autumn and again in spring. No staking is necessary. Divide plants every four or five years.

COMMON PROBLEMS None.

PROPAGATION Division in autumn or spring.

TROUBLESHOOTING Unlikely to be necessary.

SIZE Most varieties will reach about 75×50cm/$2\frac{1}{2} \times 1\frac{1}{2}$ft in three years, although a few are slightly less vigorous.

Hosta PLANTAIN LILY

Hostas are among the most popular of modern herbaceous perennials and the number of varieties proliferates. They are relatively easy to grow in most situations, but are a great favourite with slugs and snails.

SOIL Tolerates most; although traditionally associated with wet, waterside beds, hostas are in fact highly tolerant of much drier conditions. When hostas are grown in borders their leaves can become completely tattered through the ravages of slugs and snails, so one option worth exploring is to grow the plants in containers of John Innes No. 3 potting compost, then standing the pots in the borders. The pests will be deterred to some degree, and if the containers are stood on small feet on a hard surface such as a paved terrace, the problem can be almost totally overcome.

SITUATION Full sun to moderate shade.

WATERING AND FEEDING Mulch in autumn and spring. Feed with a balanced general purpose fertilizer in mid-spring and again after midsummer.

Hosta 'Tall Boy'

MANAGEMENT Cut out the flower spikes immediately after flowering – they become very hard and woody if left – and cut down the foliage as it dies in autumn. Divide plants every four or five years in spring.

COMMON PROBLEMS Slugs and snails.

PROPAGATION Division in spring.

TROUBLESHOOTING Unlikely to be necessary.

SIZE Varies considerably; most will attain about 45×30cm/$1\frac{1}{2} \times$ 1ft in three years, but the more vigorous, such as some varieties of *H. fortunei*, will reach 1×1m/3×3ft in the same time.

Kniphofia RED HOT POKER

Red hot pokers justify the large amount of space they take up when the soil is right and the area mild; then, they are always spectacularly attractive.

SOIL Rich, deep, moist but well drained; quite intolerant of heavy, waterlogged or cold soils.

SITUATION Full sun to light shade.

WATERING AND FEEDING Mulch in autumn and spring. Feed with a balanced general purpose fertilizer in mid-spring and again after midsummer.

MANAGEMENT Cut out dead flower spikes after flowering. Do not cut down the foliage in autumn, and in colder areas provide some protection from penetrating frost and water by loosely tying the leaves over the crown with raffia. Divide every five or six years in spring.

COMMON PROBLEMS None, apart from those caused by cold or frost damage.

PROPAGATION Division in spring; the species from seed.

TROUBLESHOOTING Unlikely to be necessary.

SIZE Generally $1–1.5$m $\times 40–75$cm/$3–5 \times 1–2\frac{1}{2}$ft after three years, although there are a few modern dwarf forms that barely exceed 60cm/2ft in height.

Kniphofia rooperi

Lamium DEAD NETTLE

Lamium is often dismissed as uninteresting but is in fact a very easy, useful and hardy group of more or less evergreen, ground-covering plants, tolerant of much poorer conditions than many grander things.

SOIL Most, including fairly dry and poor conditions.

SITUATION Full sun to moderate shade.

WATERING AND FEEDING Mulch in autumn and spring. Feed with a balanced general purpose fertilizer in mid-spring and again after midsummer.

MANAGEMENT Trim back to soil level in early spring. Divide every five or six years if not required as ground cover.

COMMON PROBLEMS Leaf spotting, and leaf-feeding pests.

PROPAGATION Division in spring, or from semi-ripe cuttings in summer.

TROUBLESHOOTING Unlikely to be necessary.

SIZE 25cm $\times$ 1m/10in $\times$ 3ft in three to four years.

Lamium maculatum 'Beacon Silver'

Ligularia – Lychnis

Ligularia dentata

Ligularia

A fine group of tall border perennials of two major types; both have large, lush leaves, but one (*L. dentata*) has large, single, orange, daisy-like flowers, while the other (*L. przewalskii* and *L. stenocephala*) has smaller daisy flowers massed in elongated spikes. All are essentially water-loving but otherwise easy to grow.

SOIL Rich, preferably organic and moist. The huge leaves wilt very rapidly in dry conditions.

SITUATION Full sun to light shade; ligularias are eminently suitable for waterside plantings.

WATERING AND FEEDING Mulch in autumn and spring. Feed with a balanced general purpose fertilizer in mid-spring and again after midsummer.

MANAGEMENT Cut down dead flower heads after flowering. Staking is essential in exposed sites. Divide every three or four years in spring.

COMMON PROBLEMS None.

PROPAGATION Division in spring; some varieties from seed.

TROUBLESHOOTING Not normally necessary.

SIZE Will reach 1.2–1.5m × 75cm/4–5 × 2½ft after three years.

Limonium SEA LAVENDER, STATICE

The sea lavenders are a highly individual group of brightly-coloured, low-growing perennials appreciated for their value as dried flowers. There are related, taller forms grown as annuals. As the common name suggests, coastal conditions suit them best.

SOIL Light, free-draining, tolerant of alkalinity.

SITUATION Full sun with some shelter from cold winds.

WATERING AND FEEDING Mulch in autumn and spring. Feed with a balanced general purpose fertilizer in mid-spring and again after midsummer.

MANAGEMENT Flower heads for drying should be cut when almost fully open. Leave on any heads not required for cutting, and trim back hard in spring. Divide every four years in spring.

COMMON PROBLEMS None.

PROPAGATION Division in spring, root cuttings in winter, or from seed.

TROUBLESHOOTING The plants tend to become straggly after six to eight years and are then best replaced.

SIZE Will reach 20 × 10cm/8 × 4in after three years.

Limonium latifolium

Lobelia

Although the most familiar lobelias are those dwarf forms grown as half-hardy annuals, there is one important but rather tender perennial with dark red flowers, *L. cardinalis*, that is a striking plant for milder, moist situations.

SOIL Rich, preferably organic, moist.

SITUATION Full sun with some shelter from cold winds; this is a waterside plant that will actually grow in a few centimetres of water at a pool edge.

WATERING AND FEEDING Mulch in autumn and spring. Feed with a balanced general purpose fertilizer in mid-spring and again after midsummer – unless the plants are growing in water, when no fertilizer should be given.

MANAGEMENT Cut down dead flower spikes after flowering. In all except the mildest areas, this plant is best grown in pots and lifted from its growing position for overwintering in a cool greenhouse. It may need staking where it is not supported by other plants. Divide every four or five years in spring.

COMMON PROBLEMS None.

PROPAGATION Division in spring, or from seed.

TROUBLESHOOTING None should be necessary.

SIZE 1m × 25cm/3ft × 10in in two years.

Lupinus LUPIN

Lupins are among the most familiar standbys of the herbaceous border but, although they are easy to grow, they have always had more than their fair share of pest and disease problems. This is a state of affairs likely to become worse rather than better, for the huge lupin aphid from North America is more tolerant of insecticides than seems at all reasonable.

SOIL Will tolerate most, but always best in fairly fertile, well-drained and slightly alkaline conditions.

SITUATION Full sun or very light shade.

WATERING AND FEEDING Mulch in autumn and spring. Feed with a balanced general purpose fertilizer in mid-spring and again after midsummer.

MANAGEMENT Cut down dead flower spikes immediately after flowering and cut back foliage as soon as it begins to discolour with mildew. The plants should not need staking unless growing in a very windy site. Lupins often do not divide very satisfactorily and are best renewed every four or five years by cuttings.

COMMON PROBLEMS Slugs; mildew; lupin aphid.

PROPAGATION Basal cuttings in spring, or from seed.

TROUBLESHOOTING None should be necessary, but stock will need renewing (see above).

SIZE 1–1.2m × 50cm/3–4 × 1½ft in two years.

Lychnis CAMPION, CATCHFLY

A small genus of low-growing, summer-flowering perennials, with red, pink or white flowers. Their hot colours are useful in the mixed border, while some forms are small enough to have a place in the rock garden.

SOIL Light, free-draining, not too rich, tolerant of alkalinity.

SITUATION Full sun.

WATERING AND FEEDING Mulch in autumn and spring. Feed with a balanced general purpose fertilizer in mid-spring and again after midsummer.

MANAGEMENT Cut down dead flower spikes immediately after flowering. Divide every four or five years in spring.

COMMON PROBLEMS Aphids.

Lobelia cardinalis

Lupinus Russell hybrids

Lychnis – Nepeta

Lychnis chalcedonica

PROPAGATION By division in spring or from seed, but the best method is basal cuttings taken in spring.

TROUBLESHOOTING None should be necessary.

SIZE Varies with species and variety but the largest, such as *L. coronaria* 'Abbotswood Rose' (*L. × walkeri* 'Abbotswood Rose'), will attain about 35 × 25cm/14 × 10in after three years.

Meconopsis

A stunningly lovely genus of poppies which includes the yellow-flowered *M. cambrica* and a group of mainly blue-flowered and quite magnificent Asiatic species and hybrids. The former is easy to grow; the latter tend to be difficult in some gardens and require rather specific conditions. For the best chance of success, choose a reliably perennial form such as *M. grandis* or one of the many strains of *M. betonicifolia*.

SOIL Rich, moist, organic, fully tolerant of alkaline conditions but the rich blue colour of most forms develops much more satisfactorily on acid soils.

SITUATION Light to moderate shade.

WATERING AND FEEDING Mulch in autumn and spring. Feed with a balanced general purpose fertilizer in mid-spring and again after midsummer.

MANAGEMENT Cut down dead flower spikes immediately after flowering. Divide every three or four years in spring. The flower stems are slender and difficult to stake effectively as individuals; where support is needed, the best method is to encircle the whole clump with interlocking metal stakes or canes and string.

COMMON PROBLEMS None.

PROPAGATION Division in spring, or some forms from seed.

TROUBLESHOOTING Many of the blue Asiatic species are notoriously short-lived and some are monocarpic (they die after flowering), especially if raised from seed. The best advice is to buy named and proven perennial forms from a reputable nursery.

SIZE Varies with species and variety, some being rock garden dwarfs, but the largest of the common border plants, such as *M. grandis* or *M. × sheldonii*, will attain about 1.5m × 60cm/5 × 2ft after three years.

Mentha MINT

The mints are usually thought of as inhabitants of the herb or kitchen garden, where some undoubtedly have an important place. But there are also several attractive and fragrant varieties that are useful in ornamental situations, provided they are kept within bounds.

SOIL Tolerates most, but best in rich, moist, organic soils (unlike most other herbs).

SITUATION Full sun to light shade; arguably the most shade-tolerant of culinary herbs.

WATERING AND FEEDING Mulch in autumn and spring. Feed with a balanced general purpose fertilizer in mid-spring and again after midsummer.

Meconopsis grandis

MANAGEMENT Cut down dead flower spikes after flowering. To control the invasiveness of mint, grow the plants in John Innes No. 2 potting compost in 20–25cm/8–10in diameter pots and sink the pots to just below their rims in the border. Each autumn, lift the pot and trim away any shoots or rhizomes that threaten to escape. Every third year, replace the plants with new ones raised from cuttings (provided the parent stock has remained healthy).
COMMON PROBLEMS Rust.
PROPAGATION Division in autumn or spring, or rhizome cuttings in spring.
TROUBLESHOOTING None should be necessary.
SIZE Varies with species and variety; the least vigorous common mint is probably the creeping pennyroyal (*M. pulegium*), which is a mat-forming species with upright summer shoots; it will reach about 15 × 25cm/6 × 10in in three years. The most vigorous is horsemint (*M. longifolia*), which will attain 1m × 50cm/3 × 1½ft if its roots are unconfined.

Nepeta CATMINT

One of the easiest and commonest of all herbaceous perennials, this a most useful plant for the front of the border, its soft lilac-blue flowers making a foil for hotter colours.
SOIL Tolerates most except heavy, cold and waterlogged soils.
SITUATION Full sun to light shade.
WATERING AND FEEDING Mulch in autumn and spring. Feed with a balanced general purpose fertilizer in mid-spring and again after midsummer.
MANAGEMENT Cut back to soil level at the end of summer. Divide every two years in autumn or spring, unless it is being grown in a situation where its vigour can be allowed free rein.
COMMON PROBLEMS None.
PROPAGATION Division in autumn or spring; the species can be propagated from seed.
TROUBLESHOOTING None should be necessary.
SIZE Will reach about 45 × 45cm/1½ × 1½ft in two years.

Mentha spicata

Nepeta 'Six Hills Giant'

Oenothera tetragona

Oenothera EVENING PRIMROSE

The evening primroses have a rather straggly appearance for such low-growing plants, and flowers that, individually, are very short-lived. They are nonetheless popular for the front of the border and are easy to grow in all except cold, damp sites.

SOIL Light, free-draining, preferably sandy.

SITUATION Full sun, shelter from cold winds.

WATERING AND FEEDING Mulch in autumn and spring. Feed with a balanced general purpose fertilizer in mid-spring and again after midsummer.

MANAGEMENT Cut back to soil level at the end of summer. Divide every three years in spring.

COMMON PROBLEMS None.

PROPAGATION Division in autumn or spring, or from seed.

TROUBLESHOOTING Most have a tendency to be short-lived, and once they begin to look very straggly are best replaced.

SIZE The commonest form is the low-growing, clump-forming *O. missouriensis*, which will reach about 15 × 35cm/6 × 14in in two years; the taller forms such as *O. perennis* will reach about 60 × 30cm/2 × 1ft in the same time.

Omphalodes

The best known species in this genus, the low-growing, blue-eyed Mary *(O. cappadocica)*, has truly stunning little electric-blue flowers. It is an easy, undemanding and very versatile plant, although a little slow to establish.

SOIL Tolerates most, including moderately dry soils, but best in moist, free-draining organic soils.

SITUATION Light to moderate or almost deep shade.

WATERING AND FEEDING Mulch in autumn and spring. Feed with a balanced general purpose fertilizer in mid-spring and again after midsummer.

MANAGEMENT Dead head after flowering in spring to encourage a second flush of blooms in the autumn. In most gardens, the plant remains more or less evergreen although it will look more attractive in winter if dead leaves are trimmed away. It may be divided every five or six years in spring, but is best grown where it can be left undisturbed as ground cover.

COMMON PROBLEMS None.

PROPAGATION Division in spring, or from seed.

TROUBLESHOOTING None necessary.

SIZE Will reach about 20 × 30cm/8 × 12in after three years.

Paeonia

Although many peonies, with their large and fleshy tubers, grow naturally almost at the soil surface on bare mountainsides, they benefit from much better growing conditions if they are to give of their best in gardens.

SOIL Almost any provided it is well drained, but the best blooms will come from rich, fairly organic soils. Tolerant of moderate

Omphalodes cappadocica

acidity and alkalinity. Plant the tubers with their tops at a depth of about 8cm/3in.

SITUATION Full sun to very light shade; peonies in east-facing beds sometimes suffer in late frosts because their ripe flower buds freeze, then thaw out damagingly quickly when struck by early morning sun.

WATERING AND FEEDING Mulch in spring and early autumn. Top dress with blood, fish and bone or a similar general purpose fertilizer in early spring and again around midsummer.

MANAGEMENT Cut down old flower heads promptly after flowering and also cut off any damaged heads after heavy rain, as they will rapidly attract botrytis grey mould. Cut back all growth above ground to soil level in autumn. Varieties of *P. lactiflora* benefit from staking, and interlocking metal stakes or other wrap-around support is the most satisfactory method. Peonies should be left undisturbed for as long as possible and if they must be moved or divided, this is best done in mid-spring just as shoot growth is beginning.

COMMON PROBLEMS Grey mould stem blight.

PROPAGATION The best method is semi-ripe cuttings in late summer, but careful division in spring or root cuttings in winter may also be successful.

TROUBLESHOOTING Not normally necessary.

SIZE Most varieties will reach about 1 × 1m/3 × 3ft within four or five years.

Paeonia lactiflora

Papaver POPPY

Many of the popular garden poppies are annuals but there are two important groups of perennials; the Iceland poppy (*P. nudicaule*), usually grown as a rock garden plant, and the large, showy and popular Oriental poppies (*P. orientale*), whose flowers last for all too short a time even if the plants do compensate with attractive seed-heads. These are among the least tameable of herbaceous perennials, looking particularly untidy once flowering has finished; careful siting of other plants around can overcome this.

SOIL Fairly rich, moist, but free-draining.

SITUATION Full sun to light shade.

WATERING AND FEEDING Mulch in autumn and spring. Feed with a balanced general purpose fertilizer in mid-spring and again after midsummer.

MANAGEMENT I think that most gardeners who grow Oriental poppies are resigned to having a large, unruly bunch of vegetation with vivid and blowsy flowers in the middle of it: for these poppies flop uncontrollably and there is no border perennial that is more impossible to stake. They are best renewed from root cuttings every five or six years.

COMMON PROBLEMS Aphids.

PROPAGATION Root cuttings in winter; varieties other than *P. orientale* can be propagated by seed.

TROUBLESHOOTING None necessary.

SIZE Most perennial varieties of poppy will reach about 1 × 1m/ 3 × 3ft after three years.

Papaver orientale

Penstemon – Platycodon

Penstemon 'Garnet'

Penstemon

This is a large genus that includes annuals and shrubby species, as well as a useful group of easy to grow, predominantly white-, red- or pink-flowered, semi-evergreen perennials.

SOIL Well drained but moist, rich and fertile; penstemons will be dismal in poor soils.

SITUATION Full sun or very light shade.

WATERING AND FEEDING Mulch in autumn and spring. Feed with a balanced general purpose fertilizer in mid-spring and again after midsummer.

MANAGEMENT Cut back dead flower spikes after flowering but do not cut foliage down to soil level unless it is browned by cold weather. Some staking may be needed: taller forms are best staked individually, whereas the lower-growing, more compact varieties are best supported with interlocking metal stakes or other wrap-around support.

COMMON PROBLEMS None.

PROPAGATION Semi-ripe cuttings in summer, division in spring, or the species from seed.

TROUBLESHOOTING None necessary.

SIZE Varies considerably between varieties. Most of the strictly herbaceous perennials, such as the popular *P.* 'Apple Blossom', will reach about 45×45cm/$1\frac{1}{2} \times 1\frac{1}{2}$ft by the second or third year, but there are many smaller and taller, more or less woody, semi-shrubby varieties too, so check label descriptions carefully.

Perovskia   RUSSIAN SAGE

A cross between a shrub and a herbaceous perennial, perovskia has flower spikes of a most appealing shade of blue that mixes particularly well with purples. It is not a plant for cold, damp gardens.

SOIL Fairly rich but light and free-draining.

SITUATION Full sun.

WATERING AND FEEDING Mulch in autumn and spring. Feed with a balanced general purpose fertilizer in mid-spring and again after midsummer.

MANAGEMENT Cut down to soil level either in autumn or in early spring. In a large mixed planting perovskias don't really need staking, but when grown in isolation some wrap-around support may be useful. Divide in spring every four years.

COMMON PROBLEMS None.

PROPAGATION Division or softwood cuttings in spring.

TROUBLESHOOTING None necessary.

SIZE Will reach 1.2×1m/4×3ft after three years.

Phlox

Phlox are among the classic border perennials, and require little routine maintenance. Against this, however, must be set their frustrating susceptibility to disease.

SOIL Tolerates most, but generally best in light, free-draining but fertile conditions.

Perovskia 'Blue Spire'

SITUATION Full sun to light or even moderate shade.

WATERING AND FEEDING Mulch in autumn and spring. Feed with a balanced general purpose fertilizer in mid-spring and again after midsummer.

MANAGEMENT Phlox should not require staking, but the stems should be cut back to soil level as soon as the almost unavoidable attacks of mildew begin to take their effect. The stems are rather tough and sharp, so take particular care not to poke yourself in the face when cutting them down. Divide the plants every three or four years.

COMMON PROBLEMS Mildew; stem eelworm.

PROPAGATION Division in spring, semi-ripe cuttings in summer, basal cuttings in spring, root cuttings in winter.

TROUBLESHOOTING None normally necessary, but root cuttings may be used to save valuable plants that display the leaf-narrowing symptoms of stem eelworm attack, as the pest does not penetrate the roots.

SIZE Most of the common border phlox will reach about 1–1.2m × 60–75cm /3–4 × 2–2½ft after three years.

Phlox paniculata 'Franz Schubert'

Phormium NEW ZEALAND FLAX

The phormiums are striking evergreen plants that can be useful in bold plant groupings. They succeed best where the mild, damp conditions of their native New Zealand can be provided.

SOIL Not easy to satisfy, as it must be moist and fairly rich but also light and well drained.

SITUATION Full sun and shelter from cold wind; shelter is especially important for the variegated varieties, which are appreciably less hardy.

WATERING AND FEEDING Mulch in autumn and spring. Feed with a balanced general purpose fertilizer in mid-spring and again after midsummer.

MANAGEMENT Phormiums do not require staking. In autumn cut or pull away (using strong gloves) dead foliage, and again in spring. The plants may be divided every five or six years, but given appropriate space and attention to feeding they will continue to thrive in the same position for considerably longer.

COMMON PROBLEMS None.

PROPAGATION Division in spring, or from seed.

TROUBLESHOOTING None normally necessary.

SIZE Most varieties of *P. tenax* are huge plants, reaching 3 × 2m/ 10 × 6½ft after four years. Varieties of *P. cookianum* and many of the more decorative variegated forms tend to be smaller, about 90 × 45cm/3 × 1½ft over the same timespan.

Platycodon BALLOON FLOWER

The balloon flower is a one-off, a one-species genus of low-growing, summer-flowering perennials, distinguished by bell-shaped bluish flowers and balloon-like buds. Although they are usually said to be easy, I have always found them fickle in their growing requirements.

Phormium cookianum 'Tricolor'

Platycodon – Pulmonaria

Platycodon grandiflorus

SOIL Light, free-draining; any tendency to cold and wet conditions will lead to failure.

SITUATION Full sun.

WATERING AND FEEDING Mulch in autumn and spring. Feed with a balanced general purpose fertilizer in mid-spring and again after midsummer.

MANAGEMENT Cut down to soil level in late autumn. No staking is needed unless in a very windy spot where some light, wrap-around support may be beneficial. Divide every four or five years.

COMMON PROBLEMS None.

PROPAGATION Division or basal cuttings in spring, or seed.

TROUBLESHOOTING None normally necessary.

SIZE Will reach 50×50cm/$1\frac{1}{2} \times 1\frac{1}{2}$ft in four years.

Polygonatum   SOLOMON'S SEAL

This is a wonderful arching foliage plant for difficult and shady corners; if only it wasn't a martyr to leaf-feeding pests.

SOIL Rich, moist but well drained, intolerant both of dry and waterlogged conditions.

SITUATION Light to deep shade.

WATERING AND FEEDING Mulch in autumn and spring. Feed with a balanced general purpose fertilizer in mid-spring and again after midsummer.

MANAGEMENT Cut down to soil level in autumn; staking is needed, the arching habit of the stems being a major attraction. The plants may be divided every five years or left undisturbed.

COMMON PROBLEMS Solomon's seal sawfly, which strips the leaves to a skeleton.

PROPAGATION Division in spring, or from seed.

TROUBLESHOOTING Cut back in the normal way after severe sawfly attack and the plant will grow again the following year.

SIZE The largest species is _P. commutatum_ (_P. biflorum_), which will reach 1.5m $\times 60$cm/5×2ft in three years, but there are several smaller species, particularly the widely grown _P._ × _hybridum_, attaining approximately three quarters of this height and spread.

Polygonum   KNOTWEED

Polygonums are a mixed bunch, including some invasive weeds and some astonishingly vigorous climbers, several useful ground-covering perennials, and one tall border species.

SOIL Tolerates most.

SITUATION Full sun to moderate shade.

WATERING AND FEEDING Mulch in autumn and spring. Feed with a balanced general purpose fertilizer in mid-spring and again after midsummer.

MANAGEMENT Cut down deciduous species to soil level in autumn; evergreen species such as _P. affine_ should simply have the dead flower stems trimmed back. The plants may be divided every four or five years, although when grown as carpeting ground cover they may be left undisturbed for much longer. _P. amplexicaule_ will benefit from wrap-around support.

Polygonatum × _hybridum_

COMMON PROBLEMS None.
PROPAGATION Division in autumn or spring, or from seed.
TROUBLESHOOTING None normally necessary.
SIZE The best of the ground-covering forms is *P. affine* (*Persicaria affinis*), which will reach about 30 × 30cm/1 × 1ft in two years. The upright border plant *P. amplexicaule* (*Persicaria amplexicaulis*) will attain 1.2 × 1.2m/4 × 4ft in the same time.

Polygonum affine

Pulmonaria LUNGWORT

A lovely group of deciduous or semi-evergreen ground-covering plants, grown for their bright blue, red or white spring flowers and variegated leaves. Pulmonarias are easy to establish and easy to grow, provided attention is given to supplying them with the correct soil conditions.
SOIL Tolerant of many, but must be moist; a deep, rich, fertile loam will give the best results.
SITUATION Full sun to moderate shade; shade must be given on soils prone to any drying out.
WATERING AND FEEDING Mulch in autumn and spring. Feed with a balanced general purpose fertilizer in mid-spring and again after midsummer.
MANAGEMENT Cut down to soil level in autumn. Once the leaves begin to shrivel, they may be pulled away by hand.
COMMON PROBLEMS None.
PROPAGATION Division in autumn or spring.
TROUBLESHOOTING None normally necessary.
SIZE Varies with species; the commonest of the ground-covering forms is *P. angustifolia*, of which individual plants will attain about 20 × 20cm/8 × 8in in two years.

Pulmonaria angustifolia

Ranunculus – Salvia

Ranunculus acris 'Flore Pleno'

Ranunculus BUTTERCUP

This is the large genus that embraces the wild species of buttercup but also includes a number of annual and perennial species for the border. I find the most attractive and certainly the easiest to grow are the double-flowered forms of the wild species, but care is needed for some are invasive.

SOIL Tolerates most, but best in rich and slightly moist soils.

SITUATION Full sun to light or even moderate shade.

WATERING AND FEEDING Mulch in autumn and spring. Feed with a balanced general purpose fertilizer in mid-spring and again after midsummer.

MANAGEMENT Cut down to soil level in autumn. The taller-growing forms will need some wrap-around support. Divide most forms every four or five years; ground-covering types are best left undisturbed.

COMMON PROBLEMS None.

PROPAGATION Division in autumn or spring, or from seed.

TROUBLESHOOTING None normally necessary.

SIZE Varies with species; two of the best are the double forms of the meadow buttercup, *R. acris* 'Flore Pleno', which will attain 75 × 75cm/2½ × 2½ft in three years, and the lesser celandine, *R. ficaria flore pleno*, which must only be planted where its invasiveness can be allowed free rein. Individual plants will reach 5 × 75cm/2 × 30in in about four years but each multiplies rapidly to produce a ground-covering carpet.

Romneya TREE POPPY

The Californian tree poppies always arouse interest and comment when bearing their large, poppy-like flowers in late summer, but they are fickle both in their site requirements and their early establishment. They are reliable only in milder areas.

SOIL Must be rich and deep but free-draining; they are intolerant of waterlogging.

SITUATION Full sun; intolerant of exposure to cold winds.

WATERING AND FEEDING Mulch in autumn and spring. Feed with a balanced general purpose fertilizer in mid-spring and again after midsummer.

MANAGEMENT The old shoots should be left on over the winter to provide protection, and in mild areas they may all survive until the spring, when the oldest half of them should be cut back to soil level. Usually, however, there will be considerable frost damage and all shoots should then be cut down to soil level in spring – the flowers will be borne on the new shoots. As the plants greatly resent disturbance once established, they are best not moved unless absolutely necessary. They will require some staking.

COMMON PROBLEMS None.

PROPAGATION Root cuttings in winter; some forms from seed.

TROUBLESHOOTING None normally necessary.

SIZE In good growing conditions, the shoots will attain about 1.5–2m/5–6½ft within a year, and the plant will spread to about 2m/6½ft after three or four years.

Romneya coulteri

Rudbeckia CONEFLOWER

Belonging to the group of very easily grown and rather similar border perennials in the daisy family, rudbeckias are especially useful for their mainly yellow and golden flowers in late autumn.

SOIL Tolerates almost any but always best in fairly rich and moist but free-draining soils.

SITUATION Full sun or light shade.

WATERING AND FEEDING Mulch in autumn and spring. Feed with a balanced general purpose fertilizer in mid-spring and again after midsummer.

MANAGEMENT Cut down to soil level after flowering in autumn, or in spring. They will require staking. Divide every four or five years in autumn or spring.

COMMON PROBLEMS None.

PROPAGATION Division in autumn or spring, or from seed.

TROUBLESHOOTING None normally necessary.

SIZE Varies with species; the common black-eyed Susan, *R. fulgida*, will attain about 1m × 60cm/3 × 2ft after three years, the more vigorous *R. laciniata* at least double this.

Rudbeckia fulgida

Ruta RUE

A small group of rather woody perennials verging on the shrubby, the best known being the glaucous-leaved *R. graveolens* 'Jackman's Blue'. They are aromatic herbs at home both in the herb garden and the herbaceous border.

SOIL Light, well drained, not very rich.

SITUATION Full sun or very light shade.

WATERING AND FEEDING Mulch in autumn and spring. Feed with a balanced general purpose fertilizer in mid-spring and again after midsummer.

MANAGEMENT For the bushiest plants, cut back all stems hard to new growth annually in spring, or at least cut back dead flower spikes to their woody base. No staking is needed.

COMMON PROBLEMS None.

PROPAGATION Semi-ripe cuttings in summer, or from seed.

TROUBLESHOOTING Leggy plants can be cut hard back into old wood in spring, and will rejuvenate.

SIZE *R. graveolens* 'Jackman's Blue' will reach about 75 × 60cm/ $2\frac{1}{2}$ × 2ft after two or three years.

Salvia

It is unfortunate that the best known salvias are the strident red ones only perennial in very warm climates; for there are also some easy and interesting hardy forms. There are the rosette-forming perennials derived from such species as *S. bulleyana*, the semi-shrubby types including the common sage, *S. officinalis*, and a number of more tender forms, such as *S. microphylla*.

SOIL Most forms tolerate most soils, but are best in well-drained, fairly rich conditions.

SITUATION Full sun.

Ruta graveolens 'Jackman's Blue'

Salvia – Verbascum

WATERING AND FEEDING Mulch in autumn and spring. Feed with a balanced general purpose fertilizer in mid-spring and again after midsummer.

MANAGEMENT TRUE HERBACEOUS FORMS Cut back dead flower stems after flowering and cut all growth above ground back to soil level in autumn. Divide every four or five years.

SEMI-SHRUBS For most, cut out any frost-damaged shoots in spring; otherwise no treatment is needed, although the common sage is best cut back hard in spring to its woody base.

COMMON PROBLEMS None.

PROPAGATION TRUE HERBACEOUS FORMS Division in spring. SEMI-SHRUBS Softwood or semi-ripe cuttings in early summer.

TROUBLESHOOTING Semi-shrub forms will usually regenerate if cut back hard into old wood in spring.

SIZE The rosette-forming herbaceous types will reach about 60 × 60cm/2 × 2ft in two or three years. Most of the semi-shrubs range between 60cm–1m × 50cm–1m/2–3 × 1½–3ft in the same time.

Salvia microphylla

Sanguinaria BLOODROOT

A one-species genus but nonetheless a valuable low-growing, spring-flowering plant for rather specific conditions. The double white-flowered *S. canadensis* 'Plena' is much the best form.

SOIL Must be moist but well drained, organic, and nutrient-rich if the plant is to give anything approaching its true potential.

SITUATION Full sun or light to moderate shade.

WATERING AND FEEDING Mulch in autumn and spring. Feed with a balanced general purpose fertilizer in mid-spring and again after midsummer.

MANAGEMENT Little is needed; the foliage and flowers wither away and vanish by early autumn and the only important consideration is to be sure that the position is well marked, as it is very easy to damage the clumps when planting bulbs. In most situations the plants may be left undisturbed for many years.

COMMON PROBLEMS None.

PROPAGATION Division in late summer.

TROUBLESHOOTING None normally necessary.

SIZE Will attain about 15 × 50cm/6in × 1½ft after four years.

Stachys

Among the common and popular species of this genus, *S. byzantina* has attractive woolly leaves, while *S. macrantha* features lush and richly coloured flower spikes. They are versatile plants, but not suitable for cold and wet gardens.

SOIL Tolerates most, provided it is well drained; will tolerate fairly dry and impoverished soils.

SITUATION Full sun; there are some common wild species that are woodland plants, but don't let this mislead you into planting them in shade.

WATERING AND FEEDING Mulch in autumn and spring. Feed with a balanced general purpose fertilizer in mid-spring and again after midsummer.

Sanguinaria canadensis 'Plena'

MANAGEMENT Cut back dead flower stems after flowering and cut all growth above ground back to soil level in autumn on all species except the greyish, woolly-leaved *S. byzantina*: this form is evergreen and should simply have dead or browned shoots cut back. Divide all species every three or four years.

COMMON PROBLEMS None.

PROPAGATION Division in spring.

TROUBLESHOOTING None normally necessary.

SIZE Most will reach about 45–60 × 30–45cm/1½–2 × 1–1½ft in two or three years, but *S. byzantina* is a ground-covering plant attaining about 12–15 × 50–75cm/4–6in × 1½–2½ft in the same time.

Thalictrum MEADOW-RUE

These are graceful and under-appreciated plants for lightly shaded situations, particularly useful for borders that do not receive full sun for the whole of the day; they can disappoint if their roots are allowed to dry out. The flowers are not spectacular but light, tiny and feathery with rather an individual appeal.

SOIL All of the commonly grown species require moist, fairly rich soils.

SITUATION Thalictrum tolerates full sun but always performs better in light or moderate shade.

WATERING AND FEEDING Mulch in autumn and spring. Feed with a balanced general purpose fertilizer in mid-spring and again after midsummer.

MANAGEMENT Cut down to soil level in autumn; the stems are too feeble to leave, and as soon as the winter weather arrives they look a mess. With luck and careful planting among other tall plants, you may find no staking is needed; otherwise, some wraparound support will be essential. Divide every three or four years.

COMMON PROBLEMS None.

PROPAGATION Division in autumn or spring, or from seed.

TROUBLESHOOTING None normally necessary.

SIZE Most of the popular true border species, such as *T. delavayi* and *T. aquilegiifolium*, will reach heights of 1–1.5m/3–5ft and a spread of about 60cm/2ft in two or three years; but there are also some lower-growing forms, and a rather useful ground-covering species for a woodland garden is *T. minus*, which has flower stems about 60cm/2ft tall and will spread fairly vigorously.

Verbascum MULLEIN

Some of the best mulleins are biennials or monocarpic perennials (they die after flowering), but there are a few reliably perennial species that can form majestic components to any border, especially in gentler conditions.

SOIL Tolerates most unless cold, heavy and waterlogged, but always best on slightly alkaline, free-draining but fairly rich soils.

SITUATION Full sun to light shade; shelter from strong winds.

WATERING AND FEEDING Mulch in autumn and spring. Feed with a balanced general purpose fertilizer in mid-spring and again after midsummer.

Stachys lanata

Thalictrum aquilegiifolium 'Thundercloud'

Verbascum – Ferns

Verbascum olympicum

Veronica gentianoides

MANAGEMENT Cut down the flower spike after flowering; I prefer to leave some of the old foliage until the spring and then cut it down to soil level. The tall flower spikes are stout and should not require support if protected by other plants nearby. Verbascums do not divide satisfactorily and are best renewed every four or five years.

COMMON PROBLEMS Leaf-eating insects are common but rarely very damaging. Mildew can be serious but not usually until late in the season.

PROPAGATION Semi-ripe cuttings in late summer, or root cuttings in winter.

TROUBLESHOOTING None normally necessary.

SIZE Varies with species but as a rough indication the most imposing of the perennial forms, such as *V. densiflorum*, will attain 1.5m × 75cm/5 × 2½ft in two years.

Veronica SPEEDWELL

With the shrubby hebes being so popular, there has been a tendency to forget their blue-flowered herbaceous relatives even though they are a fine group of summer-flowering perennials. Although generally more hardy than hebes, the border veronicas are almost invariably best in fairly mild conditions.

SOIL Tolerates many, but must be well drained.

SITUATION Full sun to very light shade.

WATERING AND FEEDING Mulch in autumn and spring. Feed with a balanced general purpose fertilizer in mid-spring and again after midsummer.

MANAGEMENT Cut down to soil level in autumn, and protect the crown over the winter by mounding a few centimetres of organic mulch over it. The flower spikes of some varieties tend to flop and kink but are not easily supported in an attractive manner; the best answer is to use some wrap-around support or possibly to place wide mesh netting over the top through which the stems can grow. Divide every three or four years.

COMMON PROBLEMS None.

PROPAGATION Division in spring, basal cuttings in autumn, or from seed.

TROUBLESHOOTING None normally necessary.

SIZE The least vigorous forms are more or less mat-forming rock garden plants, but the size of the more upright types ranges up to 1.2m × 60cm/4 × 2ft after three years for *V. virginica*.

Yucca

Yuccas are among the very few large, spiky-leaved monocotyledons to be really hardy, a fact that makes them useful as garden features or, as garden designers call them, 'architectural plants'. They benefit from some protection in other than very mild areas, and are often usefully grown in containers which can be moved into some protection in winter.

SOIL Must be well drained and preferably fairly rich; tolerant of alkalinity. In containers use John Innes No.2 potting compost.

SITUATION Full sun with shelter from cold winds.

WATERING AND FEEDING Mulch in autumn and spring. Feed with a balanced general purpose fertilizer in mid-spring and again after midsummer. Take care that plants in containers are not allowed to become very dry in summer.

MANAGEMENT Cut down old flower spikes as flowers fade; carefully cut away dead leaves from around the sides of the clump in late autumn. When in flower, the spike may need some improvised support although this is difficult to do unobtrusively. Plants growing in the open in colder areas are best protected by loosely wrapping hessian or a similar porous material (but not plastic sheet) around them during the coldest weather. Hardy yuccas may be left undisturbed or divided every five or six years.

COMMON PROBLEMS Fungal leaf spotting.

PROPAGATION Division in spring, root cuttings in winter, or offsets in spring.

TROUBLESHOOTING None normally necessary; if severely damaged by frost, plants may regenerate when cut back into healthy tissue.

SIZE The hardy forms will reach up to $2 \times 2m/6\frac{1}{2} \times 6\frac{1}{2}$ft after about eight or ten years.

Ferns

Hardy ferns have waxed and waned in gardening popularity and are passing through a well-justified revival. The numerous species and varieties offer a pleasing contrast to flowering plants, while the evergreen types are particularly valuable. Provided their basic site requirements can be met, there are few garden plants that need so little attention.

SOIL With very few exceptions, ferns require a moist, organic and fairly rich soil. Among common species, only the limestone fern *Polypodium vulgare* is tolerant of dry conditions; it is also one of the few that is tolerant of high alkalinity.

SITUATION Although most ferns, other than those with very fragile foliage, will survive in full sun provided the soil is very moist, they are much more successful in light to deep shade. A few of the exotic evergreen species are slightly tender and must be planted in sheltered positions and well away from winter winds.

WATERING AND FEEDING Mulch in autumn and spring. Apply a light dressing of balanced, general purpose fertilizer in mid-spring and again after midsummer.

MANAGEMENT Ferns require no staking and most will not require division more than every six or seven years in spring. Indeed, many can be left more or less indefinitely without disturbance. The dead fronds of deciduous species are best cut away (not pulled, for they may cut your hands) in late autumn. The old fronds of evergreen types may be left until they become frayed and tattered, then cut away.

COMMON PROBLEMS None.

PROPAGATION From spores, by division, or by offsets (where produced) in spring.

TROUBLESHOOTING Not likely to be necessary.

Yucca gloriosa

Phyllitis scolopendrium

Ferns – Sedges and rushes

SIZE Varies between species, so read label information carefully. The smallest forms suitable for growing in wall crevices, such as some of the *Adiantum* species, will only attain 15 × 20cm/6 × 8in in two or three years, whereas the largest of the hardy species, *Osmunda regalis*, the royal fern, will reach 2 × 1m/6½ × 3ft in the same time.

Grasses

The days when the lawn was considered the only place in the garden in which to grow grasses have now passed. Apart from the many annual species and the perennial bamboos, there are numerous ornamental herbaceous species that can be used effectively in the border or as isolated clumps. Most are fully hardy and easy to grow, although a few can be invasive. (Some so-called grasses are actually sedges or rushes, and are discussed separately.)

Grasses

SOIL Almost any, provided it is not very heavy or waterlogged. There are a few species, including the popular and rather invasive *Glyceria maxima* 'Variegata', which must have wet soil and are suitable for waterside plantings or bog gardens.

SITUATION Full sun to moderate shade, depending on species. It is important to buy named varieties of plants from a reputable nursery that will supply accurate information, because shade tolerance ranges from such species as the woodland grass *Millium effusum*, which is a deep-shade plant, to the many sun-loving forms like *Cortaderia* (pampas grass).

WATERING AND FEEDING Mulch in autumn and spring. Feed with a balanced general purpose fertilizer in mid-spring and again after midsummer.

MANAGEMENT Grasses require no staking and the clump-forming species should be divided very infrequently – in spring, once every ten years may be adequate. Where space allows you to grow the more invasive stoloniferous forms such as *Phalaris arundinacea*, these should be divided every three or four years. The soft-leaved forms are best cut down to soil level in autumn but those with stiff stems and attractive dead seed-heads should be left over the winter and then cut down in early spring. There is a belief that the best way to deal with pampas grass (*Cortaderia*) is to set fire to the clump at the end of the winter. Don't try it; you stand a good chance of killing the plant. Equip yourself with a pair of very strong gloves and pull out the dead material from the centre.

COMMON PROBLEMS None.

PROPAGATION Division in autumn or spring; some from seed.

TROUBLESHOOTING Not likely to be necessary but a common complaint is that pampas grasses fail to flower. This is almost invariably due to the plants having been raised from seed; always buy named, selected forms that flower reliably.

SIZE Varies, so read label information carefully. The smaller, clump-forming species such as *Festuca glauca* will not exceed 45 × 45cm/1½ × 1½ft in five years, while the very vigorous *Leymus arenarius* will reach 1.5 × 3–4m/5 × 10–13ft in the same time.

Sedges and rushes

Although fewer in number and generally less important than grasses as garden ornamentals, the evergreen sedge and rush families include several valuable attractive species. All are easily grown, although individual requirements vary widely.

SOIL Varies with type; among rushes, *Luzula* species require dry, more or less sandy soils, whilst *Juncus*, in general, need wetter conditions and several make very useful waterside plants. Sedges generally tend to thrive in moist soils and included among these are several species that are best grown in the water garden; check label information carefully.

SITUATION Full sun or light shade.

WATERING AND FEEDING Mulch in autumn and spring where practical – clearly this is not feasible in a bog garden. Feed with a balanced general purpose fertilizer in mid-spring and again after midsummer where the plants are growing in a conventional border; do not use fertilizer close to pools.

MANAGEMENT Little is needed; even for the varieties with very tall flower stems staking is never really successful or aesthetically pleasing. Allow dead flower stems to remain over winter and then cut them back in spring, or when they become very damaged by rain and wind. Trim back foliage lightly in spring but do not cut right back to soil level.

COMMON PROBLEMS None.

PROPAGATION Division in autumn or spring; some from seed.

TROUBLESHOOTING None normally necessary.

SIZE Varies greatly, so check label information; some of the more vigorous forms such as *Carex riparia*, the pond sedge, will attain a height of about 1–1.2m/3–4ft and spread invasively.

Carex pendula

BULBOUS PLANTS

Agapanthus
Allium
Alstroemeria
Amaryllis
Anemone
Arum
Bulbocodium
Chionodoxa
Colchicum
Convallaria
Corydalis
Crocosmia
Crocus
Cyclamen
Dahlia
Eranthis
Eremurus
Erythronium
Fritillaria

Gagea
Galanthus
Gladiolus
Hyacinthoides
Hyacinthus
Iris
Leucojum
Lilium
Muscari
Narcissus
Nerine
Ornithogalum
Schizostylis
Scilla
Sisyrinchium
Sternbergia
Trillium
Tulipa
Zantesdeschia

Principles of care

I use the term bulbous plants here to describe all those deciduous or evergreen herbaceous perennials that have a swollen underground food storage structure, whether in the form of a bulb, a corm, a tuber or a rhizome. They offer gardeners a rapid source of satisfaction, the stored food reserves virtually guaranteeing strong growth and a fine display of flowers in the first season after planting. Given the modest proviso that only high quality, plump bulbs are bought and that 'job lots' of cut-price, end-of-season mixtures are avoided, it is hard to go wrong. The only real problems with them arise in subsequent years.

PLANTING

Most bulbs require well-drained soils and most are tolerant of moderate acidity and alkalinity. The need for good drainage is particularly important from early summer onwards: although many spring-flowering bulbous plants grow in rather wet conditions in the wild, when these conditions continue throughout the year problems are likely to arise from fungal decay. It is, therefore, a sound maxim always to plant bulbs on a shallow bed of sand: place a handful of horticultural sand, to which a little bonemeal has been added, in the planting hole to minimize rot at the vulnerable bulb base.

Almost all bulbous plants make good subjects for containers either as temporary or permanent plantings, preferably in John Innes No. 2 soil-based compost. If they are fed as I recommend, hardy bulbs can usually be relied on to give a good display for about three or four years in a container. After this time they should be lifted, the compost renewed and the bulbs replanted and re-spaced.

In general, bulbous plants should be planted as soon as possible after purchase and before shoot growth begins. This will give them the best opportunity to develop a strong root system; there is no advantage in planting them more shallowly than normal towards the end of the planting period, as is sometimes supposed. A few types, of which snowdrops are the best known, will establish most successfully if bought in full leaf.

Although in the following descriptions I have indicated the approximate distances to which individual plants will spread, this is fairly academic information as most bulbs are best planted in groups of six to twelve or more (depending on size), with a space between each bulb equivalent to at least three times its diameter if the bulbs are intended as long-term plantings. You can achieve a good display, especially in containers, by planting more closely (as is often shown in the packet illustrations), but the competition for nutrients will rapidly exhaust the bulbs.

Planting depths for bulbs

PLANTING DEPTHS In general, bulbs should be planted with their bases at a depth equal to about 2½ to 3 times their average diameter, with the notable exceptions of *Lilium candidum* and cyclamen; *Fritillaria imperialis* should be planted on its side. It is better to err on the deep rather than the shallow side, but on heavier soils, where success is less certain, it may be better to plant the bulbs about thirty per cent nearer the surface.

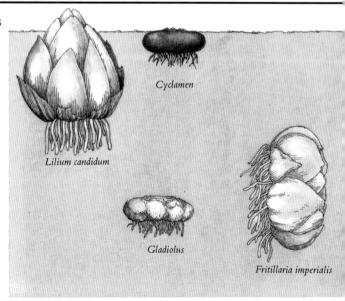

Cyclamen

Lilium candidum

Gladiolus

Fritillaria imperialis

GENERAL MANAGEMENT

Non-hardy bulbs should always be lifted at the end of the growing season and stored in a frost-free place, but most hardy types (the most significant exception to this being hybrid tulips) are best left to 'naturalize' or multiply *in situ*. If they are fed with bonemeal or a bulb fertilizer early in the season, when growth begins, and then given liquid feed after flowering, most bulbs should naturalize satisfactorily. Don't underestimate the importance of the foliage in producing food to build up the bulb's strength for flowering the following year. It might look dreary, but it should be cared for.

PROPAGATION

Natural multiplication of the bulbous structure is the most reliable method of propagation, and in most cases established clumps benefit from being lifted and split up every four or five years. Most bulbous plants may also be propagated from seed sown in pans of gritty soil-based compost, but they will take from two to seven years to flower. In a few instances, as for example with lilies, the plant will produce bulbils or bulb scales, which can be removed and grown on.

TROUBLESHOOTING

The most frequent reasons for the failure of bulbs are shallow planting and a lack of attention to feeding; some varieties, however, are not suitable for planting under turf as they are unable to compete effectively with the grass, and label information on individual species should be carefully checked. The commonest problem by far is blindness – a failure to form flowers. This is rare in the first year but thereafter can result from a variety of causes: a lack of feeding is one and, associated with it, competition between bulbs that have multiplied and become closely packed together. Lifting, dividing and replanting is the remedy in the latter case, but a bulb that has become enfeebled through lack of feeding will require three or four years of attention, with regular feeding while in leaf, before it flowers again.

Sometimes blindness arises from damage to the growing point caused by the larvae of insects such as the narcissus fly, or from damage to the whole bulb by fungal decay. If the bulbs are dug up and found to be decaying there is no point trying to salvage them; they are best discarded.

Shallowly planted bulbs or corms such as crocus can occasionally suffer from a condition known as frost heave, in which they are forced to the surface of frozen soil. They will generally survive if replanted rather more deeply. Mice and voles will also dig up and eat crocus in particular, but this problem can be circumvented by planting the corms slightly more deeply and placing fine-mesh chicken wire over them before replacing the soil.

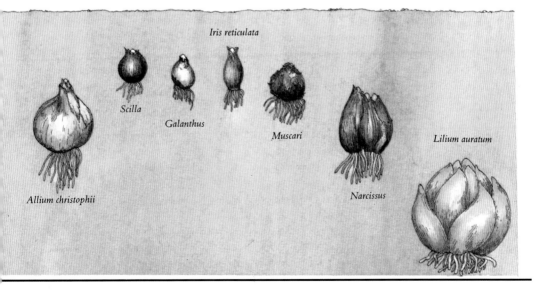

Iris reticulata

Scilla

Galanthus

Muscari

Lilium auratum

Allium christophii

Narcissus

Agapanthus – Anemone

Agapanthus AFRICAN LILY

In a mild situation the massed blue or white flowers of agapanthus are magnificent, but in cold areas they will always disappoint.

SOIL AND PLANTING Moist, well-drained, rich, organic soil, intolerant of very light or poor soils or of waterlogging. The roots should be planted with their tops covered by about 5cm/2in of soil. Agapanthus can be grown successfully in large containers of John Innes No. 3 potting compost, and this is useful in cooler areas where the plants can be moved into some shelter from frost in winter.

SITUATION Full sun, shelter from cold winds. Always most successful in mild, coastal gardens, although the narrow-leaved varieties (which are those most often offered for sale) are reliably more hardy than the broad-leaved forms, which are frost tender.

WATERING AND FEEDING Mulch in autumn and spring. Feed with a balanced general purpose fertilizer in mid-spring and again around midsummer. The autumn mulch should be mounded around the crowns to provide protection from winter frost.

MANAGEMENT Cut off dead flower spikes after flowering; divide every eight or ten years, and certainly no more frequently than about once every five or six years.

COMMON PROBLEMS None.

SIZE The forms most commonly seen are the Headbourne hybrids, which will reach about 90cm–1m × 50cm/3 × 1½ft after five years, but can eventually spread considerably more.

Agapanthus 'Castle of Mey'

Allium

A very useful group of summer-flowering bulbs with white, pink, red, mauve, blue or yellow flowers, growing to a wide range of sizes. They are related to the onion, and it is possibly the thought of an onion smell that explains why they are not more widely grown; yet in practice any smell is rare. Alliums will be more popular in the future as their value for summer flowering becomes more widely appreciated. They have a further advantage in making excellent dried heads for flower arrangements.

SOIL AND PLANTING Light, rich, fairly free-draining; tolerant of alkalinity. The bulb bases should be planted at a depth of 2½ times their average diameter.

SITUATION Always best in full sun.

WATERING AND FEEDING Mulch in autumn and apply a top dressing of bonemeal or a proprietary bulb fertilizer in early spring. Feed with a fertilizer high in potash once a week after blooming until the leaves turn yellow.

MANAGEMENT Do not lift annually but divide the clumps every five or six years. Remove the flower heads after blooming, and trim back the leaves to soil level as soon as they turn yellow.

COMMON PROBLEMS None.

SIZE The range in size between the varieties is probably greater than for any other bulb genus. At the two extremes are *A. moly* with a height and spread of 10–30 × 10–12cm/4–12 × 4–5in, and *A. giganteum* at 2m × 40cm/6½ × 1ft.

Allium aflatunense

Alstroemeria   PERUVIAN LILY

These summer-flowering, tuberous perennials come in a wide range of usually mixed colours, and are popular as cut flowers; they are hardy in most areas.

Soil and planting Light, rich, fairly free-draining. The tuber bases should be at a depth of 2½ times their average diameter.

Situation Always best in full sun, but with some shelter from cold winds.

Watering and feeding Mulch in autumn. Top dress with bonemeal or a proprietary bulb fertilizer in early spring, and feed with a liquid fertilizer high in potash once a week after blooming and until the leaves turn yellow.

Management Divide the clumps every five or six years. There is a temptation in cold areas to lift the plants annually but, as they often take at least two years to establish, this is unwise and in cold gardens it is better to mound a protective mulch over the plants in late autumn. Remove flower heads after flowering and trim back leaves to soil level when they turn yellow.

Common problems None.

Size Most forms will reach 1m × 60cm/3 × 2ft.

Alstroemeria hybrid

Amaryllis

To many gardeners, the name amaryllis conjures up an image of the huge flowering bulb more correctly called *Hippeastrum*, but most experts use the name for a single species, *A. belladonna*. It bears a group of fairly small flowers on a tall stem in late summer, and is genuinely hardy only in mild areas.

Soil and planting Light and free-draining but not impoverished. The bulbs must be planted deeply, with the bases at a depth of about 20cm/8in.

Situation Full sun or very light shade, with shelter from cold winds; close to a south- or south-west-facing wall is ideal.

Watering and feeding Mulch in autumn. Top dress with bonemeal or a proprietary bulb fertilizer in early summer, and feed with a liquid fertilizer high in potash once a week after blooming and until the leaves turn yellow.

Management The bulbs must not be lifted or disturbed, for flowering may be disrupted for two or three years.

Common problems None.

Size Up to 60cm/18in in height and spreading as the bulbs multiply to reach perhaps 30cm/12in after five years.

Anemone   WINDFLOWER

There are several groups of garden anemone, not superficially very similar. The rhizomatous forms are of two main types: the hardy, small, spring-flowering species such as *A. blanda*, in turn related to the native wood anemone *A. nemorosa*; and the 'De Caen' varieties of *A. coronaria*, which are hardy in most areas but are not reliably perennial. *A. × hybrida* is fibrous-rooted, and is discussed on page 106.

Amaryllis belladonna

Anemone – Colchicum

Anemone 'De Caen'

SOIL AND PLANTING Moist, fairly rich but free-draining soils suit all types, although *A. nemorosa* is better in free-draining organic soils. The tuber or bulb bases should be at a depth of 2½ times their average diameter.

SITUATION All are best in full sun or light shade, except *A. nemorosa*, which prefers light to moderate or even deep shade, and is a good plant for a woodland garden.

WATERING AND FEEDING SMALL PERENNIAL FORMS Mulch in autumn. Top dress with bonemeal or a proprietary bulb fertilizer in early spring, and feed with a liquid fertilizer high in potash once a week after blooming and until the leaves turn yellow.

'DE CAEN' VARIETIES Top dress the soil with bonemeal before planting. Feed with a liquid fertilizer as the flower buds form, and, if experience suggests they are perennial in your area, feed again after the flowers fade and until the foliage turns yellow.

MANAGEMENT The small perennial forms should not be lifted and seldom, if ever, require dividing. If the need arises, transplant them when dormant.

COMMON PROBLEMS None.

SIZE The small perennial forms reach a height of 15–20cm/6–8in and a spread of about 8–10cm/3–4in, with each plant slowly multiplying to form a clump perhaps 20cm/8in in diameter after five years. The 'De Caen' and similar varieties grow up to 30cm/12in tall and spread to about 5–8cm/2–3in within their first year.

Arum

The most familiar arum is the cuckoo pint or lords and ladies, *A. maculatum*, but there is also a related species, *A. pictum*, which is almost as hardy and whose handsome variegated leaves can, given the correct conditions, provide interest for much of the year.

SOIL AND PLANTING Moist, rich, organic soils always provide the best results; lushness is an important part of this plant's appeal. The tubers are horizontal and should be planted at a depth of about 5–7cm/2–3in.

SITUATION These are plants for the woodland garden and require light to moderate shade; some gardeners claim their variegation is less pronounced in deep shade.

WATERING AND FEEDING Mulch in autumn. Top dress with bonemeal or a proprietary bulb fertilizer in early spring and again after midsummer.

MANAGEMENT Leave the plants undisturbed; do not even cut down the dead flower spikes, as bright red fruits will follow.

COMMON PROBLEMS None.

SIZE Depending on the richness of the soil arums will reach a height of 15–25cm/6–10in, and a similar spread.

Bulbocodium RED CROCUS

The spring-flowering red crocus is more closely related to colchicums than true crocuses, and their requirements are similarly best satisfied in the rock garden. Of the only two species, *B. vernum* is the one likely to be seen.

Arum italicum pictum

SOIL AND PLANTING Light, preferably gritty and free-draining; tolerant of moderate acidity and alkalinity. The bulb bases should be at a depth of $2\frac{1}{2}$ times their average diameter.

SITUATION Full sun to very light shade.

WATERING AND FEEDING In early spring mulch very lightly and top dress with bonemeal or a proprietary bulb fertilizer. Liquid feed until the foliage turns yellow.

MANAGEMENT Almost none needed. Do not lift the bulbs annually and leave them undisturbed for as long as possible.

COMMON PROBLEMS None.

SIZE *B. vernum* will reach 4×4cm/$1\frac{1}{2} \times 1\frac{1}{2}$in in two or three years.

Chionodoxa   GLORY OF THE SNOW

Bulbocodium vernum

These are among my favourite small spring-flowering bulbs; they are easy to grow and have the advantages of producing their usually blue flowers early, even after severe winters, and of tolerating more shade than many similar species.

SOIL AND PLANTING Light, free-draining; tolerant of moderate acidity and alkalinity. The bulb bases should be at a depth of $2\frac{1}{2}$ times their average diameter.

SITUATION Full sun to light or even moderate shade.

WATERING AND FEEDING Mulch very lightly in early spring. Top dress with bonemeal or a proprietary bulb fertilizer in early spring; liquid feed until the foliage turns yellow.

MANAGEMENT Do not lift the bulbs annually and leave them undisturbed for as long as possible – they will self-seed freely.

COMMON PROBLEMS None.

SIZE There is some variation between species but the commonest, *C. luciliae*, will reach 10×5cm/4×2in after two years; some strains of the same species are smaller.

Colchicum

Sometimes confusingly called autumn crocuses, colchicums are quite distinct in their large, goblet-shaped flowers produced on bare stems before the leaves emerge. They are most attractive if well grown, but I never find them easy plants to manage.

SOIL AND PLANTING Will tolerate many but always best in moist, rich, organic soils. The bulb bases should be at a depth of $2\frac{1}{2}$ times their average diameter.

SITUATION Full sun to light or possibly moderate shade.

WATERING AND FEEDING Mulch in early spring. Top dress with bonemeal or a proprietary bulb fertilizer in early spring; liquid feed until the foliage turns yellow.

MANAGEMENT The tall, leafless flower stems are feeble and very readily pushed over and broken by winds and rain. I find the answer is to grow them in tall, unmown grass, which provides support. Leave the bulbs undisturbed for as long as possible.

COMMON PROBLEMS None.

SIZE The largest hybrids, such as *C.* 'The Giant', will reach a height of 20cm/8in and spread to a similar size within three years; smaller species will barely reach half this size in the same time.

Colchicum autumnale

Convallaria – Crocus

Convallaria majalis

Convallaria LILY OF THE VALLEY

One of the classic garden plants, but also one of gardening's enigmas: on some sites it becomes an ineradicable weed, while in others it obstinately refuses to establish.

SOIL AND PLANTING Tolerant of many but always best in moist, rich, organic soils. Where it is difficult to establish, try digging up and transplanting in late winter or early spring a clump that is growing well, with as much soil as possible. The horizontal rhizomes should be at a depth of about 5cm/2in.

SITUATION Best in light to moderate shade.

WATERING AND FEEDING Mulch in autumn. Top dress with bonemeal or a proprietary bulb fertilizer in early spring.

MANAGEMENT Do not lift the bulbs annually, but divide the clumps every five or six years in late winter or very early spring, unless they are growing in a semi-wild situation when they may be left undisturbed.

COMMON PROBLEMS None; if the bulbs become too invasive they may be controlled with glyphosate weedkiller.

SIZE Reaches a height of about 30cm/12in in good soils and will spread to a similar extent within three years.

Corydalis

This is a large genus of plants, surprisingly grouped in the poppy family but including many with small tuberous roots. Some are invasive to the point of becoming weeds, but there are a few choice and easy species, particularly *C. solida* and the fibrous-rooted, blue-flowered *C. cashmeriana*.

SOIL AND PLANTING Tolerates most provided the soil is well drained. Plant with the roots about 5cm/2in deep.

SITUATION Full sun to moderate shade; some forms are good plants for growing between paving slabs.

WATERING AND FEEDING Apply a light mulch where feasible in spring and autumn. Top dress with bonemeal or a proprietary bulb fertilizer in early spring and again after midsummer.

MANAGEMENT Do not lift annually but divide clumps every five or six years in late winter or early spring, unless they are growing in a semi-wild situation when they may be left undisturbed.

COMMON PROBLEMS None.

SIZE Varies with species; most of the commoner forms will reach about 20 × 10cm/8 × 4in in two or three years.

Crocosmia MONBRETIA

The monbretia is an undervalued plant, largely because the older orange-flowered forms can be invasive. Modern varieties are more compact and come in a good range of colours, so this most adaptable plant could be considered more seriously.

SOIL AND PLANTING Almost any; I have seen successful plantings on soil that resembled beach sand and others on a water-logged stream bank. Plant the corms or horizontal stolons at a depth of about 5cm/2in.

Corydalis solida

SITUATION Full sun to light shade, with shelter from cold winds.
WATERING AND FEEDING Mulch in autumn. Top dress with bonemeal or a proprietary bulb fertilizer in early spring.
MANAGEMENT Cut down the foliage as it discolours. Do not lift annually but divide clumps every five or six years.
COMMON PROBLEMS None; if it becomes too invasive it may be controlled with glyphosate weedkiller.
SIZE The modern hybrids reach a height of about 80cm–1m/ 2½–3ft and will spread to about 30cm/1ft within three years; the old, orange-flowered *C. × crocosmiiflora* reaches a similar height but spreads twice as far and continues to do so invasively.

Crocus

Of all the small bulbous plants the crocus is one of the most useful and easy to grow. Most crocuses are spring-flowering, although by careful selection of species it would be possible to have a crocus in flower for almost every month of the year.
SOIL AND PLANTING Tolerates most provided neither heavy nor waterlogged. Most species are tolerant of acidity and alkalinity if not extreme. The corm bases should be at a depth of 3–3½ times their average diameter.
SITUATION Full sun to light shade; some varieties only open completely in full sun. The large-flowered Dutch crocuses are very effective if planted in grass, especially close to deciduous trees where they will flower before the trees come into leaf.
WATERING AND FEEDING Where growing in bare soil mulch in spring and early autumn; top dress with bonemeal or a proprietary bulb fertilizer in early spring; and, if possible, liquid feed two or three times while in full leaf. Where established in grass, mulching is neither necessary nor practicable but apply a fertilizer in early spring if possible.
MANAGEMENT Almost none required, but shrivelled foliage can be pulled away about six weeks after flowering. The blooms of winter-flowering varieties can be knocked about by rain, so protect with cloches when bad weather threatens. Do not lift the corms unless they are growing in containers, when they should be carefully dried off and stored until the autumn; otherwise, leave plants undisturbed for as long as possible. Small species growing in beds may be divided after about six years. Crocuses growing in grass at lawn edges or under trees may have their foliage mown off six weeks after the flowers have faded; then it will be perfectly safe to apply weedkiller to the turf.
COMMON PROBLEMS Voles, birds, squirrels and mice will all eat crocus corms. Corms that appear above the surface of the soil can usually be left alone, as their contractile roots should soon pull them under again.
SIZE Varies with species and variety; the large Dutch crocus will reach a height of 12–15cm/5–6in and spread to about 5cm/2in within two years – although these spread figures are really academic for the corms will always be planted in groups. The smaller-flowered species typically reach about 8–10cm/3–4in in height and a spread of 3–4cm/1–1½in in the same time.

Crocosmia 'Lucifer'

Crocus chrysanthus

Cyclamen

Cyclamen hederifolium

Cyclamens are fairly unusual among the common bulbous plants in being dicotyledonous and members of the primrose family, but they are very valuable in the garden because their surface-living tubers will thrive in conditions where most true bulbs will not. In many forms, the ornamental foliage is almost as important as the flowers.

SOIL AND PLANTING Although always best in moist, organic soils, cyclamen will thrive in the thin soil beneath deciduous trees provided some organic mulch or top dressing is applied. They are tolerant of acidity and moderate alkalinity. If planting directly into the soil, place the corms with the top just showing through the soil surface; but those species with large corms are often better if grown for their first season in small pots of John Innes No. 2 potting compost.

SITUATION Full sun to moderate shade.

WATERING AND FEEDING Mulch in spring and early autumn. Top dress with bonemeal or a bulb fertilizer in early spring. If possible, liquid feed two or three times while in full leaf.

MANAGEMENT Almost none required, although plants growing in thin soil must be mulched as described above: as well as preventing them from drying out, this will also encourage self-sown seedlings. Do not lift annually but divide very overcrowded clumps every five or six years.

COMMON PROBLEMS None.

SIZE Most of the hardy forms, including the commonest, *C. hederifolium*, will reach 10 × 10cm/4 × 4in in two or three years.

Dahlia

The most important of the half-hardy, tuber-forming perennials, loved or loathed by gardeners and certainly requiring some management if they are to give of their best. For those not willing to devote the necessary time and energy, and who perhaps dislike the large-flowered varieties, the smaller-flowered bedding dahlias, grown as annuals from seed, can be very pretty and rewarding.

SOIL AND PLANTING Nutrient-rich, moist but free-draining; intolerant of extremes of acidity and alkalinity. If planted as tubers rather than young plants, they should be planted about three weeks before the last frost is likely, and with the tuber base at a depth of 15–20cm/6–8in.

SITUATION Full sun to light shade.

WATERING AND FEEDING Top dress the planting bed with bonemeal about two weeks before planting. Mulch soon after planting and again halfway through the summer, ensuring that the soil around the plants is not allowed to dry out. Liquid feed with fertilizer high in potash every week during the growing season.

MANAGEMENT Stake at planting time with a single, firm stake and tie the plant on to this as it grows. Dahlias should be stopped by having the growing tip removed about four to six weeks after growth first emerges; this will encourage the formation of side-shoots and more flowers. If the very best large blooms are required, disbud by removing all flower buds except that at the tip of each shoot, as with chrysanthemums; but most gardeners will prefer a bushy plant with more, if smaller, flowers.

In all but the mildest climates, dahlias need to be lifted and stored over winter. Once autumn frost has blackened the foliage, cut the stems down to leave about 15cm/6in. Lift the tubers very carefully with a fork, taking care not to spear them. Carefully poke away any excess soil caught in them with a small cane, and stand them upside down for about a week to drain. Dust them with sulphur fungicide and store them in a frost-free place for the winter, either in envelopes made from layers of newspaper, or, better still, in boxes packed with old, almost dry peat, coir or similar organic material; leave the tops of the tubers uncovered.

Every three or four years the stock should be renewed from cuttings taken in the spring, instead of planting out the old tubers. You will require a greenhouse or other facility where the temperature will not drop below 10°C/50°F. About three months before the last frost is likely, place the tubers in boxes of well-watered soil-less but free-draining compost, the compost to come only to the point where the roots join the tubers. Green shoots will soon emerge and are suitable for cuttings when about 10cm/4in long. They are best removed by bending them until they just break away from the tuber, but they may also be severed with a razor blade. Dip the cuttings in rooting powder and plant them in 9cm/3½in diameter pots filled with a mixture of equal parts by volume of peat and sand. Place in propagator trays. The cuttings will root in about two weeks, and should be hardened off for planting out once the danger of frost has passed.

COMMON PROBLEMS Plants may be affected by aphids; slugs; red spider mite; earwigs; virus.

SIZE A cutting should attain about 1m × 60cm/3 × 2ft in its first year; a mature plant grown from tubers may range from 1 × 1m/3 × 3ft to 2 × 1.5m/6½ × 5ft, depending on the variety.

Dahlia 'Preference' and 'Doris Day'

Eranthis WINTER ACONITE

One of the joys of early spring is the first appearance of these cheerful yellow flowers. They resemble their close relation the buttercup, but unlike them seldom become seriously invasive; they can even be tricky to establish in some gardens.

SOIL AND PLANTING Tolerates most provided the soil doesn't dry out, but always most successful in organic, woodland soils. The tubers should be approximately 5cm/2in deep. If they seem difficult to establish, try transplanting a clump from a mature colony in full leaf, taking as much soil as possible with them.

SITUATION Will tolerate full sun but much better in light to moderate shade.

WATERING AND FEEDING Where growing in bare soil, mulch in spring and early autumn. Top dress with bonemeal or a proprietary bulb fertilizer in early spring; and, if possible, give a liquid feed two or three times while in full leaf. Where established in grass, mulching is neither necessary nor practicable but apply a fertilizer in early spring if possible.

Eranthis hyemalis

Eranthis – Gagea

Eremurus elwesii

MANAGEMENT Plants growing in bare soil will benefit from mulching. Leave the tubers undisturbed for as long as possible.
COMMON PROBLEMS None.
SIZE Attains a height of about 10cm/4in within the first year and a spread of about 10cm/4in with two years – although almost invariably planted in clumps.

Eremurus FOXTAIL LILY

These must be among the tallest of all bulbous-rooted garden plants, forming elongated root tubers which are remarkably easy to break off. Well grown, these are wonderful plants but I find their conditions difficult to satisfy.
SOIL AND PLANTING Very well drained but also rich and preferably organic. Tubers should be planted carefully, spread out, and at a depth of about 8–10cm/3–4in.
SITUATION Full sun to very light shade with plenty of shelter from strong winds.
WATERING AND FEEDING It is very important to mulch in spring and early autumn as this provides frost protection for the young shoots, which can emerge very early in mild seasons. Feed with a balanced general purpose fertilizer in early spring and again after midsummer.
MANAGEMENT They must be staked carefully, either with wrap-around support if the clump is large enough, or with individual canes. Cut down flower spikes as the flowers fade and cut all growth down to soil level after the autumn frosts.
COMMON PROBLEMS None.
SIZE This varies between species and hybrids but can reach up to $2–3 \times 1m/6\frac{1}{2}–10 \times 3ft$, so only plant them where they really do have room to grow.

Erythronium DOG'S TOOTH VIOLET

Erythroniums are among the great under-appreciated delights of the bulbous plant world, principally I think because they are fairly expensive, but also because they tend to be disappointingly short-lived in some gardens.
SOIL AND PLANTING Moist, rich, organic and preferably slightly acidic. Plant tubers approximately 5cm/2in deep.
SITUATION They are intolerant of full sun and require light to moderate shade.
WATERING AND FEEDING Mulch in spring and early autumn and top dress with bonemeal or bulb fertilizer in early spring; if possible, liquid feed two or three times while in full leaf.
MANAGEMENT None required; ideally, erythroniums should be grown in an undisturbed woodland garden or shady bed. I think they tend to be shorter-lived when they have been disturbed and where the soil is not naturally organic and rich in leaf mould.
COMMON PROBLEMS None.
SIZE This varies slightly but most forms will reach a height of about 20–25cm/8–10in within two years and spread to 10–15cm/4–6in in the same time.

Erythronium dens-canis

Fritillaria

Although the genus *Fritillaria* is a very large one with over one hundred species, two rather contrasting types far outweigh all others in garden importance. The small snake's head fritillary (*F. meleagris*) is a rare European native plant of damp pastures, whereas the tall and very distinctive crown imperials (*F. imperialis*) are most at home in the herbaceous border; both share certain important cultivation features. Details about the relatively few other species commonly offered should be checked at the time of purchase, for while most can be treated in the same way as crown imperials, others require well-drained, alpine-bed conditions.

SOIL AND PLANTING Moist but free-draining and fairly rich for *F. imperialis*, wetter although not quite waterlogged for *F. meleagris*. Snake's head bulbs should be planted approximately 5cm/2in deep; crown imperial bulbs should be planted approximately 15cm/6in deep on their sides: this is important to prevent water from collecting in the hollow where the stem emerges.

SITUATION Full sun to light shade.

WATERING AND FEEDING Mulch in spring and early autumn (except where snake's heads are growing in grass, making this impossible). Top dress with bonemeal or a proprietary bulb fertilizer in early spring; if possible, give all types a liquid feed two or three times after blooming and while in full leaf.

MANAGEMENT Crown imperials may require light, wrap-around support if grown in an exposed site; their fleshy stems may be cut back six weeks after the flowers have faded, although by this time they will generally be rotting at the base and can easily be pulled away from below soil level. Snake's heads are best grown in fairly long grass which should not be mown until at least six weeks after the flowers fade. Fritillarias should not be moved once established as they will take several years to flower fully again.

COMMON PROBLEMS None.

SIZE The snake's head fritillary will reach about 30cm/12in in height after two years and spreads slowly to reach perhaps 20cm/8in after seven or eight years. Crown imperials will reach a height of 1–1.5m/3–5ft after two years and spread to around 30cm/1ft after four or five years.

Fritillaria imperialis

Gagea

Small, spring-flowering bulbs with bright yellow, star-shaped flowers. Their growing conditions are perhaps best met by growing them in a rock garden or alpine bed.

SOIL AND PLANTING Light, preferably gritty and free-draining; tolerant of moderate acidity and alkalinity. The bulb bases should be at a depth equal to 2½ times their average diameter.

SITUATION Full sun but not too hot; they are best planted with the shelter of a large rock or larger clump-forming plant nearby.

WATERING AND FEEDING Apply a very light mulch in spring and early autumn. Top dress with bonemeal or a proprietary bulb fertilizer in early spring; if possible, give a liquid feed two or three times after blooming and while in full leaf.

Gagea lutea

Gagea – Hyacinthoides

Galanthus nivalis

MANAGEMENT Allow foliage to die down naturally. The bulbs should not be lifted annually and are best left undisturbed for as long as possible.

COMMON PROBLEMS None.

SIZE They will reach $5–15 \times 2.5–5cm/2–6 \times 1–2in$ after three or four years, depending on the species.

Galanthus SNOWDROP

Among the top half-dozen bulbous plants by almost anyone's reckoning, snowdrops are undemanding in their requirements and easy to grow once they are over the initial, slightly tricky, phase of establishment.

SOIL AND PLANTING Tolerant of most but always best in moist but free-draining and fairly rich organic soils. The bulbs should be planted with their bases at a depth equal to $2\frac{1}{2}–3$ times their average diameter, but they may be difficult to establish from dormant bulbs and are better planted while in full leaf. Nurseries may sell snowdrops in this way, referred to as 'in the green'.

SITUATION They will tolerate full sun but are better in light to moderate or even deep shade.

WATERING AND FEEDING Mulch in spring and early autumn. Top dress with bonemeal or a proprietary bulb fertilizer in early spring; if possible, give a liquid feed two or three times after blooming and while in full leaf.

MANAGEMENT Do not cut back the foliage until at least six weeks after the flowers have faded, by which time it will be beginning to shrivel and before long can be pulled away like straw. In semi-natural situations the foliage may simply be left to die away. The bulbs should not be lifted annually.

COMMON PROBLEMS None.

SIZE Height and vigour vary considerably between species. The commonest, *G. nivalis*, will attain about $15 \times 8–10cm/6 \times 3–4in$ after four years, but some forms are shorter and others, most notably *G. × atkinsii* and *G.* 'S Arnott', are much taller, reaching $35 \times 8–10cm/14 \times 3–4in$ within two years.

Gladiolus

A plant that possibly divides the passions even more than the dahlia, but still almost certainly the most important non-hardy, corm-forming garden genus. There is nothing difficult about growing gladioli and in most gardens they will thrive and give a good display, in return for relatively little effort.

SOIL AND PLANTING Tolerant of most, provided it is not heavy and clayey, but always best in a fairly rich but free-draining soil. Plant the corms with their bases at a depth equal to about 3 times their average diameter, and in succession from about ten to six weeks before the likelihood of the last frost. This will result in a succession of blooms, for gladioli flower on average one hundred days after planting.

SITUATION Full sun to very light shade, preferably with some shelter from cold winds.

WATERING AND FEEDING Work in a dressing of bonemeal or a proprietary bulb fertilizer about one week before planting, then mulch lightly over the corms after planting. Give a liquid feed high in potash every two weeks during the summer, both before and after flowering.

MANAGEMENT In all but the mildest areas, gladioli should be lifted and overwintered. Around the time of the first autumn frosts is safest, but it is also important to leave the corms in place for about six weeks after the flowers have been cut. If the first frosts are not too severe and mild weather returns, it may therefore be advantageous to leave the later-flowering plants in the ground for a few more weeks before lifting them. Once lifted, cut back the foliage to about 10cm/4in above the corms and allow them to dry in a warm but airy place, out of full sun. Peel away the dead leaves and carefully remove any small daughter cormlets. Store corms and cormlets in separate paper bags in a frost-free place. In the spring pot up the cormlets into pots of John Innes No. 2 potting compost. Gladioli will require staking and this is done most neatly and effectively by tying them individually to slender canes, inserted close to each plant.

COMMON PROBLEMS Fungal corm rots; virus; thrips; slugs.

SIZE There are many dwarf species of gladiolus suitable for the alpine garden but these tend to be grown only by specialists. The common, large-flowered garden hybrids will mostly attain 1–1.5m × 15–30cm/3–5ft × 6–12in within the season, depending on variety. The smaller-flowered butterfly varieties will reach about half to two thirds of these sizes.

Gladiolus Butterfly hybrid

Hyacinthoides BLUEBELL

This is the name now used to describe the genus that was formerly *Endymion* but best known as the bluebell. It is easy – too easy – in most gardens and should be planted in semi-natural situations where its invasiveness can be used to greatest effect.

SOIL AND PLANTING Tolerates most but, unlike the majority of bulbs, performs best in heavy soil and is a valuable carpeting species on clayey sites. Ideally, the bulbs should be planted with their bases at a depth equal to about 2½ times their average diameter, but in practice the bluebell is a very obliging plant and will usually establish well even if planted very carelessly.

SITUATION Tolerates full sun but performs much better in light to fairly deep shade; it is a plant of woodland glades.

WATERING AND FEEDING If practical, mulch in spring and early autumn. Top dress with bonemeal or a proprietary bulb fertilizer in early spring.

MANAGEMENT Very little is required. The dead foliage and flower stalks may be pulled away as they discolour, but in a semi-natural planting they will fade away of their own accord and self-mulch the bulbs.

COMMON PROBLEMS Rust.

SIZE Will attain a height of about 20cm/8in and spread to about 10cm/4in individually within two or three years; the groups will spread continuously to form a ground-covering carpet.

Hyacinthoides non-scripta

Hyacinthus HYACINTH

Hyacinthus 'Delft Blue'

Perhaps because the hyacinth is best known as an indoor pot plant it is often neglected as a garden bulb; it is, however, a useful subject for a formal planting and is also attractive when grown in large containers.

Soil and planting Intolerant of waterlogging and requires a fairly rich but free-draining soil. In containers, use either a soil-less compost or John Innes No. 2 potting compost. The bulbs should be planted with their bases at a depth equal to $2\frac{1}{2}$ times their average diameter.

Situation Full sun; the plants will soon deteriorate in anything deeper than very light shade.

Watering and feeding Mulch in spring and early autumn. Top dress with bonemeal or a proprietary bulb fertilizer in early spring; if possible, give a liquid feed two or three times after blooming and while in full leaf.

Management Pull away the dead foliage and flower stalks as they discolour. Once the top growth has died down, the bulbs may be lifted, dried off and stored for replanting, or left *in situ*; in my experience, there is little difference in the results. Plants grown in containers can be lifted to make room for summer-flowering subjects. After indoor plants have finished flowering, cut down the old flower stalk and continue to give a liquid feed until the leaves turn yellow. Then stop feeding, allow them to dry off and remove them from the compost; they can be planted outdoors in the autumn, but will not achieve the same quality of bloom, nor flower so early.

Common problems Fungal bulb rots; slugs.

Size About 20–25 × 10cm/8–10 × 4in within the first year.

Iris

Iris is a large genus of about 250 species and many garden hybrids. Water-loving and alpine varieties are described on pages 186 and 173–4, but the most important group comprises the bearded irises and one or two slightly lesser-known groups grown as border perennials, such as *I. foetidissima*. All are easy to grow provided a few guidelines are adhered to.

Soil and planting Rich, fairly moist but must be free-draining; tolerant of alkalinity, but contrary to a widespread belief this is not essential for success – the low-growing Pacific hybrids actually fare better in a slightly acid soil, although this too is not essential. *I. foetidissima* will thrive in very dry conditions. The rhizomes of bearded irises must be planted very carefully at the surface, so that the lateral roots are buried and anchored but the fleshy rhizomes themselves protrude. Other rhizomatous irises should be planted between 5 and 15cm/2 and 6in deep, depending on their size. The bulbs of the Xiphium irises (which include the so-called Spanish and English irises) should be planted with their bases at a depth equal to about $2\frac{1}{2}$ times their average diameter.

Situation Full sun, except for *I. foetidissima* which tolerates moderate or even deep shade.

WATERING AND FEEDING Mulch lightly in spring and early autumn, taking care not to bury the rhizomes of bearded varieties completely. Top dress with bonemeal or a proprietary bulb fertilizer in early spring, and, if possible, give a liquid feed two or three times after blooming and while in full leaf.

MANAGEMENT Irises should not require staking. Cut down the dead flower stem to the base and cut away any dead foliage as it appears during the summer. On bearded irises, cut back the fan of leaves in late autumn to about 20cm/8in above the base, and divide clumps every three or four years; dwarf Pacific hybrids, which in my experience take a long time to establish, should be left for six or seven years provided they are not showing signs of deterioration. Cut back the foliage of Xiphium irises as soon as it discolours – the new leaves arise very soon afterwards. Divide them every five or six years. The evergreen *I. foetidissima* is best when simply tidied up in early spring and dead leaves cut away; it too should be divided every five or six years.

COMMON PROBLEMS On bearded irises, fungal rhizome rots; viruses; slugs; leaf spots. Other types are more or less trouble free.

SIZE This varies considerably. The dwarf bearded irises range from about $10 \times 10cm/4 \times 4in$ up to $70 \times 30cm/2 \times 1ft$ after three years. Medium-size irises range from about $30 \times 15cm/1ft \times 6in$ to $80 \times 20cm/2\frac{1}{2}ft \times 8in$. Tall forms range upwards from about $90–120 \times 20–30cm/3–4ft \times 8–12in$. The Pacific hybrids reach about $25 \times 15cm/10 \times 6in$ after three or four years. *I. foetidissima* reaches $60 \times 15cm/2ft \times 6in$ in the same time; and the Xiphium irises about $80–90 \times 25cm/2\frac{1}{2}–3ft \times 10in$.

Iris Californian hybrid

Leucojum SNOWFLAKE

A quite superb small genus of plants that should be represented in every garden, especially by the variety called *L. aestivum* 'Gravetye Giant'. They are usually called snowflakes and they flower when their similar, but much smaller, relatives the snowdrops fade.

SOIL AND PLANTING Tolerates most but performs best in moist, free-draining, but rich soil; tolerant of moderate acidity and alkalinity. Bulbs should be planted with their bases at a depth equal to about $2\frac{1}{2}–3$ times their average diameter.

SITUATION Tolerates full sun but performs best in light to moderate shade.

WATERING AND FEEDING Mulch in spring and early autumn. Top dress with bonemeal or a proprietary bulb fertilizer in early spring; if possible, give a liquid feed two or three times after blooming and while in full leaf.

MANAGEMENT Do not cut back foliage until at least six weeks after the flowers have faded, when it will still be fairly lush. The bulbs should not be lifted annually. Leucojums, especially the tall varieties, require some form of wrap-around support. Divide the clumps every four or five years.

COMMON PROBLEMS None.

SIZE The smaller forms of *L. aestivum* will reach about $50 \times 10cm/ 1\frac{1}{2}ft \times 4in$ in three years but the tall forms, including 'Gravetye Giant', will be at least double this.

Leucojum aestivum 'Gravetye Giant'

Lilium Citronella

Lilium LILY

Lilies need no introduction beyond dispelling their reputation for being difficult to grow. Many of the older varieties were certainly prone to deterioration through virus and other disease, but modern hybrids have few such vices; and there remain many species that form magnificent garden plants, although in my experience they are best grown in pots – even if these are stood among the borders for the flowering period.

SOIL AND PLANTING The soil must be deep, rich and free-draining without ever drying out. In pots, use a mixture of equal parts by volume of John Innes No. 2 potting compost and well-rotted leaf mould. They will tolerate moderate acidity and alkalinity. Bulbs should be planted with their bases at a depth equal to 3 times their average diameter, except *L. candidum*, which should be planted just below the surface.

SITUATION Full sun to moderate shade, depending on the variety, so check information carefully when buying. Some shelter from strong winds is desirable, not because the plants are at all tender but because they are so tall.

WATERING AND FEEDING Mulch in spring and early autumn with well-rotted leaf mould to which bonemeal has been added; liquid feed two or three times after blooming and before the foliage yellows.

MANAGEMENT Do not cut back the stems until at least six weeks after the flowers have faded. The bulbs should not be lifted annually and in the open ground they may be left for seven or more years before the clumps are divided. In pots, divide every four years. Most lilies require staking, either with wrap-around, interlocking metal stakes or with individual slender canes; in all cases take care not to spear the bulbs.

COMMON PROBLEMS Virus; lily beetle; botrytis grey mould.

SIZE This differs according to the variety; the lower-growing lilies, such as many of the modern hybrids, will reach about 1m × 30cm/3 × 1ft after two years' growth; others, such as *L. henryi*, can be as much as 3m × 30cm/10 × 1ft in favourable conditions after the same time, so check label information carefully.

Muscari GRAPE HYACINTH

Small, pretty and decidedly invasive, most muscaris are not trustworthy plants for confined spaces. They are exceptionally easy to grow, however, and if you need a plant to fill paving cracks over a wide area, then this is it.

SOIL AND PLANTING Will tolerate all. The bulbs should ideally be planted at a depth equal to 2½ times their average diameter, but in practice you can simply drop them and they will establish.

SITUATION Full sun to light shade.

WATERING AND FEEDING Scarcely necessary, but if you want particularly lush plants of selected varieties mulch in spring and early autumn; top dress with bonemeal or a proprietary bulb fertilizer in early spring; and, if possible, give a liquid feed two or three times after blooming.

Muscari latifolium

MANAGEMENT None necessary, apart from pulling out all the unwanted seedlings.

COMMON PROBLEMS None.

SIZE All of the common species, including *M. neglectum* which is the really invasive one, will attain 15 × 10cm/6 × 4in after three years, but bear in mind that they self-seed prolifically and each seedling will have the same growth potential.

Narcissus

By far the most important genus of garden bulbs, embracing a huge number of varieties that are popularly divided into the long-trumpeted daffodils and the short-trumpeted narcissi – although experts recognize many more divisions. Most are easy to grow and undemanding and most will also naturalize well, although some varieties raised for the show bench are fickle things. In general, the more costly the individual variety, the more likely it is to fail as a garden plant; although conversely, cheap or job-lot mixtures will probably be of the right variety but of poor quality.

SOIL AND PLANTING Tolerant of most, even very wet soil provided it drains freely in the summer. Tolerant of moderate acidity or alkalinity. In containers, use John Innes No. 2 potting compost. Bulbs should be planted with their bases at a depth equal to $2\frac{1}{2}$ times their average diameter.

SITUATION Full sun to light shade; tolerant of strong winds.

WATERING AND FEEDING Mulch in spring and early autumn. Top dress with bonemeal or a proprietary bulb fertilizer in early spring. Give a liquid feed two or three times after blooming and while in full leaf.

MANAGEMENT Do not cut back the stems until at least six weeks after the flowers have faded, and never tie the leaves in knots. The bulbs may be lifted, dried and stored for replanting in the autumn, and this will be necessary with container-grown plants. They may also be left to naturalize with no disturbance at all; if necessary divide large clumps every five or six years in autumn. Daffodils and narcissi do not need supporting.

Narcissus bulbocodium

Narcissus – Sisyrinchium

COMMON PROBLEMS Blindness (lack of flowers), caused by too-shallow planting, not feeding, or attack by narcissus fly.
SIZE Most daffodils and larger narcissi will reach 30–40 × 20cm/12–15 × 8in after three years, but there are also some charming dwarf species and varieties.

Nerine

Close relatives of narcissi but needing much gentler conditions and careful planting. *N. bowdenii* is the species most likely to succeed outdoors.
SOIL AND PLANTING Light, free-draining but fairly rich; they will not succeed in impoverished conditions. The bulbs must be planted shallowly with their tips just protruding.
SITUATION Full sun; nerines will not be successful in shaded situations or when exposed to cold winds.
WATERING AND FEEDING Mulch lightly in spring and early autumn, taking care not to bury the bulbs deeply. Top dress with bonemeal or a proprietary bulb fertilizer in early spring; liquid feed two or three times after blooming and while in full leaf.
MANAGEMENT Do not cut back the foliage until six weeks after the flowers have faded, and leave the bulbs undisturbed for as long as possible. Nerines should not need supporting.
COMMON PROBLEMS None.
SIZE Will reach about 50 × 15cm/1½ft × 6in after three years.

Nerine bowdenii

Ornithogalum STAR OF BETHLEHEM

Most ornithogalums are useful little white-flowered bulbs for filling in odd corners. Never plant the species *O. umbellatum* however, as it will very soon become an ineradicable weed.
SOIL AND PLANTING Almost any, although least successful in very heavy, wet conditions. Bulbs should be planted with their bases at a depth equal to 2½ times their average diameter.
SITUATION Full sun to light shade.
WATERING AND FEEDING Mulch in spring and early autumn. Top dress with bonemeal or bulb fertilizer in early spring; if possible, liquid feed two or three times after blooming.
MANAGEMENT None necessary; allow foliage to die down naturally and do not lift the bulbs each year.
COMMON PROBLEMS None.
SIZE Most varieties will reach about 20 × 10cm/8 × 4in after two years, although there are a few much taller, less common species such as *O. saundersiae*, so check label information when buying.

Schizostylis KAFFIR LILY

A distinctive, relatively easy to grow and vigorous member of the iris family, yet more closely resembling gladioli with its flower spikes and grassy leaves.
SOIL AND PLANTING Well-drained, rich, moist and preferably fairly organic. Tolerant of moderate acidity and alkalinity. Plant the rhizomes at a depth of about 10cm/4in.

Ornithogalum saundersiae

SITUATION Full sun to very light shade.

WATERING AND FEEDING Mulch in spring and early autumn. Top dress with blood, fish and bone or a similar general purpose fertilizer in early spring and again around midsummer.

MANAGEMENT Cut down old flower heads after flowering and cut back all growth above ground to soil level in autumn. Schizostylis should not require staking but they are vigorous and should be divided every three years in spring.

COMMON PROBLEMS None.

SIZE Will reach about 60 × 25–20cm/2ft × 10–8in in three years.

Scilla SQUILL

Among the prettiest and certainly the bluest of spring bulbs, scillas are extremely easy to grow and require the minimum of attention; no garden should be without them.

SOIL AND PLANTING Well drained, preferably fairly rich and moist. Tolerant of moderate acidity and alkalinity. Bulbs should be planted with their bases at a depth equal to 2½ times their average diameter.

SITUATION Full sun to very light shade.

WATERING AND FEEDING Mulch in spring and early autumn. Top dress with bonemeal or a proprietary bulb fertilizer in early spring; if possible, give a liquid feed two or three times after blooming. Do not lift annually but divide the clumps every five or six years after flowering.

MANAGEMENT None necessary; allow the foliage to die down naturally and do not lift the bulbs each year.

COMMON PROBLEMS None.

SIZE They will reach about 15 × 5cm/6 × 2in after four years.

Sisyrinchium

These are barely bulbous in the strict sense, having very short or non-existent rhizomes, but as members of the iris family they are most conveniently dealt with here. *Sisyrinchium* is a large genus with relatively few garden representatives: the majority of these are small plants with grass-like leaves often grown in the alpine garden, a fact that betrays their site requirements.

SOIL AND PLANTING Well drained, gritty, moderately rich. Tolerant of moderate acidity and alkalinity. Plant rhizomes or roots with their tops at a depth of about 5–8cm/2–3in, depending on their size.

SITUATION Full sun to light or even moderate shade.

WATERING AND FEEDING Mulch in spring and early autumn. Top dress with bonemeal or a proprietary bulb fertilizer in early spring; if possible, give a liquid feed two or three times after the bulbs have finished blooming.

MANAGEMENT None necessary; allow the foliage to die down naturally and do not lift the plants each year.

COMMON PROBLEMS None.

SIZE Depending on species and variety ranges between 15 × 10cm/6 × 4in and 60 × 30cm/2 × 1ft in three or four years.

Schizostylis coccinea
Scilla siberica
Sisyrinchium striatum

Sternbergia

An important, if neglected, genus of predominantly autumn-flowering bulbs, looking rather like crocuses and with mainly yellow flowers. They are not difficult to grow, although their site requirements are certainly much more demanding than those of real crocuses.

SOIL AND PLANTING Sternbergias will tolerate most soils, but with the very important proviso that it must dry out thoroughly in summer. Bulbs should be planted with their bases at a depth equal to about $2\frac{1}{2}$ times their average diameter.

SITUATION Full sun with shelter from cold winds; the bulbs must be subjected to very hot and dry conditions during the summer if they are to flower satisfactorily.

WATERING AND FEEDING Mulch in spring and early autumn. Top dress with bonemeal or a proprietary bulb fertilizer in early spring; if possible, give a liquid feed two or three times after the bulbs have finished blooming.

MANAGEMENT None necessary; allow the foliage to die down naturally and leave the bulbs undisturbed.

COMMON PROBLEMS None.

SIZE Depending on species and variety ranges between 2×5cm/1×2in and 8×10cm/3×4in in three years.

Sternbergia lutea

Trillium WOOD LILY

Wood lilies or Trinity flowers (so called because most of their parts occur in threes) are members of the lily family but are barely bulbous in the strict sense for they simply have a thick, stubby rhizome. They are easy to grow given the right conditions but will disappoint otherwise.

SOIL AND PLANTING Moist, well drained, organic and preferably rich in leaf mould. Tolerant of moderate acidity or alkalinity. Rhizomes should be planted approximately 5cm/2in deep.

SITUATION Light to fairly deep shade with shelter from winds; the plants are called wood lilies for good reason.

WATERING AND FEEDING Mulch in spring and early autumn. Top dress with bonemeal or a proprietary bulb fertilizer in early spring; if possible, liquid feed two or three times after blooming.

MANAGEMENT None necessary; allow the foliage to die down naturally and leave the bulbs undisturbed.

COMMON PROBLEMS None.

SIZE The most common species, *T. grandiflorum*, will reach about 30×30cm/1×1ft after three or four years.

Tulipa TULIP

After daffodils, these are the major spring-flowering bulbs. As far as cultivation is concerned, they can be conveniently divided into two major groups: the dwarf species; and the generally taller hybrid varieties – of which the Darwin hybrids are the best known. They can all, however, be grown in more or less the same soil and site conditions.

Trillium grandiflorum

SOIL AND PLANTING Tolerant of most except those that are very heavy, clayey, cold or waterlogged. Tolerant of moderate acidity or alkalinity. In containers, use John Innes No. 2 potting compost. Bulbs should be planted with their bases at a depth equal to $2\frac{1}{2}$ times their average diameter.

SITUATION Full sun to light shade. The low-growing species are tolerant of strong winds but the hybrids, especially the very tall ones, must have some shelter.

WATERING AND FEEDING Mulch in spring and early autumn. Top dress with bonemeal or bulb fertilizer in early spring; liquid feed two or three times after blooming and while in full leaf.

MANAGEMENT Do not cut back the foliage until at least six weeks after the flowers have faded. The species are best left in the ground to naturalize (so should be planted where they may be left undisturbed), and their foliage will gradually die away and shrivel. The foliage on the taller hybrids, however, tends to die down slowly and gracelessly and in general they are better lifted after the flowers have faded and temporarily transplanted to an inconspicuous spot. When the foliage has finally died down, they should be lifted and the bulbs dried off and stored. The species tulips need no support and the tall hybrids never look attractive when staked; but if it is impossible to plant them with good wind protection, use slender, green, split canes and tie each plant to these as unobtrusively as possible.

COMMON PROBLEMS Slugs; virus; fire disease; bulb rots.

SIZE This differs greatly depending on species and variety, so check label information carefully. Most of the species will attain about $10–30 \times 20cm/4–12 \times 8in$ in their first year, but some of the taller hybrids can be at least $60 \times 25cm/2ft \times 10in$.

Tulipa tarda

Zantedeschia ARUM LILY

A genus that could appear in a number of categories for it is sometimes grown as a border perennial and in water gardens; it is also a popular house plant and cut flower. Undeniably beautiful, the plants frequently cause disappointment as their site requirements are strict.

SOIL AND PLANTING Moist but free-draining border soil, or if grown in pots moist John Innes No. 2 potting compost, offers the best conditions, although the plant will grow in water gardens in several centimetres of water. Tubers should be planted 10–15cm/ 4–6in deep.

SITUATION Full sun to light shade, with shelter from cold winds. In colder areas, the plant is best grown in pots or lifted in the autumn and potted up for winter protection.

WATERING AND FEEDING Mulch in spring and early autumn. Top dress with bonemeal or bulb fertilizer in early spring; liquid feed two or three times after blooming and while in full leaf.

MANAGEMENT As these are evergreen plants, do not cut back the foliage. They should not require staking.

COMMON PROBLEMS Leaf spot; tuber rots.

SIZE Differs with variety but the more common forms will reach $50cm–1m \times 45–75cm/1\frac{1}{2}–3 \times 1\frac{1}{2}–2\frac{1}{2}ft$ after three or four years.

Zantedeschia aethiopica

ROCK PLANTS

Alyssum	Lewisia
Androsace	Myosotis
Arabis	Oxalis
Armeria	Primula
Aubrieta	Pulsatilla
Campanula	Raoulia
Crassula	Saponaria
Dianthus	Saxifraga
Dodecatheon	Sedum
Gentiana	Sempervivum
Helianthemum	Silene
Iberis	Viola
Iris	

Principles of care

In order to avoid giving the impression that the plants in this chapter are subjects only for the specialist, I have chosen to define them loosely as rock plants rather than alpines. The term 'alpines' covers a vast spectrum of species, almost all of them exquisite but many of them demanding in their cultivation and only really able to thrive in the protection of an alpine greenhouse. 'Rock plant', on the other hand, suggests something a little more robust and easily capable of being grown in a rock garden, trough, hollow wall, or similar site outdoors.

SOIL AND SITE REQUIREMENTS
Most rock plants come from mountainous areas (though certainly not all from the Alps), and the one feature that almost all have in common is a need for a gritty, free-draining soil. They will not grow in clay, and if that is your natural garden soil then you will need to resort to containers or raised beds. Unfortunately, the conventional treatment for clay, the digging in of large quantities of organic matter, will be counter-productive for rock plants because of their proneness to the fungal decay that such organic matter can encourage. For most species in containers I use a mixture of equal parts of John Innes No. 2 potting compost and coarse horticultural grit, with a layer of coarse gravel or chips on the surface.

Most rock plants also share a need for sun, and, while a few are tolerant of light shade, certainly none will thrive in really deep shadow. As may be expected, they are tolerant of very low winter temperatures, but not of cold, clinging damp. Some may therefore require protection in the form of cloches or glass coverings during the worst spells of cold, wet lowland weather. If you live in a particularly damp region you will be wise to avoid growing rock plants with silvery, hairy or woolly leaves, which are especially prone to rotting. Strong winds in general present no problems, although the less robust species need some shelter from winter gales.

GENERAL MANAGEMENT
Apart from the occasional need for shelter, a very little fertilizer in autumn and spring and, with a few of the more vigorous types, a light clipping after flowering, there is not a great deal to be managed. Be sure regularly to remove any dead leaves that accumulate around the plants as these absorb moisture which in turn leads very quickly to rotting of the crown. As far as fertilizer is concerned, I would recommend using bonemeal in the autumn, which slowly releases phosphate and so encourages root development but also contains a little nitrogen for leaf growth. A very light dressing with the rather richer blood, fish and bone mixture in spring completes the feeding routine, although care should be taken during any drought periods in summer to water regularly. Organic mulches should never be used.

Provided that damp conditions can be avoided, there should be little trouble with botrytis or other fungal moulds. There are few difficulties with pests, although slugs and aphids can be troublesome. The use of coarse grit over the soil surface will help to deter the former while vigilance and a contact insecticide spray should cope with the latter.

Rock garden sites

CHOOSE a site for each plant that is appropriate to its needs: some prefer soil-filled crevices, some will tolerate the shade cast by the rocks themselves.

Alyssum

Although some of the annual and perennial alyssums have changed their names in recent years, this is still the name by which most people know and buy them.

Soil Light, well drained, fairly rich.

Situation Full sun.

Watering and feeding Lightly top dress with bonemeal in autumn, and apply a very light dressing of fish, blood and bone in early spring.

Management The larger forms, especially the yellow-flowered *A. saxatile*, may be trimmed back fairly hard after flowering to maintain a neat appearance.

Common problems None.

Propagation Softwood cuttings in spring, or grow from seed (the best and most compact forms of *A. saxatile* do not, however, come true from seed).

Size The compact forms of *A. saxatile* will reach about 20 × 30cm/8 × 12in after three years, but other perennial species, such as *A. montanum*, are even more compact.

Alyssum saxatile

Androsace ROCK JASMINE

This genus includes some of the best-loved alpine plants, even if they need more care than many others. They will benefit from some protection in most areas.

Soil Light, well drained, fairly rich, preferably slightly acidic.

Situation Full sun, shelter from cold winds and damp.

Watering and feeding Lightly top dress with bonemeal in autumn, and apply a very light dressing of fish, blood and bone in early spring.

Management The enemy of androsaces is clinging damp. The best way to prevent moisture from accumulating in the leaf rosette is to protect the plants with small cloches in the coldest, wettest part of the winter.

Common problems Botrytis grey mould will attack tissues damaged by damp; aphids can also be troublesome.

Propagation Softwood cuttings in late spring, or some forms from seed.

Size Most will reach about 5–8 × 10–15cm/2–3 × 4–6in in three or four years, although some are more wide spreading.

Androsace carnea

Arabis

There are several genera of attractive little rock garden plants that belong, improbably, to the cabbage family, but arabis is one of the best. There are a few straggly and invasive forms, but the finest, such as *A. blepharophylla*, are delightful and easy.

Soil Light, well drained, moderately rich; arabis prefers a slightly alkaline soil.

Situation Full sun.

Watering and feeding Top dress lightly with bonemeal in autumn; very lightly with fish, blood and bone in early spring.

Arabis caucasica

Armeria maritima

MANAGEMENT A neat appearance will be encouraged by trimming back lightly after flowering.

COMMON PROBLEMS None.

PROPAGATION Softwood cuttings in summer, or from seed.

SIZE *A. blepharophylla* is fairly typical in forming a compact mat of 10–15 × 10–15cm/4–6 × 4–6in after about three years.

Armeria

Included in this genus are some of the easiest to grow of rock garden plants; the forms derived from the wild sea thrift, *A. maritima*, are the most common, and are particularly rewarding.

SOIL Light, free-draining, intolerant of clay; armeria is tolerant of high alkalinity.

SITUATION Full sun.

WATERING AND FEEDING Lightly top dress with bonemeal in autumn, and apply a very light dressing of fish, blood and bone in early spring.

MANAGEMENT Immediately after flowering trim back dead flower heads with shears and lightly trim the shoot tips.

COMMON PROBLEMS None.

PROPAGATION Basal cuttings in late summer, or from seed.

SIZE Reaches about 10 × 15cm/4 × 6in in five years.

Aubrieta

These are very familiar spring-flowering perennials, with red, mauve and bluish flowers. They are most commonly grown as mixtures from seed but many good, named varieties are available.

SOIL Tolerant of most, but always best when the soil is light and free-draining. Wall crevices provide exactly the right conditions.

SITUATION Full sun or very light shade.

WATERING AND FEEDING Lightly top dress with bonemeal in autumn, and apply a very light dressing of fish, blood and bone in early spring.

MANAGEMENT Trim back dead flower heads with shears immediately after flowering, trimming well into the plant even if the result is bare and unsightly: this will restore the rounded clump shape.

COMMON PROBLEMS Mildew; flea beetles.

PROPAGATION Basal cuttings in summer, or some from seed.

SIZE Reaches about 8 × 30cm/3 × 12in over three years.

Campanula BELLFLOWER

Campanula is a large, diverse and distinctive genus with annuals and border perennials (see page 111) among its species. For the rock garden, there are neat, compact delights like *C. cochleariifolia*, as well as some very invasive forms, most notably *C. portenschlagiana* and *C. poscharskyana*: these can become a menace, but are lovely where they can be allowed free rein through a stone wall.

SOIL Light, well drained, moderately rich, and preferably slightly alkaline.

Aubrieta 'Riverslea'

SITUATION Tolerates full sun but better in light shade; part of the value of campanulas is that shade tolerance is rare in alpines.
WATERING AND FEEDING Top dress lightly with bonemeal in autumn; very lightly with fish, blood and bone in early spring.
MANAGEMENT None usually necessary, but the more vigorous forms may be lightly trimmed back after flowering.
COMMON PROBLEMS None.
PROPAGATION Division in early spring, softwood cuttings in summer, or some forms from seed.
SIZE The more desirable and compact species, such as the popular *C. carpatica*, will reach about 10 × 30cm/4 × 12in after three years, but there is a wide range in vigour among the rock garden species so check label information.

Campanula cochleariifolia

Crassula

There are many tender species of *Crassula* grown as house plants, but also a few that are well worth growing in mild areas. Do choose carefully, however, and if necessary take expert advice for I have often seen species offered for sale that will be most unlikely to survive for long outdoors.
SOIL Light, very well drained soil, preferably gritty and slightly alkaline.
SITUATION Full sun or light shade, depending on the species; the hardiest, such as *C. sarcocaulis*, are better in full sun with shelter from cold winds and damp.
WATERING AND FEEDING Lightly top dress with bonemeal in autumn, and apply a very light dressing of fish, blood and bone in early spring.
MANAGEMENT None necessary.
COMMON PROBLEMS None.
PROPAGATION Softwood cuttings in summer, or some forms from seed.
SIZE *C. sarcocaulis* is a tiny shrubby species, reaching 25–30 × 25–30cm/10–12 × 10–12in after three or four years. The other hardy species tend to be smaller, forming compact rosettes of fleshy leaves.

Dianthus PINK

A large and important genus, including rock garden forms as well as several good plants for the front of the border (border carnations and some of the larger pinks especially). They must all have sun and rather precise soil conditions.
SOIL Light and free-draining; tolerant of high alkalinity and never really successful in acid soils.
SITUATION Full sun or very light shade. Many species are suitable for rock crevices and a few, such as *D. pavonius* (*D. neglectus*) are tolerant of being walked on, so make good subjects for growing between paving slabs.
WATERING AND FEEDING Lightly top dress with bonemeal in autumn, and apply a very light dressing of fish, blood and bone in early spring.

Crassula sp.

Dianthus – Iris

Dianthus deltoides

Dodecatheon meadia

Gentiana asclepiadea

MANAGEMENT Immediately after flowering, trim back any dead flower heads, using shears on large plants. On the larger-growing forms trim two or three centimetres into the shoots to encourage bushiness. Many forms – especially the larger border species – soon become straggly and should be replaced with new plants every four years. It is a mistake to consider dianthus as long-lived.
COMMON PROBLEMS Slugs; fungal leaf spots.
PROPAGATION Shoot tip cuttings (pipings) or basal cuttings in summer after flowering; layering or basal cuttings in late summer; some forms from seed.
SIZE Varies considerably; border carnations and some of the pinks will reach about 75×30cm/$2\frac{1}{2} \times 1$ft after three years, whereas many of the true rock garden species will barely exceed 5×5cm/2×2in in twice that time.

Dodecatheon SHOOTING STAR

These are exquisitely lovely and always arouse attention, but they are not widely grown, probably more because they tend to be expensive rather than because they are difficult. Like cyclamen, they are members of the primrose family.
SOIL Moist, fairly rich, but well drained.
SITUATION Full sun to light or moderate shade.
WATERING AND FEEDING Lightly top dress with bonemeal in autumn, and apply a very light dressing of fish, blood and bone in early spring.
MANAGEMENT None needed.
COMMON PROBLEMS None.
PROPAGATION Division in early spring, or from seed.
SIZE The commonest species is *D. meadia*, which will reach about 20×15cm/8×6in after three years, although there are smaller and more compact forms too.

Gentiana

One of the most exquisite and important rock garden genera with some easy and some extremely difficult species. The correct soil conditions are especially critical, for some are lime tolerant and some emphatically not.
SOIL Varies with species. Most require moist but fairly well-drained, organic acid soils, preferably with a high natural peat content. The late summer-flowering *G. septemfida* can be successful on rather heavier and alkaline soils. *G. angustifolia* and *G. clusii* are lime tolerant. The exquisite *G. acaulis* is lime tolerant but notoriously and inexplicably reluctant to flower.
SITUATION Full sun or very light shade. As a general guide, the Asiatic gentians are better in very light shade whereas the European and New Zealand types are best in full sun.
WATERING AND FEEDING Top dress lightly with bonemeal in autumn; very lightly with fish, blood and bone in early spring.
MANAGEMENT None needed, although dead flower heads may be carefully snipped off immediately after flowering.
COMMON PROBLEMS Fungal leaf spots.

PROPAGATION Basal cuttings in spring, division in spring, or some forms from seed.

SIZE Varies between species; the largest, such as the willow gentian, *G. asclepiadea*, have arching stems that reach 75cm/2½ft or more and spread to perhaps 30cm/1ft in three or four years. The more typical, mound-forming gentians become a hummock of 15–30cm/6–12in diameter, from which flowering stems rise to about 20–30cm/8–12in.

Helianthemum SUN ROSE

This is not the only genus with this common name but it is appropriate, for helianthemums must have dry, warm conditions to succeed. Most tend to be too vigorous for container planting, but in larger rock gardens in mild areas they are admirable.

SOIL Light, well drained, gritty; helianthemums are tolerant of moderate alkalinity or acidity.

SITUATION Full sun, preferably with shelter from cold winds.

WATERING AND FEEDING Top dress lightly with bonemeal in autumn; very lightly with fish, blood and bone in early spring.

MANAGEMENT Trim back lightly after flowering to maintain a neat, compact habit.

COMMON PROBLEMS None.

PROPAGATION Semi-ripe cuttings in early summer, or some forms from seed.

SIZE Most of the common species and varieties will reach about 20–30 × 20–30cm/8–12 × 8–12in after three or four years.

Helianthemum 'Wisley Pink'

Iberis

A genus from the cabbage family that includes a few choice rock garden species. Most form miniature sub-shrubs.

SOIL Light, well drained, preferably slightly alkaline.

SITUATION Full sun.

WATERING AND FEEDING Top dress lightly with bonemeal in autumn; very lightly with fish, blood and bone in early spring.

MANAGEMENT Larger plants may be trimmed lightly after they have finished flowering to maintain a neat appearance.

COMMON PROBLEMS None.

PROPAGATION From seed; the shrubby species from semi-ripe cuttings in spring.

SIZE The common shrubby species such as *I. sempervirens* will reach about 30 × 60cm/1 × 2ft after three years, although more compact forms exist of this and other species.

Iris

Water-loving and bulbous forms of iris are covered on pages 158 and 186, a reflection of the size, importance and diversity of this genus. For the rock garden, the important and easiest species are the small bulbous irises, especially the bluish *I. reticulata* and *I. histrioides* and the yellow *I. danfordiae*, although the specialist alpine gardener will wish to try other, rarer species.

Iberis sempervirens

Iris – Primula

Iris danfordiae

SOIL Well drained, moist, fairly rich; tolerant of moderate alkalinity and acidity. The bulbs should be planted with their bases at a depth equal to at least 3 times their average diameter.

SITUATION Full sun or very light shade.

WATERING AND FEEDING Top dress lightly with bonemeal in autumn; very lightly with fish, blood and bone in early spring.

MANAGEMENT None needed, although dead flower heads may be carefully snipped off immediately after flowering and the long grassy leaves cut back at least six weeks later. *I. danfordiae* is notoriously reluctant to bloom after the first or second season, for it forms masses of small daughter bulbs that take many years to reach maturity. The only success seems to come from planting them very deeply; with the bulbs 20cm/8in deep, I have had flowers for three years.

COMMON PROBLEMS None.

PROPAGATION Not feasible, other than by the natural multiplication of the bulbs.

SIZE Flower stems range in height from about 10cm/4in for *I. danfordiae* to about 20cm/8in for some of the blue-flowered hybrids, and the flimsy, grassy leaves may be 60cm/2ft long. All will spread to about 5–6cm/2in after three years.

Lewisia

Almost the archetypal alpine, small with a rosette of leaves (evergreen in some species), pretty in a very individual way, and demanding, not to say odd, in the conditions it requires. Lewisias are among the most admired of rock garden plants but their quirky needs can make them frustratingly difficult.

SOIL Very well drained, especially after flowering; intolerant of any alkalinity.

SITUATION Full sun. Lewisias are quite intolerant of any water lying in the leaf rosette, and are best planted almost vertically in soil-filled crevices in the sides of rocks.

WATERING AND FEEDING Top dress lightly with bonemeal in autumn; very lightly with fish, blood and bone in early spring.

MANAGEMENT Dead flower heads may be carefully snipped off immediately after flowering, and some protection provided by a sheet of glass during cold wet weather in winter.

COMMON PROBLEMS None.

PROPAGATION Most are best from seed, although basal cuttings taken carefully in summer may also be successful.

SIZE Varies with species, ranging from 5 × 5cm/2 × 2in to 15 × 15cm/6 × 6in in three years.

Myosotis FORGET-ME-NOT

There are forget-me-nots suitable for the border, some annual forms and some aquatic species. The most choice, however, are the alpines, such as the blue-flowered European *M. alpestris*, and a small group of white-flowered New Zealand species.

SOIL Well drained, fairly gritty, tolerant of moderate acidity and alkalinity. Non-alpine species are tolerant of wet conditions.

Lewisia cotyledon

SITUATION Full sun or light shade.

WATERING AND FEEDING Top dress lightly with bonemeal in autumn; very lightly with fish, blood and bone in early spring.

MANAGEMENT Dead flower heads may be trimmed back.

COMMON PROBLEMS Mildew.

PROPAGATION Most are best from seed although basal cuttings taken carefully in summer may also be successful.

SIZE The alpine forms reach 12–20 × 8–10cm/5–8 × 3–4in in about three years. Non-alpine species are of a similar height but are more spreading and straggly.

Myosotis alpestris

Oxalis

Oxalis is a real Jekyll-and-Hyde genus, for it includes some very pretty and easy to grow alpines (and some rather larger forms suitable for borders), as well as a few of the most invasive and ineradicable of all garden plants. *O. adenophylla* is one of the best, and *O. latifolia* and *O. pes-caprae* are the ones to avoid.

SOIL Well drained, fairly gritty soil; is tolerant of moderate acidity and alkalinity.

SITUATION Full sun to light shade; these are among the more shade-tolerant alpines.

WATERING AND FEEDING Lightly top dress with bonemeal in autumn, and apply a very light dressing of fish, blood and bone in early spring.

MANAGEMENT None needed.

COMMON PROBLEMS None.

PROPAGATION Most are best from seed, although basal cuttings, offsets or division in early summer are also successful. The invasive weed species spread by means of bulbils.

SIZE Varies slightly between species but *O. adenophylla* will reach about 5 × 10cm/2 × 4in in three years.

Primula

One of the loveliest and most important genera of ornamental garden plants, included in this chapter because most of the major species are small and appropriate for an alpine or rock garden.

SOIL AND SITUATION The requirements vary widely:

'Candelabra' primulas including *P. aurantiaca*, *P. bulleyana*, *P. chungensis*, *P. helodoxa* (*P. prolifera*), *P.* 'Inverewe', *P. japonica*, *P. pulverulenta*; also *P. rosea* and *P. sikkimensis*: constantly moist soil and full sun or light shade.

Border auriculas (derived from *P. auricula*), the drumstick primula (*P. denticulata*), Gold Lace primulas, polyanthus, the common primrose (*P. vulgaris*) and the many double forms and hybrids derived from it and related species, including the popular variety 'Wanda', the cowslip (*P. veris*), and *P. vialii*: moist but well-drained soil in full sun or light to moderate shade. I find *P. veris* is always better in full sun and slightly drier conditions.

P. alpicola, *P. bhutanica*, the oxlip (*P. elatior*), and the bird's eye primrose (*P. farinosa*): peaty or acid, gritty soil in full sun or partial shade.

Oxalis adenophylla

Primula – Sedum

Primula auricula

WATERING AND FEEDING Those species growing in well-drained soils require a light top dressing of bonemeal in autumn and a very light dressing of fish, blood and bone in early spring. Those in more moist soil should be lightly mulched in autumn and spring and given a balanced general fertilizer in early spring.

MANAGEMENT Primulas are at their best when allowed to self-seed, so don't cut back the dead flower heads. Divide every three years after flowering (this is most important with primulas of the primrose and polyanthus type).

COMMON PROBLEMS Leaf-eating pests; virus.

PROPAGATION Most are best from seed although division immediately after flowering is also successful.

SIZE Varies considerably; in general, the moisture-loving species are the largest. *P. florindae*, for example, will reach 1m × 60cm/3 × 2ft after three years; while many of the alpine species will barely exceed 5 × 8cm/2 × 3in in the same time.

Pulsatilla PASQUE FLOWER

These are like low-growing anemones (to which they are closely related) with very hairy flowers and feathery foliage. Their richly coloured and spectacular flowers are among the delights of the alpine garden in spring.

SOIL Moist but free-draining, fairly rich.

SITUATION Full sun.

WATERING AND FEEDING Lightly top dress with bonemeal in autumn, and apply a very light dressing of fish, blood and bone in early spring.

MANAGEMENT None necessary; do not disturb once established.

COMMON PROBLEMS None.

PROPAGATION Best from seed; root cuttings in winter are also successful but disturbing established plants risks losing some.

SIZE Varies slightly between species but most will reach 15–30 × 20cm/6–12 × 8in after three or four years.

Pulsatilla vulgaris

Raoulia

Uniquely appealing, forming a neat, very dense mat; some species are more like a fine green carpet than any other living thing.

SOIL Light, gritty, well drained but not dry.

SITUATION Full sun to light shade with shelter from cold winds and damp.

WATERING AND FEEDING Lightly top dress with bonemeal in autumn, and apply a very light dressing of fish, blood and bone in early spring.

MANAGEMENT They are prone to rot in damp conditions, especially the more woolly forms such as *R. tenuicaulis*, and will benefit from a sheet of glass or similar protection over them in the worst winter weather.

COMMON PROBLEMS None.

PROPAGATION Division in spring, or some forms from seed.

SIZE Most of the common species will reach 2.5 × 10–30cm/1 × 4–12in after three or four years, depending on the conditions.

Raoulia tenuicaulis

Saponaria SOAPWORT

Easy and attractive, low-growing plants with small, pink or red flowers and a long flowering season. In addition to their value in rock gardens, they are useful when allowed to tumble over stone walls or down sunny banks.

SOIL Light, fairly nutrient-rich, but free-draining.

SITUATION Full sun.

WATERING AND FEEDING Lightly top dress with bonemeal in autumn, and with fish, blood and bone in early spring.

MANAGEMENT The plants can be lightly trimmed in early spring to maintain their shape.

COMMON PROBLEMS None.

PROPAGATION Semi-ripe cuttings in late spring, or from seed.

SIZE The commonest species, *S. ocymoides*, will reach about 8–10 × 30–40cm/3–4 × 12–15in in three years, but some others are more compact and form tiny clumps.

Saponaria ocymoides

Saxifraga

One of the largest and most important genera of rock garden plants, the saxifrages come in an astonishing array of shapes, forms and colours. There is important variation too in their site requirements so read label information carefully.

SOIL Light, fairly nutrient-rich but free-draining soil will suit most types. The mossy saxifrages are the most tolerant, while the encrusted forms are the most choosy, needing very well-drained, alkaline soil – the ideal places to grow them would be in pockets between limestone rocks.

SITUATION Varies considerably; the encrusted forms need full sun, most others benefit from light shade.

WATERING AND FEEDING Lightly top dress with bonemeal in autumn, and with fish, blood and bone in early spring.

MANAGEMENT Dead leaves should be carefully pulled away. If possible, protect the buds of early-flowering forms from rain damage with a sheet of glass or a cloche.

COMMON PROBLEMS None.

PROPAGATION By offsets in early spring, or some forms can be propagated by seed.

SIZE Varies considerably. The mossy saxifrages are the most vigorous; a few forms such as *S. × urbium* will reach as much as 30cm/1ft in height and provide good ground cover with a vigorous spread of up to 60cm/2ft within four years. Most other forms develop neat clumps of about 10 × 15cm/4 × 6in.

Sedum STONECROP

The sedums include some very effective and attractive rock garden plants – and one or two notoriously invasive species too. For example, although it is still widely recommended, I would steer well clear of *S. acre*, which can be very difficult to keep in check. The popular *S. spectabile*, the ice plant, is grown as a border perennial, where it is useful for its late-summer colour.

Saxifraga × urbium

Sedum – Viola

Sedum spurium

Soil Tolerates most well-drained soils, and tolerant too of moderate acidity and alkalinity.

Situation Full sun to very light shade.

Watering and feeding Lightly top dress with bonemeal in autumn, and with fish, blood and bone in early spring.

Management None necessary, although unwanted seedlings should be removed regularly.

Common problems None.

Propagation Offsets, division or softwood cuttings in spring; in many instances, these can be short lengths of segmented stem which easily break off the parent plant. Some forms can be propagated from seed.

Size Varies considerably from neat clumps that attain around 5 × 5cm/2 × 2in after three years, to larger, more spreading plants of about 30 × 30cm/1 × 1ft, so check label information carefully. *S. spectabile* and other border forms will reach 45 × 45cm/1½ × 1½ft.

Sempervivum HOUSELEEK

The houseleeks are compact, rather spiky, rosette-producing plants of distinctive form. Easy to grow and at home in the rock garden, they are also very effective grown separately in a trough, where their foliage colours can be appreciated.

Soil Very well-drained, gritty soil; in trough gardens, use John Innes No. 2 potting compost mixed with an equal volume of coarse grit. Bear in mind that the adopted home of sempervivums is on roofs, the tops of walls and similar places where the soil is all but non-existent.

Situation Full sun to very light shade.

Watering and feeding Lightly top dress with bonemeal in autumn, and with fish, blood and bone in early spring.

Management Sempervivums are very slow growing (hence their name) and will not flower for many years, although this matters little since most forms are grown for their decorative foliage. Each rosette dies after flowering but perpetuates itself by offsets, which are best removed and planted separately, and the dead clump cleared away.

Common problems None.

Propagation By offsets, or some forms from seed.

Size Most rosettes will reach 10–15 × 15–30cm/4–6 × 6–12in after about eight years.

Silene CATCHFLY

These are a mixed group including some bedding annuals and border perennials, but the most splendid and important species are the rosette-forming, rock garden perennials. They are easy, bright, and should be represented in every collection.

Soil Tolerates most types of well-drained, fairly rich soil; best in slightly alkaline conditions.

Situation Full sun to very light shade.

Watering and feeding Lightly top dress with bonemeal in autumn, and with fish, blood and bone in early spring.

Sempervivum arachnoideum

MANAGEMENT None necessary.

COMMON PROBLEMS None.

PROPAGATION Softwood cuttings in early spring, or some forms from seed.

SIZE The more vigorous forms will reach about 10 × 20cm/4 × 8in after three or four years, but others are smaller and more compact.

Silene schafta

Viola

This is a large and much-loved genus of plants that embraces all the invaluable pansies and violas grown as bedding or container annuals. Their deserved popularity has tended to obscure the many little perennial species that are so easily grown in the rock garden and elsewhere.

SOIL Tolerates most; some species will thrive in quite heavy clays, although most are best in lighter, free-draining and quite poor soils.

SITUATION Full sun to light or moderate shade.

WATERING AND FEEDING Top dress lightly with bonemeal in autumn; very lightly with fish, blood and bone in early spring.

MANAGEMENT None needed, although some forms such as the sweet violet, *V. odorata*, self-seed very readily and it may be necessary to remove excess seedlings.

COMMON PROBLEMS None.

PROPAGATION Softwood cuttings in spring; by division; or some forms from seed.

SIZE Most of the clump-forming types, such as *V. gracilis*, will reach about 5–10 × 5–10cm/2–4 × 2–4in after two or three years but some, including *V. odorata*, are more invasive and spread by runners or rhizomes, so check label information carefully.

Viola cornuta

WATER PLANTS

Principles of care

For most of us water gardens hold a particular attraction and water plants a rather special appeal. As a group, they are less diverse than those used for more conventional plantings; there are, for instance, no really aquatic shrubs or perennials with genuine bulbs, and certainly none for garden use. Most of those that grow in or close to the water's edge are fibrous-rooted or rhizomatous herbaceous perennials (some of which are evergreen), while there are a few that fall into special categories. True water plants are rooted in the mud within the pool and have leaves and flowers that rise to the surface. Floating plants merely dangle their roots into the water, and submerged species, as their description implies, scarcely see the fresh air at all. Because of their growing habits water plants in general make certain demands in terms of management, but perhaps the most important consideration to bear in mind is that many varieties are fairly invasive, so plants for small pools should be chosen with special care. It is worth pointing out that in some areas, especially in parts of the United States, the growing of some water plants is legally restricted because their aggressive growth can pose a threat to water courses.

SOIL AND SITE REQUIREMENTS

With very few exceptions, water plants require full sun and there is little variation in their soil requirements. Plants grown at the water margin (so-called marginals) must be in constantly waterlogged soil and will generally tolerate 15–20cm/6–8in of water over their roots. True water plants such as water lilies, which can be planted in fairly deep water, and those marginals that will grow in shallow standing water, require special treatment. The easiest way to deal with them is to plant them in purpose-made planting baskets that can be lowered into water of appropriate depth. The baskets should be filled with soil that has had no compost, manure or other organic matter added, and has not been treated with any fertilizer. Once the baskets are planted up, it is wise to cover the soil surface with a layer of coarse grit before lowering them into the pool; this will prevent fish from stirring up the soil and clouding the water.

Large planting baskets may also be used for vigorous marginal plants even when they are not actually growing in standing water; the baskets may restrict their growth to some extent and in any event will facilitate lifting the plants for periodic division.

GENERAL MANAGEMENT

As with other herbaceous perennials, deciduous water plants should have their dead foliage and flower stems cut back in the autumn, although this is obviously not essential if they are growing· some distance from the banks. In small pools, however, it is very important to remove any dead plant material promptly before it becomes waterlogged, sinks and decays to foul the water.

In my experience, water plants require no feeding since they obtain all the nutrients necessary from the soil in which they grow. Purpose-made sachets of slow-release fertilizer are available for insertion into planting baskets and may well be of benefit, but never under any circumstances should you use conventional garden fertilizer.

There are few pest and disease problems with water plants, although aphids can be troublesome on some species. Very little can safely be done to discourage them, however, for insecticides and fungicides should never be sprayed in or close to water. (This of course means sprays should also not be used on normal plants growing in containers placed close to the water's edge. If you need to use a spray on them, move the containers right away.) On water plants, using a hosepipe to wash the aphids into the water where the fish will feed on them is as much as should be attempted.

PROPAGATION

As with other perennials, water plants – unless they are growing in or close to large expanses of water, where they may be allowed freer rein – benefit from periodic division. They should always be divided in spring, just as growth is recommencing, because if they are disturbed in the autumn they will be prone to damage from winter cold. Ice on a garden pool is most unlikely to cause harm to water plants but it is important to use a pool heater or other device to keep a small area unfrozen, allowing oxygen to enter and any foul gases to escape, for the benefit of any fish.

Environments for water plants

POND SITES With careful construction, butyl rubber sheeting can be used to create a pond that offers a variety of environments for water plants. Grow the plants in soil held firm by rocks, or in planting baskets. From left to right: marginal plants: *Caltha* (marsh marigold), *Menyanthes* (bogbean), *Alisma* (water plantain), *Sagittaria* (arrowhead). Floating plant: *Stratiotes* (water soldier). True water plant: *Nymphaea* (water lily). Submerged plant: *Elodea* (Canadian pondweed).

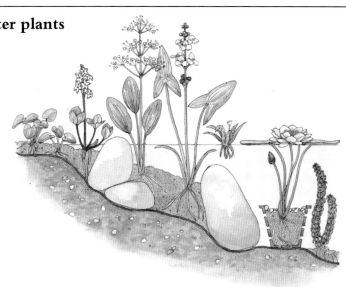

Acorus SWEET FLAG

One of several aquatic members of the arum family, although this is not very obvious from its appearance. It is grown principally for its scented, deciduous, iris-like leaves which were once used as an aromatic floor covering. In mild areas, the insignificant brownish-green flowers develop into attractive red fruits.

PLANTING AND SITUATION Marginal/submerged, needing 10–30cm/4–12in water depth. Full sun.
MANAGEMENT Cut back dead foliage in autumn. The plants are fairly vigorous, so in smaller pools divide them every three or four years.
COMMON PROBLEMS None.
PROPAGATION Division in spring.
SIZE Will reach about 75 × 60cm/2½ × 2ft in three or four years.

Acorus calamus 'Variegatus'

Alisma WATER PLANTAIN

For the shallow parts of large pools *A. plantago-aquatica* is a very attractive deciduous subject, with gypsophila-like, pink-white flowers, but its self-seeding invasiveness will create dreadful problems in smaller ones.

PLANTING AND SITUATION Marginal, needing 0–20cm/0–8in water depth. Full sun.
MANAGEMENT Cut back dead flower stalks and foliage in autumn. Unless the pool is very large, it will be worth cutting off the flower stalks before the seed matures as it self-seeds very freely. Divide every three or four years.
COMMON PROBLEMS None.
PROPAGATION Division in spring, or from seed.
SIZE The flowers will reach 75–90cm/2½–3ft in height, and an individual plant spreads to about 50cm/20in in three years; but it is the seedlings that cause the problems.

Alisma plantago-aquatica

Aponogeton distachyos

Aponogeton WATER HAWTHORN

One of the few aquatic plants to offer the combination of attractive foliage, flowers and perfume but without a grossly invasive habit (although it is still not a plant for a small pool). It is fairly shade tolerant and in mild areas will be in leaf and flower for much of the year.

PLANTING AND SITUATION A true water plant, requiring 15–60cm/6–24in water depth. Full sun to light or moderate shade.

MANAGEMENT Tidy up dead foliage in autumn or as it arises and cut off the seed-heads (if within reach) if you wish to limit the spread. Divide every three or four years in spring.

COMMON PROBLEMS None.

PROPAGATION Division in spring, or from seed.

SIZE *A. distachyos* will reach 10–15cm × 1–1.2m/4–6in × 3–4ft in about five years.

Azolla FAIRY MOSS

The unique *A. caroliniana* is a tiny floating fern with minute green fronds that turn red-brown in autumn and produce overwintering 'buds' that sink to the pool bottom. It is a tempting thing but can become a problem, as once established it is all but irremovable. It is best used only in small pools, where you can easily net excess growth and remove it. Another plant that can occasionally get into ponds is the duckweed (*Lemna*). It too is irremovable and any introductions of plants or fish should be carefully examined to ensure they do not contain any fronds.

Azolla caroliniana

PLANTING AND SITUATION Floating; simply scatter the fronds on to the water surface. Full sun.

MANAGEMENT None required, but it can be checked, to a degree, by netting in summer.

COMMON PROBLEMS None.

PROPAGATION Not necessary; simply remove a few fronds to begin a new colony.

SIZE Will cover about 1 square metre/1 square yard after a year and increase rapidly thereafter.

Butomus umbellatus

Butomus FLOWERING RUSH

A deciduous, rush-like plant with umbels of tiny pink flowers. It is attractive *en masse* in a large pool but is too large and not intrinsically pretty enough for a small one.

PLANTING AND SITUATION Marginal, needing 0–20cm/0–8in water depth. Full sun.

MANAGEMENT Cut back dead foliage in autumn. *Butomus* is a fairly vigorous plant and can be divided every three or four years, but it is really best grown in a situation large enough for it to be left undisturbed.

COMMON PROBLEMS None.

PROPAGATION Division in spring, or from seed.

SIZE Will reach about 1m × 50cm/3 × 1½ft after three or four years.

Calla BOG ARUM

Hardier than its larger and more showy relative *Zantedeschia*, which is also grown as a water garden plant. It is an obvious member of the Araceae family, and perhaps the one best suited to smaller, more informal pools.

PLANTING AND SITUATION Marginal, needing 0–20cm/0–8in water depth. Full sun.

MANAGEMENT In mild areas, the plant remains evergreen and requires no management other than dividing every four or five years. In colder regions, the foliage may be killed by autumn frosts and should then be cut back.

COMMON PROBLEMS None.

PROPAGATION Division in spring, or from seed.

SIZE Will reach about 30 × 30cm/1 × 1ft after two or three years.

Calla palustris

Caltha MARSH MARIGOLD

One of the most familiar and best loved water garden plants, suitable for informal water's edge plantings beside all except very small pools. Both golden- and white-flowered forms exist of *C. palustris*, but for more natural water garden plantings, the golden form is generally the most appropriate choice.

PLANTING AND SITUATION Marginal, needing 0–20cm/0–8in water depth. Full sun.

MANAGEMENT The foliage tends to turn yellow and die back during the summer (often aided by mildew) and it should then be cut back.

COMMON PROBLEMS Mildew.

PROPAGATION Division in spring, or from seed, except for the very attractive, fully double form *C. palustris* 'Plena', which does not produce seed.

SIZE The single-flowered form will reach about 60 × 50cm/ 2 × 1½ft; the double-flowered variant, perhaps half this.

Caltha palustris

Cyperus SEDGE

There are several cultivated species of *Cyperus* but *C. longus* is the one most frequently used for waterside plantings as it is the hardiest of those that tolerate waterlogged conditions. It is also fairly invasive so is best used beside large, informal pools. One of the so-called umbrella or papyrus sedges, *C. papyrus* 'Nanus', is also sometimes grown in water gardens, but as it is tender it should be kept in pots for removal every autumn.

PLANTING AND SITUATION Marginal, needing 0–20cm/0–8in water depth. Full sun.

MANAGEMENT The plant is evergreen so requires no more than a tidying up of damaged foliage in the autumn. It may be divided every five or six years if space is limited but it is better to leave it if at all possible, as it will usefully stabilize soft banks.

COMMON PROBLEMS None.

PROPAGATION Division in spring, or from seed.

SIZE Will reach 1.2–1.5m × 50cm/4–5 × 1½ft in three years.

Cyperus papyrus 'Nanus'

Iris – Sagittaria

Lysichiton americanus

Iris

Irises, also described in other sections of the book, certainly make indispensable and beautiful waterside plants.

PLANTING AND SITUATION Marginal, but of the two common water garden species, only *I. laevigata* should be considered truly aquatic, tolerating 0–20cm/0–8in water depth. *I. kaempferi* will tolerate 0–10cm/0–4in of water in summer but is likely to rot if its rhizomes are fully submerged in winter. All types need full sun.

MANAGEMENT Cut back foliage to just above water level in autumn and cut flower spikes back after flowering to the point where they emerge from the leaf fan. The plants may be divided every five or six years if space is limited.

COMMON PROBLEMS Aphids.

PROPAGATION Division in spring.

SIZE Varies between varieties but most forms will reach 60cm–1m × 60cm/2–3 × 2ft in three to four years.

Lysichiton   SKUNK CABBAGE

Striking members of the arum family with vivid white or yellow spathes in spring. At this stage, they seem only moderately large, but don't be deceived as the remainder of the summer is spent producing large leaves that would completely swamp a small water garden.

PLANTING AND SITUATION Marginal, requiring 0–15cm/0–6in water depth. Full sun or light shade.

MANAGEMENT Cut back dead foliage in autumn. They may be divided every five or six years in limited space but tend to perform much better when left undisturbed, as they resent upheaval and can be difficult to re-establish.

COMMON PROBLEMS None.

PROPAGATION Division in spring, or from seed.

SIZE Both of the two common species, the yellow *L. americanus* and the white *L. camtschatcensis*, will reach 1m × 75cm/3 × 2½ft in about three years, although *L. americanus* usually tends to be the more vigorous.

Menyanthes   BOG BEAN

Not a plant for a small pool because of its vigour but a very useful and attractive, fairly early-flowering deciduous species for the margins of a larger one. The common name derives not from the flowers or fruits but from the broad-bean-like leaves.

PLANTING AND SITUATION Marginal, requiring 5–15cm/2–6in water depth. Full sun or very light shade.

MANAGEMENT Pull away dead flower heads after flowering and dead foliage in autumn before it rots. Divide every four or five years if it threatens to outgrow its space.

COMMON PROBLEMS None.

PROPAGATION By division, softwood cuttings in spring, or from seed.

SIZE Will reach about 25 × 25–30cm/10 × 10–12in in three years.

Menyanthes trifoliata

Nymphaea WATER LILY

The prize plants of almost everyone's pool. Water lilies are not difficult to grow provided varieties are chosen appropriate to the size of pool and depth of water. Perhaps more than any other type of pool plant, they are unremitting in their demand for a bright sunny position.

PLANTING AND SITUATION A true water plant, requiring a depth of water of at least 15cm/6in, and up to 1m/3ft, depending on the variety. Full sun.

MANAGEMENT Pull away dead leaves as they brown and die and also pull away dead flower heads before they become fully water-logged and sink. Both of these operations are very important in a small pool, for such large pieces of vegetation will rot rapidly and help to foul the water. Divide every four or five years.

COMMON PROBLEMS Aphids; water lily beetle; various fungal leaf spots.

PROPAGATION Division in spring.

SIZE Differs greatly with variety and is generally correlated with the required water depth; those types needing deeper water usually spread furthest. Check label information very carefully and, if necessary, buy plants from a specialist water plant stockist who is more likely to have varieties suited to your own particular pool conditions. As a general guide, varieties exist in each of the common colours (pink, red, white and yellow) that will spread within three years to distances ranging in diameter from 30cm to 2.5m/1ft to 8ft.

Nymphaea 'Atropurpurea'

Pontederia PICKEREL WEED

Beautiful for both their rich glossy foliage and their spikes of soft-blue flowers, pontederias should be along the margins of every large pool. Sadly, their invasive rhizomes are probably too much to cope with alongside smaller pools unless they are grown in large containers, sunk to their rims.

PLANTING AND SITUATION Marginal, requiring 5–20cm/2–8in water depth. Full sun.

MANAGEMENT Cut away flower stalks as the flowers fade – more blooms will continue to be produced throughout the summer – and cut away dead foliage in autumn.

COMMON PROBLEMS None.

PROPAGATION Division in spring, or from seed.

SIZE Will reach 60–75 × 45cm/2–2½ × 1½ft after three or four years.

Sagittaria ARROW HEAD

'Arrow leaf' would be a more accurate name for this vigorous but lovely marginal species with white flowers (almost grotesquely double in some forms). Other than by a very large pool, however, it really must be restrained.

PLANTING AND SITUATION Marginal, requiring 5–15cm/2–6in water depth. Full sun. Because it is so vigorous once established, it is usually best planted in a large container for ease of lifting.

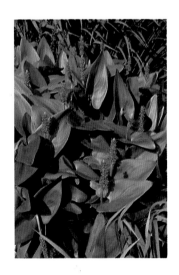

Pontederia cordata

Sagittaria – Submerged plants

Sagittaria sagittifolia

MANAGEMENT Cut away dead flower heads as they fade. Divide every three or four years in spring; this is greatly facilitated if the plant is grown in a container.

COMMON PROBLEMS None.

PROPAGATION Division or offsets in spring.

SIZE The European *S. sagittifolia* will reach about 45×30–$45cm/1\frac{1}{2} \times 1$–$1\frac{1}{2}ft$ within two years; the double-flowered form 'Flore Pleno' (sometimes called *S. japonica* 'Flore Pleno') is a little less vigorous.

Scirpus CLUBRUSH

Of a number of true aquatic rushes, some of the forms of *S. lacustris*, especially the variegated 'Zebrinus', are the most attractive. They are very hardy and very easy to grow but, like so many other marginal plants, must be placed with care if they are not to swamp the habitat.

PLANTING AND SITUATION Marginal, requiring 5–15cm/2–6in water depth. Full sun. Best planted in a large container to restrain its spread.

MANAGEMENT The plants are evergreen, so little annual management is needed apart from cutting out any damaged or browned foliage. Divide every three or four years in spring; this is greatly facilitated if the plant is grown in a container.

COMMON PROBLEMS None.

PROPAGATION Division in spring.

SIZE Most of the commonly grown forms will reach about $1.5m \times 75cm/5 \times 2\frac{1}{2}ft$ in three or four years.

Scirpus lacustris

Typha REEDMACE

These are the plants popularly but erroneously called bulrushes, distinguished by the brown, club-like flowering and seeding heads. They are impressive and stately plants, but even the small species tend to be invasive, so should really only be planted by a large pool.

PLANTING AND SITUATION Marginal, requiring 5–15cm/2–6in water depth. Full sun. Only plant them alongside large pools and even then choose the lesser species, *T. angustifolia* and *T. minima*, in preference to the much taller *T. latifolia*.

MANAGEMENT Tidy up dead foliage in autumn, but leave the seed-heads which are the primary appeal. Divide every three or four years in spring. Unfortunately, these distinguished plants are invasive and problematic on three counts. They produce prodigious quantities of feathery seeds that blow in the wind and germinate freely where they land, they are intrinsically vigorous and invasive, and the roots have sharp points that can easily penetrate a plastic pool liner.

COMMON PROBLEMS None.

PROPAGATION Division in spring, or from seed.

SIZE *T. minima* will reach $45 \times 30cm/1\frac{1}{2} \times 1ft$ in three years, *T. angustifolia* $1.8m \times 50cm/6 \times 1\frac{1}{2}ft$, and *T. latifolia* $2.5m \times 75cm/8 \times 2\frac{1}{2}ft$ in the same time.

Typha latifolia

Floating plants

There are several genera of water plants that float on or just below the surface, their roots unattached to either bed or bank. Among the most common of these are *Hottonia* (water violet), *Hydrocharis* (frogbit), *Stratiotes* (water soldier) and *Eichhornia* (water chestnut); the latter is too tender to survive outdoors over winter, except in very mild areas. Apart from this, the treatment of all forms is similar.

PLANTING AND SITUATION Floating. Although these plants will float in any depth of water, they should not be grown in a pool deeper than about 1m/3ft because their overwintering buds sink to the bottom in the autumn and will not thrive in, or re-emerge from, very deep water. Full sun or very light shade. *Stratiotes*, although hardier than *Eichhornia*, is less so than the other two species and, like *Eichhornia*, can be invasive in warmer climates; for this reason, there are restrictions on their sale in parts of the United States and elsewhere.

MANAGEMENT Pull out or net excess plants in the summer.

COMMON PROBLEMS None.

PROPAGATION Use a net to remove a few individual plants for transfer elsewhere.

SIZE This varies with climatic conditions, but a few individual plants will usually spread to cover an area of about 1 square metre/1 square yard within two years by the redistribution of their overwintering buds.

Stratiotes aloides

Submerged plants

Although little is seen of these plants, they play an invaluable role in oxygenating the water for the well-being of other aquatic life. They are sometimes loosely rooted in the basal mud but otherwise float just above the pool bottom. Those most commonly seen are *Ceratophyllum*, *Myriophyllum* and two species of *Elodea* (both of which have experienced name changes but are still usually sold under their old names). In my experience it is the first two plants which make the best oxygenators. Their whorls of tiny leaves offer a larger surface area than the broader-leaved *Elodea*, while still offering effective shelter to various forms of sub-aquatic life, and they have the advantage of being much less prone to acting as a base for the build up of algal blanket weed.

PLANTING AND SITUATION They can be submerged in any except very deep water, although they flourish best in well-lit conditions down to about 2m/6ft depth. Although it is possible in shallower water to anchor them in the mud, they will very soon be uprooted by fish. Full sun.

MANAGEMENT Pull out or net excess plants in the summer.

COMMON PROBLEMS None.

PROPAGATION Use a net to remove a few individual plants for transfer elsewhere.

SIZE Varies with climatic conditions but a few individual plants will usually spread to furnish a water volume of about $\frac{1}{2}$ cubic metre/$\frac{1}{2}$ cubic yard within three years.

Myriophyllum aquaticum

TREES

Abies	Ilex
Acacia	Juniperus
Acer	Koelreuteria
Amelanchier	Laburnum
Araucaria	Magnolia
Betula	Malus
Catalpa	Parrotia
Cedrus	Picea
Cercidiphyllum	Pinus
Chamaecyparis	Populus
Cupressus	Prunus
× Cupressocyparis	Pyrus
Cornus	Robinia
Corylus	Salix
Crataegus	Sorbus
Davidia	Taxodium
Eucalyptus	Taxus
Fagus	Thuja
Ginkgo	Tsuga
Gleditsia	

TREE FRUIT

Apple	Nectarine
Pear	Apricot
Plum	Cherry
Peach	Fig

Principles of Care

Because of their size, trees are likely to be the most dominant plants in any garden, be it a large one with an area of woodland or a tiny one with a single tree. (As a general guideline, I call a garden small if it is under about 200 square metres/240 square yards, medium-sized if between about 200 and 2000 square metres/ 240–2400 square yards, and large if over 2000 square metres/2400 square yards.) A tree's foliage, growth habit and other aesthetic qualities are all important factors to consider when choosing a tree for a particular spot, but of greater importance is its ultimate height and spread. Making an unwise or hasty decision will have a lasting impact not only on your own garden and house, but on neighbouring gardens too.

CHOOSING AN APPROPRIATE TREE

I hold very strongly to the view that planting a tree in a garden simply because you like the look of it, and cutting it down if it happens to grow larger than you wish, is the wrong approach. It can also lead to complications, because in many areas there are legal impediments to the felling of trees over a certain size.

I have been accused in the past of being too cautious in my general advice not to plant a tree closer to a building than a distance approximately equal to its ultimate height. I concede that this would exclude from many gardens trees that would be unlikely to cause serious damage if they fell, and I have no wish to cause alarm to the many gardeners who already have trees much closer than this to their houses (as I do myself). Nonetheless, when you are starting afresh, it is wise to be cautious, and there are a

Understanding a tree

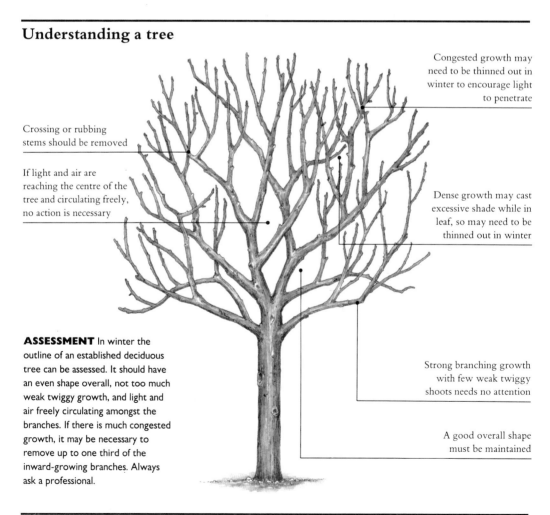

Congested growth may need to be thinned out in winter to encourage light to penetrate

Crossing or rubbing stems should be removed

If light and air are reaching the centre of the tree and circulating freely, no action is necessary

Dense growth may cast excessive shade while in leaf, so may need to be thinned out in winter

ASSESSMENT In winter the outline of an established deciduous tree can be assessed. It should have an even shape overall, not too much weak twiggy growth, and light and air freely circulating amongst the branches. If there is much congested growth, it may be necessary to remove up to one third of the inward-growing branches. Always ask a professional.

Strong branching growth with few weak twiggy shoots needs no attention

A good overall shape must be maintained

Simple tree surgery

REMOVING A BRANCH Make a sloping saw cut close to (not flush with) the trunk, leaving the collar at the base of the branch intact.

WIND OR SNOW DAMAGE
Always clean up the jagged end of a branch broken by wind or snow, as an untidy wound may admit decay organisms. Saw the end off or remove the branch.

number of reasons, both practical and aesthetic, for choosing a tree proportionate to the size of your garden.

If, for instance, a potentially tall, spreading tree is planted close to a house (as happens surprisingly often) it will not only take light from the building, and from all the plants around it, it will also of course be deprived of light and nourishment itself and be unable to form a good shape. And the same is true of trees planted too close to others in a large garden: the struggle to compete will produce straggly, lopsided specimens that are unable to fulfil their potential. Trees can be the most beautiful as well as the most dominant features in a garden, but they must be well placed in order to thrive.

FEEDING AND WATERING

There is no standard guideline to distinguish shrubs from trees in terms of size, but a simple definition of a tree is a woody plant that attains a height of more than about 6m/20ft on a single stem. There is a tendency to think of trees as self-sufficient simply on account of their size. In practice, in their early years they require as much feeding, watering (and mulching), and protection from competition with weeds as do shrubs and herbaceous perennials. It is particularly important not to allow grass or other vegetation to grow up to the stems of young trees, and a circle of turf approximately 1m/3ft in diameter should be removed from around

the base of trees planted in lawns. Fertilizer and organic mulch applied to this area will quickly penetrate the soil and reach its intended target.

Small trees (those up to about 4–5m/13–16ft) may be grown in containers of soil-based John Innes No. 3 potting compost; a container of 75–100cm/2½–3ft in diameter will be needed. The tree will require regular watering during the summer, and varieties with a high water demand should be avoided. Trees that I consider suitable include fruit trees on dwarfing rootstocks, the smaller types of Japanese cherry, laurel, Japanese maple, hawthorn and magnolia.

STAKING

Until their stems are strong enough to provide them with full support, trees require staking. It is impossible to give a precise age at which the stake may be dispensed with for trees grow at such differing rates, but a tree more than about 4m/13ft tall is unlikely to require staking in most situations. In certain instances, most notably for 'trees' formed artificially by training a single stem from a tall shrub, or apple trees grafted on to dwarfing rootstocks (see pages 18–19 and 225), a permanent stake will be necessary. Stakes should always be placed on the side of the stem facing the prevailing wind (so that the stem is blown away from and not towards it) and secured with purpose-made, belt-pattern tree ties. Hitherto, traditional tree

Principles of Care

Tree braces

▶ **SUPPORTING LOW BRANCHES** The branches of trees such as damsons and magnolias often dip so low to the ground around the tree that mowing is severely hindered. Prop the branches attractively with rough-hewn crutches forked at the top to cradle the limb. If necessary tie the crutches on securely to avoid the possibility of the wind blowing the branch off and perhaps breaking it.

▲ **INTERNAL WIRING** Branches in danger of being torn away from the tree can be internally wired to the main trunk with purpose-made supports, cushioned with foam to prevent chafing.

◀ **WIRING CONIFERS** Heavy snowfalls can weigh down the branches of conifers and cause them to open outwards. Rescue them by tying wires firmly and permanently around the outside, pulling all the branches in. The foliage will quickly hide the wires.

stakes have been of cylindrical, unbarked, treated timber about 6cm/2½in in diameter, driven into the soil for about 75cm/2½ft and protruding to a height of about 2m/6½ft. This is the type that I still prefer, although recently short stakes (only about 75cm/2½ft tall) have gained favour and are now widely used by local authorities, on the principle that the tree gains the best wind tolerance when it is blown to and fro.

TROUBLESHOOTING

With the exception of fruit trees, very few trees require routine pruning, and the subject only really arises if they are large or old. In general I believe that a tree in need of pruning on account of its size has been planted in the wrong place, although I accept that problems may occur when buildings have been erected on old woodland or near established trees. Damaged or diseased branches can usually be removed with a fine-toothed saw, cutting neatly just above the basal collar where the branch joins the main trunk. Never use wound-sealing paints on these cut surfaces as they give no benefit and may be harmful.

Removal of a tree should really be the last resort. Even a very large specimen that is casting deep shade or otherwise creating difficulties can often be saved: crown thinning – the selective removal of some of the branches from the

Rejuvenating malnourished trees

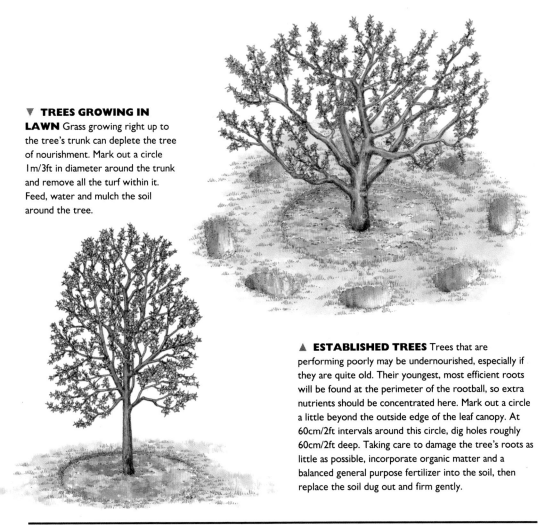

▼ TREES GROWING IN LAWN Grass growing right up to the tree's trunk can deplete the tree of nourishment. Mark out a circle 1m/3ft in diameter around the trunk and remove all the turf within it. Feed, water and mulch the soil around the tree.

▲ ESTABLISHED TREES Trees that are performing poorly may be undernourished, especially if they are quite old. Their youngest, most efficient roots will be found at the perimeter of the rootball, so extra nutrients should be concentrated here. Mark out a circle a little beyond the outside edge of the leaf canopy. At 60cm/2ft intervals around this circle, dig holes roughly 60cm/2ft deep. Taking care to damage the tree's roots as little as possible, incorporate organic matter and a balanced general purpose fertilizer into the soil, then replace the soil dug out and firm gently.

crown of the tree – is very often beneficial but must be done in such a way as to preserve the aesthetic and, most importantly, the physical balance. If an entire tree must be removed, it should generally be taken down piecemeal, one large branch at a time, again maintaining the balance in the process. Stumps should be removed if at all possible, especially those of broad leaved (non-coniferous) trees, as they may provide the entry point for honey fungus. Relatively small stumps should be dug out, larger ones winched or ground out with specialist equipment. (Chemical products claimed to degrade stumps are by and large ineffective.) But do remember that the removal, or even the

pruning, of large trees is not a matter to be undertaken lightly. I cannot emphasize too strongly that major work on a large tree, or even on a small one close to buildings, should be performed by a qualified professional operator who will not only be familiar with the techniques and equipment necessary but will also have third-party insurance.

In addition to these words of warning, it is vital to bear in mind that felling a tree in effect means removing the equivalent of a large water pump from your garden, with the possible consequence that the soil will become saturated and begin to heave. Remember the statistic that on a warm day 1 square metre/1 square yard of

Principles of Care

Root pruning a tree

AUTUMN Trees that have outgrown their allotted space may need the drastic measure of root pruning to stop them from growing any bigger. Never root prune plums or other species of *Prunus*, *Rhus typhina*, willows or poplars, as root damage to these trees will encourage the production of suckers.

Begin by marking out a circle around the tree to a radius equal to 12cm/5in for every 1cm/½in of trunk diameter. Dig a trench along this line, about 45cm/1½ft deep, to reveal the tree's roots. With loppers or a small saw, cut the thick main roots right through, leaving the fibrous roots intact. Refill the trench.

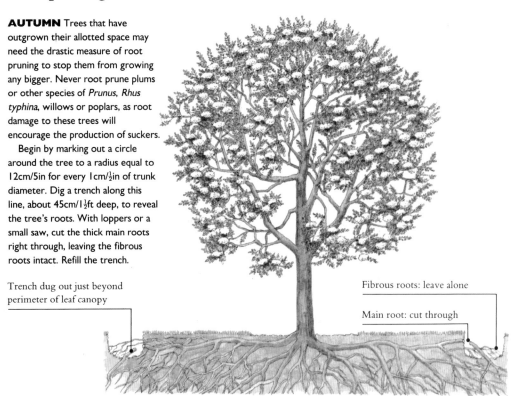

Trench dug out just beyond perimeter of leaf canopy

Fibrous roots: leave alone

Main root: cut through

leaf cover will lose over 5 litres/1 gallon of water. Even the severing of major roots without actual removal of the tree can give rise to soil swelling on some sites.

Something that often gives rise to concern is the development of suckers (shoots that arise from the roots, often at some distance from the main plant). This is most likely to occur when the plant has been grafted on to a rootstock of different type and vigour, but plants growing on their own roots are also quite capable of forming suckers. Usually it happens when the roots have been damaged in some way, perhaps by being severed with a spade or even attacked unseen, by some soil-inhabiting pest. The most notorious producers of suckers are *Prunus* species, including plums, and the stagshorn sumac, *Rhus typhina*, so special care should be taken not to damage or disturb the roots of these trees. Suckers are best pulled rather than cut away in order to discourage others from growing in their place. On lawns they may be mown off. Using weedkillers is unsatisfactory; contact weedkillers simply leave a dead sucker to remove later, while systemic weedkillers may damage the main plant.

The appearance of fungal fruiting bodies on tree branches indicate decay of the wood within, and if such growths arise on the main trunk it is likely that the decay is already extensive. Expert advice should be sought, as gales could tear off branches or blow the tree over.

Surface rooting is sometimes a problem with established trees and can make lawn mowing difficult or cause paths to lift. Little can be done to remedy this: heaping more soil or other material over the raised area will merely create awkward humps and can only serve as a temporary expedient until the roots grow upwards again. Simply allowing the mower to slice the top off surface roots in a lawn will do the tree no harm and is probably the only solution.

Like shrubs, trees can sometimes be moved. The success of this depends rather less on the type of tree than on its size and the nature of the soil and general growing conditions, which in turn affect the spread of the root system. In most areas, I would not hesitate to transplant a broad leaved tree up to about 4m/13ft in height (rather less for a conifer), following the procedure for moving shrubs (see page 22).

COPING WITH ESTABLISHED TREES

One of the most beautiful features of a mature garden is often its ancient trees; without them its whole aspect would be changed, and we naturally value highly any that we are lucky enough to inherit. Though every species has a character of its own, with specific requirements and susceptibilities, they hold in common the fact that great age and height tend to make them vulnerable to damage, and I am frequently asked for advice on their management. I have selected five species here to represent the problems most frequently encountered with old, established trees.

Fraxinus The common ash, which can reach a height of 30m/100ft, is better suited to the wild than to gardens as it tends to become gaunt and untidy (and prone to wood decay fungi) in later life. However, it recovers well after surgery if damaged branches are cut back to the basal collar. The popular weeping variety, *F. excelsior* 'Pendula', whose attraction lies largely in its habit – it forms a giant umbrella with a spread of up to 10m/33ft – loses so much of its appeal after surgery that overgrown or damaged trees are generally best removed.

Juglans Fully mature walnut trees are large (up to 30m/100ft high), wide spreading and, in the right place, magnificent – even if they rarely produce good nuts. As long as they are sheltered from the prevailing wind, they suffer few problems, and broken branches, once cleaned up, don't usually make the tree unsightly; if all else fails and a *Juglans* must be felled, remember that walnut timber is highly prized.

Pseudotsuga A coniferous tree for very large gardens, the Douglas fir may reach a height of over 50m/150ft. Mature specimens can have broken branches cut back to just above the basal collar or leading shoots cut back to healthy wood, but a young tree disfigured by storm damage is probably beyond salvation.

Quercus Big old oaks are tough trees, and although they may lose branches (occasionally through fungal decay), they rarely become unstable; unlike beeches, and many other large species, they are deeply and securely rooted. Torn limbs should be cut clean to just above the basal collar, but the tree itself should be allowed to stand as long as it retains its natural dignity.

Ulmus Once a common farmland tree throughout Britain, the elm is now largely a thing of the past; I include it here because where it survives it can be a cause of problems. Its habit of shedding large branches without warning has always made it a potential hazard, and damaged limbs should be cut back to above the basal collar. Dead trees must be felled promptly for they constitute a breeding ground for the bark beetle vector of the elm disease fungus.

Abies SILVER FIR

Among the less well-known garden conifers but, given plenty of space, the silver firs make fine specimens. Very few species are suitable for small gardens, although there are a few mutant dwarf forms (see page 79). Their cones are borne upright on the branches, but usually near to the top and out of sight.

SOIL Deep, preferably well drained, most are fairly intolerant of alkaline conditions.

SITUATION Open situation to allow room to grow; intolerant of smoky industrial atmosphere.

WATERING AND FEEDING Normally only necessary until well established: mulch in autumn and spring, and feed with a balanced general fertilizer in mid-spring.

PRUNING None; cannot be trimmed to form a hedge.

COMMON PROBLEMS Adelgids (aphid-like insects); frost, particularly late frost, may cause damage or death.

PROPAGATION Not feasible.

Abies koreana 'Lutea'

Abies – Amelanchier

Acacia dealbata

TROUBLESHOOTING Not necessary; large trees badly damaged by storms are best removed for they will never recover their appealing pyramidal shape.

SIZE Many species will reach around 5m/16ft after ten years and 30m/100ft or more ultimately. A notable exception is *A. koreana*, which may eventually attain 12m/40ft but is very slow growing in the early years and will bear bluish cones when only 1m/3ft tall.

Acacia

The evergreen mimosa, *A. dealbata*, is always greatly admired, but its tenderness can lead to disappointment in colder areas.

SOIL Light, free-draining, intolerant of high alkalinity.

SITUATION Shelter is essential and they will never reach much more than shrub size unless there is little likelihood of frost. Small specimens can be grown in large containers and moved under cover in winter.

WATERING AND FEEDING Mulch in autumn and spring. Feed with a balanced rose or similar potash-rich fertilizer in mid-spring, and again around midsummer.

PRUNING None.

COMMON PROBLEMS None.

PROPAGATION Semi-ripe cuttings in summer.

TROUBLESHOOTING Plants damaged by winter cold will regenerate if cut back at least 30cm/1ft into undamaged wood. Frost-damaged plants usually shoot naturally from soil level.

SIZE Fast growing, capable of attaining at least 8m/26ft in five years, but rarely reaching much more than 10m/33ft ultimately except in frost-free climates.

Acer MAPLE

This is a large and quite invaluable group of small, medium-sized and, in a few instances, large trees. There is a maple appropriate for almost any size of garden, but the smallest tend to be the most expensive and also the most difficult to grow.

SOIL Tolerates most, but the smaller, shrub-sized species need a free-draining soil and are best in slightly acid conditions.

SITUATION The large maples will grow almost anywhere and the sycamore (not a plant I recommend for any garden) is tolerant of the worst that the climate can throw at it. The small ornamental species are quite intolerant of exposure to cold winds but make good subjects for large containers which can be positioned in a sheltered spot.

WATERING AND FEEDING With large species, normally only necessary until well established, but with small forms must be continued throughout their lives: mulch in autumn and spring, and feed with a balanced general fertilizer in mid-spring.

PRUNING None.

COMMON PROBLEMS Coral spot.

PROPAGATION Hardwood cuttings in winter for the large species; the small ornamental types are almost all grafted (a major reason for their high price) and will not strike from cuttings.

Acer palmatum 'Senkaki'

TROUBLESHOOTING On large trees, cut back damaged or broken branches with a clean saw cut just above the basal collar. On small species, cut out cold-damaged or diseased shoots at least 10cm/4in into healthy wood. It may be necessary to trim some healthy shoots also to restore an attractively balanced shape. Very often, unsatisfactory growth of the small ornamental maples is the result of planting them in poor, heavy or waterlogged soil. By moving them to a more suitable position or even into a container with a proprietary soil-based compost, recovery can be remarkably successful.

SIZE Varies enormously, so check label information. As a guide, the commonest of the really large ornamental species, *A. platanoides* 'Crimson King', will reach about 5 × 4m/16 × 13ft after five years and an ultimate height of around 8 × 5m/26 × 16ft after 25 or more years. The popular medium-sized trees, such as the paper-barked *A. griseum*; the snake barks, like *A. grosseri hersii*; and the Japanese maple, *A. palmatum*, will all reach about 2 × 1m/6½ × 3ft after five years and around 10 × 4m/33 × 13ft after 25 years. The shrubby Japanese maples and other species, most notably the staggeringly lovely and popular fern-leaved *A. palmatum* 'Dissectum' types, generally grow very slowly to reach perhaps 1.5 × 1.5m/ 5 × 5ft after twenty years.

Amelanchier SNOWY MESPILUS

The deciduous amelanchier remains, after many years, my favourite small garden tree. It has aesthetic appeal at almost all times of the year: white spring blossom, dainty summer leaves, delightful autumn colours and a delicate tracery of twigs through the winter. Moreover, it will tolerate the toughest of conditions.

Amelanchier lamarckii

Amelanchier – Catalpa

Araucaria araucana

SOIL Any, including heavy clay.

SITUATION Almost any; tolerant of full sun and moderate shade, and unharmed by strong winds.

WATERING AND FEEDING Until the tree is very well established mulch in autumn and spring, and feed with a balanced general fertilizer in mid-spring.

PRUNING To maintain a tree-like appearance, cut away suckers that arise from the stem base at least once a year; otherwise, the plant will grow as a multi-stemmed shrub.

COMMON PROBLEMS None.

PROPAGATION Very difficult from cuttings; the best method is carefully to remove a rooted sucker.

TROUBLESHOOTING Should not be necessary, but cut back any branches accidentally damaged to just above the basal collar.

SIZE Trained as a tree on a single stem, will attain 3×1.5m/10×5ft after five years and 8×3m/26×10ft after 25 years.

Araucaria MONKEY PUZZLE

A coniferous tree that is too well known to justify description, beyond saying that its spiky appearance is unique. It was extensively planted in the nineteenth century and many people with old gardens have inherited large specimens.

SOIL Any, provided it is sufficiently deep.

SITUATION Almost any; tolerant of full sun and moderate shade but always produces the best growth in moist, milder areas.

WATERING AND FEEDING Until the tree is well established mulch in autumn and spring, and feed with a balanced general fertilizer in mid-spring.

PRUNING The lower branches tend to brown and die back unattractively; they should then be pruned to within a few centimetres of the main stem. There is no justification, however, for regularly cutting off healthy lower branches to produce a long, bare bole as is sometimes done in public parks.

COMMON PROBLEMS None.

PROPAGATION Impossible from cuttings.

TROUBLESHOOTING Old trees in urban areas often have a ragged appearance through having shed many limbs, a characteristic to which they are prone when affected by atmospheric pollution. Isolated trees may also be damaged by gales. As the tree will not satisfactorily regenerate a new leading shoot or side branch to replace those lost, a decision must be taken on whether the amount of pruning necessary to tidy it up will not result in an even worse mess. A really badly damaged tree is better felled.

SIZE About 3×2m/10ft $\times 6\frac{1}{2}$ft after ten years but up to 30m/100ft after about 30 years.

Betula BIRCH

Birches can be wonderful trees, given room. But their delicate tracery of twigs, autumn leaf colours and often beautiful bark are so alluring that they are often planted in small gardens where they soon outgrow their allotted space.

SOIL Almost any, although usually best in acid conditions and generally intolerant of waterlogging. *B. pendula* and *B. pubescens* are especially tolerant of rather poor growing conditions, although these do not make the best garden trees.

SITUATION Almost any; tolerant of full sun and moderate shade.

WATERING AND FEEDING Until the tree is well established mulch in autumn and spring, and feed with a balanced general fertilizer in mid-spring.

PRUNING None. On the species with white bark, it is important to rub out any buds that appear low down on the stem, or at least trim off any twigs that appear; the longer these are left, the greater will be the disfiguring scar.

COMMON PROBLEMS Some species, most notably *B. pendula*, are prone to heavy aphid infestation which results in an almost constant drip of honeydew on to anything underneath. Partly for this reason, it is often difficult to establish other plants beneath *B. pendula*. This species and *B. pubescens* are also prone to attack by wood-decaying fungi.

PROPAGATION Almost impossible from cuttings.

TROUBLESHOOTING Some birches, especially *B. pendula* and *B. pubescens*, are not very long-lived and succumb to fungal attack. The white-barked Asian and American types seem less prone to this. Once bracket-like fungal growths are seen on the trunk, the tree's future life will be relatively short and a careful watch should be kept for signs of instability. Severely attacked trees should be felled. On otherwise healthy trees, storm-damaged branches should be removed with a clean saw cut just above the basal collar, but the exposure of woody tissue will increase the likelihood of fungal attack.

SIZE Up to 6 × 1.5m/20 × 5ft after about five years, and about 20–25 × 5m/65–82 × 16ft after 25 to 30 years.

Betula jacquemontii

Catalpa INDIAN BEAN TREE

C. bignonioides is one of the easiest of the more exotic ornamental deciduous trees for medium-sized gardens. The huge leaves and runner-bean-like pods are eye-catching and it also has the great merit of being surprisingly drought tolerant, provided site requirements can be satisfied.

SOIL Deep, rich and preferably moist loam; *Catalpa* is not tolerant of high alkalinity.

SITUATION Full sun to light shade.

WATERING AND FEEDING Until the tree is well established mulch in autumn and spring, and feed with a rose or similar potash-rich fertilizer in mid-spring.

PRUNING None.

COMMON PROBLEMS None.

PROPAGATION Semi-ripe cuttings in late summer.

TROUBLESHOOTING Unlikely to be necessary, although damaged trees will regenerate fairly well if cut back into wood up to five or six years old.

SIZE About 4 × 3m/13 × 10ft after five years, 8 × 5m/26 × 16ft after ten years, and an ultimate height of about 15m/50ft.

Catalpa bignonioides

Cedrus – Chamaecyparis

Cedrus CEDAR

There are three species of true cedar commonly seen in gardens: the cedar of Lebanon (*C. libani*), the deodar cedar (*C. deodara*), and the Atlas cedar (*C. atlantica*), usually in its blue-foliaged form. All are quite magnificent trees, hardy and tolerant of a wide range of conditions; but in most gardens, they are also totally inappropriate. These are plants for very large gardens or for parkland.

SOIL Almost any, although best in deep, rich, moist loams.

SITUATION Almost any; tolerant of full sun and moderate shade, although being so large, it is usually they which cast the shade.

WATERING AND FEEDING Until the tree is well established mulch in autumn and spring, and feed with a balanced general fertilizer in mid-spring.

PRUNING None.

COMMON PROBLEMS None.

PROPAGATION Almost impossible from cuttings.

TROUBLESHOOTING Cedars have fairly brittle wood and gales and heavy falls of snow can easily snap off the top or break branches. Commonly a broken branch tears away a cup-shaped portion of wood from the main trunk, leaving a wound almost impossible to clean up and therefore prone to invasion by wood-decaying fungi. Nonetheless, any jagged branches must be sawn clean, either just above the basal collar if the damage is extensive, or just above the point of emergence of a side branch if less severe.

SIZE Cedars will reach up to 8 × 3m/26 × 10ft after ten years, 12 × 4m/40 × 13ft after twenty years and, note this carefully, 35 × 6m/115ft × 20ft ultimately.

Cedrus deodara 'Pendula'

Cercidiphyllum

An infrequently grown deciduous tree that in some seasons produces spectacular autumn colours. In good soil and mild areas it will attain a large size, and should really only be planted where it has room to achieve its full potential.

SOIL Tolerates most, but is best on moist, rich, deep, well-drained loams, preferably slightly acidic.

SITUATION Light shade, which in practice probably means a woodland situation with even taller trees close by. Shelter from late frosts is desirable to avoid shoot tip damage.

WATERING AND FEEDING Until the tree is well established mulch in autumn and spring, and feed with a balanced rose or similar potash-rich fertilizer in mid-spring.

PRUNING None needed. The plant is naturally multi-stemmed, but if a single-stemmed tree is desired all the other stems can be cut back to soil level.

COMMON PROBLEMS None.

PROPAGATION By layering.

TROUBLESHOOTING Should not be necessary; if serious damage occurs to one stem of a multi-stemmed plant, that stem should be cut back to soil level.

SIZE Will reach about 8 × 6m/26 × 20ft after ten years and multi-stemmed trees up to 12 × 10m/40 × 33ft after 30 years.

Cercidiphyllum japonicum

Chamaecyparis, Cupressus, × Cupressocyparis

These are the three genera of important coniferous garden trees popularly called cypresses, × *Cupressocyparis* being an intergeneric hybrid between the other two and containing one particularly important tree known as Leyland cypress. Although some cypress varieties are useful as ornamental specimens, many grow far too large and can lose their attractive shape as they age. They all tend to be used more as hedging plants, although here too there are important considerations of size and vigour.

SOIL Almost any, although best in fairly deep, moist loams.

SITUATION Tolerant of a wide range of situations but unsuccessful when exposed to very icy or salt-laden winds and therefore inappropriate for coastal planting. Cypress hedges alongside main roads can be browned by road salt in winter.

WATERING AND FEEDING Until the tree is well established mulch in autumn and spring, and feed with a balanced general fertilizer in mid-spring.

Chamaecyparis nootkatensis 'Pendula'

PRUNING None. When grown as a hedge, clip twice, first around midsummer and again in early autumn; or clip once only in late summer, although this will look tidy for a shorter time.

COMMON PROBLEMS Apart from the browning from wind damage, red spider mite and fungal root decay (including honey fungus) may cause problems in gardens.

PROPAGATION Almost impossible from cuttings without a misting facility.

TROUBLESHOOTING Once cypresses have grown more than about 2–3m/6½–10ft above their desired height, they will almost inevitably remain misshapen after cutting back, because they do not regenerate sufficiently well from old wood. For the same reason, moderately large trees broken by storms or broken or bent by heavy falls of snow are aesthetically usually beyond salvation and are better felled. The commonest problems arise with the upright, columnar or pyramidal varieties of Lawson cypress (*Chamaecyparis lawsoniana*), such as 'Ellwoodii' or 'Ellwood's Pillar'. These tend to open out naturally as they mature and are very prone to spreading outwards like peeled bananas after snowfalls. They can sometimes be rescued by wiring (see page 194) but, because this opening out is such a frequent occurrence, I think it is sensible to wire all of these varieties anyway as a precaution.

SIZE Varies enormously, so read label information. Unfortunately, there is still a tendency for some nurseries to sell as 'dwarf conifers' cypress varieties that will ultimately become rather tall trees, and while there are some fairly slow-growing varieties, such as 'Ellwoodii', that will only attain about 5m/16ft after twenty years, there are also some almost unstoppable monsters. Leyland cypress certainly has its value in producing rapid shelter, but if it isn't regularly and enthusiastically restrained, it can become a major problem. As the hybrid has only existed since the turn of the century, its full growth potential can only be guessed at but it easily grows 1m/3ft per year for a considerable time, and 35–40m/115–130ft ultimately is not improbable.

Cornus – Crataegus

Cornus kousa chinensis

Cornus DOGWOOD

The cornuses most frequently grown in gardens are those shrubby species whose stems are cut back hard each year to encourage young, brightly coloured bark (see page 33). There are also a few tree-sized species grown principally for their flowering appeal: *C. mas* for its winter flowers on bare twigs, *C. kousa* for its beautiful white bracts, and *C. alternifolia* and *C. controversa* for their tiers of small white flowers and, in selected forms, variegated foliage. All of them are easy to grow.

SOIL Tolerates most, although best on moist, well-drained loams; tolerant of moderate acidity and alkalinity.

SITUATION Full sun to light shade, with shelter from cold winds.

WATERING AND FEEDING Until well established mulch in autumn and spring; feed with a balanced rose or similar potash-rich fertilizer in mid-spring, and again around midsummer.

PRUNING None needed, although to maintain the effect of the tiered species it is wise to cut out any intermediate branches as the tree matures.

COMMON PROBLEMS None.

PROPAGATION Semi-ripe cuttings in summer, or by layering.

TROUBLESHOOTING Should not be necessary, and although regeneration will usually occur when old branches are cut out, the shape of the tiered forms will be lost.

SIZE *C. kousa* will reach about $2 \times 2m/6\frac{1}{2} \times 6\frac{1}{2}$ft after ten years and $3–4 \times 3–4m/10–13 \times 10–13$ft after about twenty years; the other species will attain about twice this size over the same period.

Brutting hazel

LATE SUMMER Break the strongest side-shoots about half way along their length, but leave them hanging. This concentrates the plant's energies into producing a better crop.

Corylus HAZEL

The hardy, deciduous hazels are often underappreciated as trees for larger gardens, although they are perhaps better described as large shrubs for they seldom develop naturally on a single stem. Rather untidy in habit, there are varieties offering attractive foliage, curiously twisted stems, and a crop of edible nuts.

SOIL Any.

SITUATION Almost any, from full sun to deep shade.

WATERING AND FEEDING Until the tree is well established mulch in autumn and spring, and feed with a balanced general fertilizer in mid-spring. Trees grown for nuts will crop better if a potash-rich fertilizer is used instead of a general blend.

PRUNING Varies, depending on the use to which the plants are put. The ornamental purple- and golden-leaved varieties need no pruning, but leaf size and colour are improved by cutting back the oldest third of the shoots to soil level each spring. In smaller gardens or restricted spaces, cut these forms back to soil level every four or five years.

The variety of *C. avellana* called 'Contorta', with twisted stems, is slow growing and less vigorous than the other forms, and is best left unpruned.

Varieties grown for their filberts, cob or hazel nuts will produce some crops if left unpruned but careful pruning is needed to yield good quality nuts. The tree should be trained initially much as an open-centred bush apple (see page 224). Once the plant has reached about 2m/6½ft in height, all leading shoots should be pruned back by half in early winter, but the pruning of the side-shoots is best left until the flowers are evident in spring. By mid-spring, the male catkins and reddish female flower tufts will be visible and then the more slender side-shoots bearing catkins and flowers are retained, although they may be cut back to a point just above the flower or catkin itself. Stronger side-shoots with no flowers are cut back to two buds above their bases. Any misplaced or weak, flowerless side-shoots should be cut out completely.

A process called brutting (see below left) will also help the fruiting process, by encouraging better ripening of the wood at the base of the strongest side-shoots. Brutting consists of breaking (not cutting) these longest, strongest side-shoots in late summer – about half way along their length – and then leaving them hanging until they are cut back to two buds from their bases in winter, at the same time as the winter pruning of leading shoots.

C. avellana can be grown with other shrubs to form a tall, mixed, rural-style hedge, and in this case the pruning needs to keep the plant within bounds, at the expense of fruit. Clip the plant over in mid-spring, leaving on a few catkins for effect.

COMMON PROBLEMS On ornamental varieties, none; on fruiting varieties, squirrels and nut weevil.

PROPAGATION By layering or suckers.

TROUBLESHOOTING Old, overgrown or otherwise misshapen trees can be rejuvenated by cutting them back to soil level. This process of coppicing was once an important commercial operation for producing fencing poles.

SIZE Pruned as described, nut trees will attain a height of about 2.5m/8ft. Unpruned, they will reach about $4 \times 2m/13 \times 6½ft$ after ten years and twice this after 25 years.

Crataegus HAWTHORN

Hawthorns are usually thought of solely as hedging plants, but there are several varieties that make quite excellent ornamental flowering trees, offering in succession flowers, attractive berries and good autumn colours.

SOIL Any, except where very dry.

SITUATION Full sun to moderate shade.

WATERING AND FEEDING Until the tree is well established mulch in autumn and spring, and feed with a balanced rose or other potash-rich fertilizer in mid-spring.

PRUNING None necessary. When grown as a hedge, clip several times starting just after the time when the last frost is likely to occur, and stop at the first autumn frost.

COMMON PROBLEMS Fireblight.

PROPAGATION Impossible from cuttings.

TROUBLESHOOTING Old or damaged trees will regenerate well, although slowly, if cut back hard into old wood.

SIZE Attains about $4 \times 1.5m/13 \times 5ft$ after five years, $6 \times 4m/20 \times 13ft$ after 25 years, and eventually, and very slowly, perhaps $12 \times 6m/40 \times 20ft$.

Crataegus laevigata

Davidia – Ginkgo

Davidia involucrata

Davidia DOVE TREE

Once described as the finest deciduous tree to grow in a temperate climate, *D. involucrata* is definitely one for milder areas and patient gardeners, for the fabulous white-bracted flowers that inspired the common name are usually only produced after twenty years or more.

SOIL Tolerates most, although best on moist, deep, rich, well-drained loams; tolerant of moderate acidity and alkalinity.

SITUATION Full sun to light shade, with shelter from cold winds.

WATERING AND FEEDING Until the tree is well established mulch in autumn and spring, and feed with a balanced rose or similar potash-rich fertilizer in mid-spring.

PRUNING None needed, although some shoot death usually occurs in winter and should be cut out in spring.

COMMON PROBLEMS None.

PROPAGATION By layers.

TROUBLESHOOTING Should not be necessary; damaged branches should be cut back neatly to just above the basal collar.

SIZE The dove tree will reach about 6 × 3m/20 × 10ft after ten years and in good growing conditions may attain about 15 × 8m/50 × 26ft or more after 25 years.

Eucalyptus

Most species of *Eucalyptus*, the gum trees of Australia, are not hardy in northern climates, and even those that will survive never attain the huge size reached in warmer areas. They are, nonetheless, attractive and useful in appropriate situations for their steely-blue and often appealingly shaped leaves.

SOIL Will tolerate most, but least successful in waterlogged conditions; best in free-draining, rich loams.

SITUATION Full sun, but tolerates light shade and requires some shelter from cold winds.

WATERING AND FEEDING Until the tree is well established mulch in autumn and spring, and feed with a balanced general fertilizer in mid-spring.

PRUNING None necessary, but hard pruning is desirable because large plants almost invariably suffer sooner or later from wind or cold damage, and also because the rounded juvenile foliage, so beloved of flower arrangers, is only produced on young shoots. The tree is best pruned every other year: cut back half of the shoots to about 15cm/6in above soil level, or to the junction with the permanent main stem.

COMMON PROBLEMS Aphids.

PROPAGATION Impossible from cuttings; almost always raised from seed.

TROUBLESHOOTING Old or damaged trees will be rejuvenated by cutting them hard back, to soil level if necessary.

SIZE Pruned as described, the hardiest species, *E. gunnii*, attains about 3 × 1m/10 × 3ft in two years and will remain at about this size; unpruned, it might achieve 20 × 5m/65ft × 16ft after twenty years and 30m/100ft in height eventually.

Eucalyptus gunnii

Fagus BEECH

One of the loveliest and most typical of hardy, deciduous, British native trees, the beech, even in its coloured-leaved variants, is sadly a plant only for large gardens as a free-standing specimen. It does, however, make a superb hedge in appropriate conditions. Hornbeam (*Carpinus betulus*) is a comparable (although unrelated) hedging plant, and may be treated similarly.

SOIL Most, but much the best growth is on rich, free-draining soils; tolerant of alkaline conditions.

SITUATION Full sun or light shade; when in leaf, it casts a deeper shade than almost any other tree.

WATERING AND FEEDING Until the tree is well established mulch in autumn and spring, and feed with a balanced general fertilizer in mid-spring.

PRUNING None necessary but can be clipped very satisfactorily as a hedge: clip twice, the first time two or three weeks after mid-summer, the second in early autumn; or clip once only in late summer, although this will give a tidy appearance for a shorter time. Frost- or wind-damaged shoots will soon be attacked by coral spot disease and so should be cut out promptly.

COMMON PROBLEMS Aphids (especially as a hedge); beech bark disease (as a specimen tree); coral spot; wood-decaying fungi.

PROPAGATION Impossible from cuttings.

TROUBLESHOOTING Overgrown hedges will rejuvenate well if cut back into the old wood. The job is best done in early spring, after the danger of the hardest frost has passed. Mature beech trees are very prone to damage from storms, largely because they suffer from a number of wood-decaying fungi which render them un-stable; and, no matter how carefully the damage is cleaned up with saw cuts, the very existence of the wounds will admit further decay organisms. While cutting back to sound tissue just above the basal collar is worthwhile, therefore, the plant is likely to become increasingly unstable. Beech are shallow rooted, and large trees growing close to buildings and exposed to the prevailing winds should be examined by an expert.

SIZE Attains about 5 × 5m/16 × 16ft after five years, 15 × 12m/50 × 40ft after twenty years, and an eventual height of 40m/130ft.

Fagus sylvatica

Ginkgo MAIDENHAIR TREE

Part of the appeal of this strange deciduous relative of the conifers lies in its extraordinary history as the sole surviving member of a group of plants extinct millions of years ago. It is also a quite superb specimen plant for a large garden, being extremely hardy and with a fascinating leaf shape and fine yellow colours in autumn. For more confined spaces the rarer upright forms, such as *G. biloba* 'Fastigiata', are well worth hunting for.

SOIL Tolerates most, but always best on rich, deep loams.

SITUATION Full sun to light shade.

WATERING AND FEEDING Until the tree is well established mulch in autumn and spring, and feed with a balanced general fertilizer in mid-spring.

Ginkgo biloba

Ginkgo – Koelreuteria

Gleditsia triacanthos 'Sunburst'

PRUNING None necessary, although on upright forms cut off any shoots that show a tendency to spread.

COMMON PROBLEMS None.

PROPAGATION Impossible from cuttings.

TROUBLESHOOTING Rarely necessary, but damaged branches may be cut back to the basal collar and new shoots will regenerate, much as with broad-leaved trees and quite unlike true conifers.

SIZE Up to $3 \times 1m/10 \times 3ft$ after five years; $5 \times 3m/16 \times 10ft$ after ten years and $30 \times 12m/100 \times 40ft$ eventually, although 'Fastigiata' should never exceed about 2.5m/8ft in spread.

Gleditsia HONEY LOCUST

The deciduous honey locust has become one of the more popular ornamental trees of recent years, although its brittle twigs and intolerance of exposure are significant drawbacks.

SOIL Tolerates most, but best on rich, deep loams.

SITUATION Full sun to light shade; must be sheltered from winds because the twigs are brittle and very easily broken, resulting in a misshapen and unattractive plant.

WATERING AND FEEDING Until the tree is well established mulch in autumn and spring, and feed with a balanced general fertilizer in mid-spring.

PRUNING None necessary.

COMMON PROBLEMS None.

PROPAGATION Almost impossible from cuttings.

TROUBLESHOOTING Damaged branches may be cut back to the basal collar and new shoots will regenerate fairly well, but the shape will never recover satisfactorily.

SIZE The selected forms grown in gardens, such as the golden-foliaged *G. triacanthos* 'Sunburst', are slower and lower growing than the true species and will reach $3 \times 1m/10 \times 3ft$ after five years and about $8 \times 5m/26 \times 16ft$ after twenty years.

Ilex HOLLY

As a group, the hollies are valuable garden evergreens. They are very hardy, slow growing and appealing both in their foliage and berries. Among the numerous foliage variants are some with more or less spineless leaves, and these are particularly valuable in smaller gardens.

SOIL Tolerates most.

SITUATION Full sun to moderate shade.

WATERING AND FEEDING Until the plant is well established mulch in autumn and spring, and feed with a balanced general fertilizer in mid-spring, although on fruiting forms (hollies have the sexes on separate plants), substitution of a potash-rich rose or other fertilizer is desirable.

PRUNING None necessary. When grown as a hedge, clip twice, the first time two or three weeks after midsummer, the second in early autumn; or clip once only in late summer, although this will give a tidy appearance for a shorter time.

COMMON PROBLEMS None.

Ilex aquifolium

PROPAGATION Impossible from cuttings.

TROUBLESHOOTING Damaged branches may be cut back to the basal collar and new shoots will regenerate fairly well, but as growth is so slow, the attractive shape of the undamaged plant will seldom return satisfactorily.

SIZE Varies greatly, so check label information carefully. Some species and varieties remain as little more than dwarf shrubs, while the commonly grown *I. aquifolium* attains 3–4 × 1m/10–13 × 3ft after five years, 10–12 × 4m/33–40 × 13ft after twenty, and eventually up to 15–20m/50–65ft in height.

Juniperus JUNIPER

Although relatively few conifers should find a place in gardens other than as dwarf forms or hedging plants, junipers are among the exceptions; such varieties as *J. scopulorum* 'Skyrocket' contribute a useful conical or spire-like effect among other plants.

SOIL Tolerates most, including fairly dry soils, although best on moist, deep, rich, well-drained loams; tolerant of moderate acidity and alkalinity.

SITUATION Full sun to light shade, with shelter from cold winds.

WATERING AND FEEDING Until the tree is well established mulch in autumn and spring, and feed with a balanced general purpose fertilizer in mid-spring.

PRUNING None needed; although junipers may be trimmed lightly, they will not regenerate when cut back into old wood.

COMMON PROBLEMS Red spider mite.

PROPAGATION Semi-ripe cuttings in summer, or hardwood cuttings in winter; it is often very difficult to induce rooting without a misting facility.

Juniperus scopulorum 'Skyrocket'

TROUBLESHOOTING Difficult because of the juniper's inability to regenerate from old wood. Broken or diseased branches should be cut back neatly to the basal collar, but it is important not to cut away any more growth than is absolutely necessary.

SIZE Varies greatly between species and varieties, and as there are so many it is impossible to generalize. Suppliers regularly underestimate the sizes of conifers, whether sold as 'dwarf' or 'tall' varieties, so check the ultimate height of your chosen plant in at least two reference sources.

Koelreuteria

A hardy, deciduous flowering tree that could be more widely grown, although its golden-yellow flowers and bladder-like fruits are only produced reliably in warmer climates.

SOIL Will tolerate most, although best on moist, deep, rich, well-drained loams; tolerant of moderate acidity and alkalinity.

SITUATION Full sun, with shelter from cold winds; this tree is at its best in areas with reliably warm summers.

WATERING AND FEEDING Until the tree is well established mulch regularly in autumn and spring, and feed with a balanced rose or similar potash-rich fertilizer in mid-spring, and again around midsummer.

Koelreuteria – Malus

Koelreuteria paniculata

PRUNING None needed.

COMMON PROBLEMS None.

PROPAGATION Root cuttings in winter, or from seed.

TROUBLESHOOTING Unlikely to be necessary; although damaged branches should be cut back to the basal collar, there will be little regeneration from old wood. This is not a long-lived tree, and many succumb to disease and decay after about 30 years.

SIZE The normal species will attain about $5 \times 2m/16 \times 6\frac{1}{2}ft$ after five years and perhaps $12 \times 7m/40 \times 23ft$ after about 25 years.

Laburnum

Laburnums are very hardy and in the best selected forms very beautiful, but they age rather gracelessly and old trees are invariably misshapen. The seeds are also poisonous, and it is perhaps not wise to plant a laburnum in a garden with very young children.

SOIL Will tolerate most, but especially successful in well-drained alkaline conditions.

SITUATION Full sun to light shade.

WATERING AND FEEDING Until the tree is well established mulch in autumn and spring, and feed with a rose or similar potash-rich fertilizer in mid-spring.

PRUNING None.

COMMON PROBLEMS None.

PROPAGATION Very difficult, but hardwood cuttings in winter may be successful.

TROUBLESHOOTING Damaged branches may be cut back to the basal collar but regeneration is poor or non-existent and the tree will almost inevitably look disfigured. Laburnums are not long-lived and tend to succumb to fungal decay and generally lose their attractive appearance after 30 to 40 years. They also tend to have shallow root systems and should be well staked throughout most of their lives.

SIZE The variety to grow is the long-flowered Voss's laburnum, *L. × watereri* 'Vossii', which will reach $4 \times 1.5m/13 \times 5ft$ after five years, $7 \times 4m/23 \times 13ft$ after twenty years and, if you are lucky and it lives long enough, perhaps 10m/33ft tall eventually.

Magnolia

Although some magnolias are barely more than shrubs in many gardens, this quite magnificent genus of mainly deciduous plants does include some superb tree-sized species. In general, the larger the species, the more tender it tends to be, and the finest and biggest specimens are in mild, moist areas.

SOIL Tolerates most and, contrary to widely held belief, will thrive in moderately alkaline conditions – although it is also true that the best plants tend to be on deep, rich, rather acid loams.

SITUATION Full sun to light or moderate shade. The superb evergreen *M. grandiflora* is often trained against a tall wall but while it thrives in this situation, it only really needs shelter in colder, more exposed gardens and can be grown as a good freestanding specimen.

Laburnum × watereri 'Vossii'

WATERING AND FEEDING Until the tree is well established mulch in autumn and spring, and feed with a rose or similar potash-rich fertilizer in mid-spring.

PRUNING None.

COMMON PROBLEMS None.

PROPAGATION Tip cuttings in spring.

TROUBLESHOOTING Damaged branches or misplaced branches may be removed, but any pruning should be kept to a minimum because magnolias tend to produce masses of small twigs from the position of any cuts. *M. grandiflora* is prone to damage from heavy snowfalls; broken branches should be cut clean and, if necessary, the plant supported with wires and stakes to aid the recovery of shape. Wall-trained plants of *M. grandiflora* should be regularly checked for the tightness of ties and retied. A common problem with the multi-stemmed *M. × soulangeana* is that the branches bend down to ground level and so impede lawn mowing when, as often, the plant is grown in grass. It may be worth using wires to hold the branches up (see page 194).

SIZE Varies greatly, so check label descriptions. As a guideline, *M. grandiflora* and *M. × soulangeana* will reach about 3 × 2m/10 × 6½ft after five years and 8–9 × 4–5m/26–30 × 13–16ft after twenty or more years, but others, such as *M. stellata*, seldom exceed 4m/13ft in height.

Magnolia × soulangeana

Malus ORNAMENTAL APPLE

The genus *Malus* plays its most important role in gardens by including the apple-producing species, but there are several valuable ornamental blossoming species too, generally grouped as flowering crab apples. Many are much prettier than the more popular flowering cherries, but they tend to suffer from the same pests and diseases as true apples.

SOIL Almost any, although least successful on very heavy, cold, wet clays.

SITUATION Full sun to very light shade.

WATERING AND FEEDING Until the tree is well established, mulch in autumn and spring, and feed with a rose or similar potash-rich fertilizer in mid-spring.

PRUNING None necessary on varieties grown solely for their blossom, but cut out diseased or crossing branches in winter. Varieties such as 'John Downie' or 'Golden Hornet', grown equally for their fruit, may either be left unpruned or treated in the same way as bush apples (see page 224).

COMMON PROBLEMS Scab; canker; mildew; aphids.

PROPAGATION Not feasible by cuttings.

TROUBLESHOOTING Damaged or overgrown trees may be treated in the same way as apples (see page 228), but much of the appeal of old garden trees comes from their distorted shape. They respond to hard pruning by producing masses of new shoot growth which will itself require pruning.

SIZE Almost all ornamental *Malus* species and varieties may be obtained grafted on to the same rootstocks used for apples, and the rootstock dictates the overall size of the tree (see page 228).

Malus 'Golden Hornet'

Parrotia – Pinus

Parrotia   PERSIAN IRONWOOD

A deciduous tree or large shrub with coarse leaves, grown principally for its glorious autumn colour. Its drawbacks are a relatively
dull appearance in summer, rather exacting soil requirements and
fairly vigorous growth.

SOIL Moderately acidic, organic soil gives the best results and
growth will never be as satisfactory in alkaline conditions.
SITUATION Full sun.
WATERING AND FEEDING Until the tree is well established
mulch in autumn and spring, and feed with a balanced general
fertilizer in mid-spring.
PRUNING None necessary, but may be trimmed in spring if
grown against a wall or in other restricted space.
COMMON PROBLEMS None.
PROPAGATION Not feasible by cuttings but may be layered.

Parrotia persica

TROUBLESHOOTING Unlikely to be necessary, but will regenerate fairly well if cut back in spring into moderately old wood.
SIZE Attains about $2.5 \times 2m/8 \times 6\frac{1}{2}ft$ in five years and continues
approximately to double every five years until reaching around
10m/33ft tall with a spread of 8m/26ft.

Picea   SPRUCE

The coniferous genus *Picea* is most familiar in the shape of *P. abies*,
the Norway spruce or Christmas tree, and this is the one most
likely to be seen as a garden plant. By and large, this is a genus of
forest trees, although a few mutant dwarf forms are both useful
and attractive (see page 79).

Soil Intolerant of poor, alkaline or dry soils.

Situation Open situation to allow room to grow; intolerant of more than light shade.

Watering and feeding Until the tree is well established mulch in autumn and spring, and feed with a balanced general fertilizer in mid-spring.

Pruning None; cannot be trimmed to form a hedge.

Common problems Adelgids (aphid-like insects), some of which produce small, pineapple-shaped galls.

Propagation Not feasible; cuttings need a misting facility.

Troubleshooting Not necessary. Trees badly damaged by storms are best removed, for they will never recover their appealing pyramidal shape.

Size Few gardeners plant Norway spruce as a specimen tree, for it grows very rapidly, especially in the early stages, attaining 4×2m/$13 \times 6\frac{1}{2}$ft after five years. Ultimately, it becomes very tall – perhaps 30m/100ft. When used as a Christmas tree, the best plan is to have two trees and to dig them up and pot them for use every other year until they become too large. Then they are better discarded or given to someone with room for them to grow.

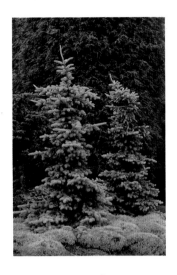

Picea pungens 'Koster'

Pinus PINE

A famous tree nursery once described the pines as the conifers with the most class and, undoubtedly, their long needles (very long in some instances) confer a distinction lacking in other genera. Nonetheless, few species are distinctive enough to be grown as specimen trees, and few species small enough to be considered other than for fairly large gardens; although there are some dwarf forms (see page 79).

Soil Free-draining; preferably – but not essentially – acidic.

Situation Open situation to allow room to grow; intolerant of more than light shade. The most attractive ornamental species are the long-needled pines, some of which are rather tender and must have shelter from cold winds and late frosts.

Watering and feeding Until the tree is well established mulch in autumn and spring, and feed with a balanced general fertilizer in mid-spring.

Pruning None; cannot be trimmed to form a hedge.

Common problems None.

Propagation Not feasible; cuttings need a misting facility.

Troubleshooting Not normally necessary. Trees badly damaged by storms are best removed for they will never recover their appealing shape. Trees with more limited damage may be tidied by having broken branches cut back to just above the basal collar, but there will be no regeneration of new shoots.

Size Varies considerably, so check label information. The best of the species for larger gardens are *P. peuce* and *P. leucodermis*, both with fine shapes and, in the latter case, beautiful blue cones when mature (both 4×1m/13×3ft after ten years, 10×3m/33×10ft after twenty years). Another species, *P. montezumae*, with its long, almost shaggy needles, attains 6×2m/$20 \times 6\frac{1}{2}$ft after ten years, 12×5m/40×16ft after twenty years.

Pinus montezumae

Populus – Pyrus

Populus candicans 'Aurora'

Populus POPLAR

As garden plants, poplars have a fondness for water and grow much larger than their owners expect, although they do have the advantage of thriving in soils that few other trees will tolerate. There are, however, a few useful ornamental varieties.

SOIL Almost any, but especially successful in very wet soils.

SITUATION Full sun to moderate shade.

WATERING AND FEEDING Until well established mulch in autumn and spring, and apply a general fertilizer in mid-spring.

PRUNING None necessary, although a denser, bushier plant will result from cutting it back hard every five or six years in the spring. Some gardeners regularly pollard poplars by cutting new growth back each spring to the main trunk.

COMMON PROBLEMS Canker; rust; leaf-attacking insects.

PROPAGATION Hardwood cuttings in winter.

TROUBLESHOOTING Will regenerate very well if cut back hard to remove broken or misshapen branches, and this usually results in a more attractive plant.

SIZE Varies slightly between species and varieties, so check label information. Among screening species, the Lombardy poplar will reach $5 \times 1m/16 \times 3ft$ after five years, $10 \times 2m/33 \times 6\frac{1}{2}ft$ after ten years and up to $35 \times 8m/115 \times 26ft$ eventually. Other species spread much more widely, and even the popular ornamental *P. candicans* 'Aurora' becomes a very big tree, attaining perhaps $20 \times 8m/65 \times 26ft$ over 25 or 30 years.

Prunus

The genus *Prunus* includes all of the garden stone fruits – plums, damsons, cherries, peaches, nectarines and apricots, and these are covered in detail on pages 229–34. But it also embraces the vast tribe of so-called flowering cherries, both the Japanese varieties, overplanted almost everywhere, and a number of choice species. They are fairly undemanding in their soil and site requirements, but in my view their flowers and foliage aren't always beautiful enough to compensate for their tendency to disease and their habit of surface rooting and suckering.

SOIL Almost any, although least successful on very heavy, cold, wet clays.

SITUATION Full sun to very light shade.

WATERING AND FEEDING Until the tree is well established mulch in autumn and spring, and feed with rose or similar potash-rich fertilizer in mid-spring.

PRUNING None necessary on varieties grown solely for their blossom, although diseased or crossing branches should be cut out in winter. The winter cherry, in particular, is prone to a great deal of twig death and it pays to cut out the worst of this in the cause of tidiness. If any pruning is necessary, delay until summer to reduce the risk of silver leaf infection.

COMMON PROBLEMS Bacterial canker; various dying back conditions – the variety 'Kanzan' is especially prone to one from which the tree seldom recovers; aphids; silver leaf disease.

Prunus × *subhirtella* 'Autumnalis'

PROPAGATION Not feasible by cuttings.

TROUBLESHOOTING Mature ornamental cherries are troublesome trees because they are prone to several diseases of the bark and wood that cause die-back. The temptation is to cut out the damaged branches but this invariably compounds the problem, rendering the tree even more unsightly and possibly allowing further infection by fungi and bacteria. Damaged or diseased ornamental cherries seldom recover and are better removed.

Most are grafted on to *P. avium* rootstock, which is very prone to surface rooting. This causes problems in lawns, where the roots foul mower blades, and also under paths and driveways. Little can be done about this, as mounding soil over the top or cutting the roots off is only a temporary measure; more roots surface, and the damage often throws up suckers.

SIZE Varies considerably. Most of the popular double-flowered cherries reach about $3–4 \times 2–3m/10–13 \times 6\frac{1}{2}–10ft$ after five years and perhaps $10 \times 7m/33 \times 23ft$ after 25 years, after which they begin to decline. The narrowly upright 'Amanogawa' reaches a similar height, but will remain about 1m in width until it reaches the age of fifteen to twenty years, when it tends to open out most unattractively. The height of the weeping 'Kiku-shidare-zakura' is largely determined by the height of its graft on to the *P. avium* rootstock, but whatever the initial size, the rootstock will itself grow to produce a plant perhaps 4m/13ft tall in twenty years. The winter-flowering cherry, *P. subhirtella* 'Autumnalis', is a useful tree but often planted in far too small a space; it may reach $8 \times 6m/26 \times 20ft$ in 20 to 25 years. Ornamental flowering or foliage forms of plum and peach will attain a similar size, but tend to be lower growing if grafted on to the rootstock 'Pixy'. The Tibetan cherry, *P. serrula*, reaches about $3 \times 2m/10 \times 6\frac{1}{2}ft$ after five years and perhaps $10 \times 5m/33 \times 16ft$ ultimately.

Pyrus ORNAMENTAL PEAR

The best known *Pyrus* is the pear tree, but there are a few ornamental garden species too, most notably and commonly the weeping, silvery, willow-leaved pear, *P. salicifolia* 'Pendula', which has some of the appeal of genuine weeping willows and rather less significant drawbacks, making it an attractive garden tree.

SOIL Tolerates almost any, but the richer the better.

SITUATION Full sun.

WATERING AND FEEDING Until well established mulch in autumn and spring, and apply a general fertilizer in mid-spring.

PRUNING None, but plants must be staked as they tend to have feeble root systems.

COMMON PROBLEMS Scab.

PROPAGATION Not feasible by cuttings.

TROUBLESHOOTING As the tree ages, the branches tend to become a congested mass; thin them out by removing whole branches every few years, in winter. Any damaged by scab or other problems should be cut out at the same time.

SIZE About $2.5 \times 2m/8 \times 6\frac{1}{2}ft$ after five years; $6–8 \times 5–6m/20–26 \times 16–20ft$ after twenty or more years.

Pyrus salicifolia 'Pendula'

Robinia – Taxodium

Robinia pseudoacacia

Robinia

There are several species of fairly hardy deciduous robinias, often called the hardy or false acacias, grown for their pink and white flowers or, in one particular instance, for golden foliage (*R. pseudoacacia* 'Frisia'). Like their relatives the true acacias, they often fail because the site is not appropriate.

SOIL Tolerates most, but best on free-draining fertile sites and least successful on heavy, waterlogged soils.

SITUATION Full sun to very light shade, but must have shelter from winds, which damage the foliage of some varieties and can break the brittle twigs.

WATERING AND FEEDING Until the tree is well established mulch in autumn and spring, and feed with a rose or similar potash-rich fertilizer in mid-spring.

PRUNING None.

COMMON PROBLEMS None.

PROPAGATION Not feasible by cuttings.

TROUBLESHOOTING Problems are only likely to arise when plants have been damaged by wind. They will regenerate if cut back a short way into sound wood in spring, but the problem will recur while the plant remains in an exposed site.

SIZE 3 × 2.5m/10 × 8ft after five years, up to 15 × 8m/50 × 26ft after twenty or more years, although the pink-flowered *R. hispida* is smaller, reaching barely half this size and growth rate.

Salix WILLOW

I believe that the best of the garden willows are the shrub-sized species, but there are a few tree species that are useful for their ability to grow in otherwise difficult sites: the plant usually called *S. matsudana* 'Tortuosa', *S. alba argentea*, and *S. a. vitellina*.

SOIL Will tolerate most, although particularly successful in wet or even waterlogged soils.

SITUATION Full sun to moderate shade. Because all large willows have water-seeking and invasive roots, they should not be planted where they may damage drains or the foundations of buildings. It is inadvisable to plant any tree-sized willows closer to a building than a distance equal to twice their ultimate spread.

WATERING AND FEEDING Until well established mulch in autumn and spring, and apply a general fertilizer in mid-spring.

PRUNING None necessary, but as many of the species are grown for their coloured shoots, pruning to stimulate some new growth each year is desirable. No matter how hard willows are cut back, they will regenerate. They are among the few trees for which regular pollarding to a crown may look attractive.

COMMON PROBLEMS Many species suffer from leaf-attacking insects and fungal leaf spots, which may cause some disfigurement as summer progresses. The commonest so-called weeping willow, (usually called *S. babylonica*, but more accurately *S.* 'Chrysocoma') suffers from anthracnose disease, which causes leaf spots and shoot die-back. It is one further reason why this most invasive of willows should not be planted in gardens.

Salix alba

PROPAGATION Hardwood cuttings in winter, layers or suckers; willows root extremely readily from cuttings.

TROUBLESHOOTING Old willows almost invariably suffer from broken and damaged branches, but often look the better for it. They regenerate and heal so successfully that cutting out of damaged parts may be as hard or light as aesthetics dictate. If a large tree must be felled, especially if close to a building, take expert advice first because willows draw more water from the soil than almost any other tree and the removal of such a natural water pump can lead to waterlogging and consequent problems.

SIZE All big willows grow quickly. *S.* 'Chrysocoma' reaches 5 × 5m/16 × 16ft in five years and up to 20 × 20m/65 × 65ft in twenty years. The other tree species, including the popular twisted *S. matsudana* 'Tortuosa', are unlikely to achieve half this size and growth rate.

Sorbus 'Joseph Rock'

Sorbus

This is a most useful genus of medium-sized and hardy, deciduous trees, grown principally for their attractively coloured berries but with good blossom and, in many instances, spring or autumn foliage appeal also.

SOIL Almost any, including strongly alkaline soils.

SITUATION Full sun to moderate shade; most are tolerant of exposure to wind.

WATERING AND FEEDING Until the tree is well established mulch in autumn and spring, and feed with a rose or similar potash-rich fertilizer in mid-spring.

PRUNING None; as many varieties are grafted suckers may arise, which should be promptly cut away.

COMMON PROBLEMS None, although some species may be attacked by leaf-spotting fungi, and insects.

PROPAGATION Not successful from cuttings.

TROUBLESHOOTING Should not be necessary, although will regenerate fairly well if cut back lightly into old wood in spring.

SIZE Varies slightly between varieties of the main species, which are usually grouped into the mountain ashes or rowans and the whitebeams. Most, however, attain about 2.5 × 1.5m/8 × 5ft after five years, double this after ten years and 12–15 × 5–8m/40–50 × 16–26ft eventually.

Taxodium SWAMP CYPRESS

A strange but lovely tree, *T. distichum* is one of the few deciduous conifers. Its common name is misleading for it will grow in a variety of soils, but although many gardeners are attracted by young specimens, it will grow too large for most gardens.

SOIL Tolerates most except very dry conditions, and has the advantage of tolerating, although not requiring, very heavy, wet, or even waterlogged clays.

SITUATION Full sun with shelter from cold winds; the key to success with this tree is not to plant it in a swamp but to grow it somewhere with warm summers.

Taxodium distichum

Taxodium – Tsuga

WATERING AND FEEDING Until the tree is well established mulch in autumn and spring, and feed with a balanced general purpose fertilizer in mid-spring.

PRUNING None needed.

COMMON PROBLEMS None.

PROPAGATION Hardwood cuttings in winter, or from seed.

TROUBLESHOOTING If a plant threatens to outgrow its space it may be cut to about 2m/6½ft above soil level; it will look unsightly for a time but should produce new shoots from the old wood. Dead or damaged branches may also be cut back in the expectation that they will regenerate.

SIZE Will attain 5 × 2m/16 × 6½ft after ten years and perhaps 30 × 10m/100 × 33ft after 30 years.

Taxus YEW

A uniquely special tree, living to a phenomenal age and possessed of a peculiar majesty, although best known in gardens for producing the densest and most beautiful of hedges. While the wild form is unlikely to be planted in gardens, there are a few selected forms and colour variants that are most attractive, if slow growing. Yew is exceedingly poisonous and its various parts should not be eaten by animals or people, but it will not poison the soil nor harm other plants; it is simply a very effective competitor because of the dense shade it casts.

SOIL Almost any, but best on deep, rich loams; excellent in strongly alkaline conditions.

SITUATION Full sun to fairly deep shade; tolerant of fairly exposed conditions, but stunted by severe and constant wind.

WATERING AND FEEDING Until well established mulch in autumn and spring, and apply a general fertilizer in mid-spring.

PRUNING None. When grown as a hedge, clip twice, the first time around midsummer, the second in early autumn; or clip once only in late summer, although this will give a tidy appearance for a shorter time.

COMMON PROBLEMS None.

PROPAGATION Hardwood cuttings in winter.

TROUBLESHOOTING Should not be necessary on free-standing trees, although a yew will regenerate very well if cut back hard into old wood in spring – and thus old and overgrown hedges may be rejuvenated very successfully. It is worth remembering however, that much of the appeal of ancient yew trees is their wizened, gnarled appearance.

SIZE Both of these features of the yew, together with its great age potential, have aroused considerable and often erroneous speculation. Although the selected forms such as the fastigiate Irish yew and the golden-foliaged varieties are slow growing, *T. baccata* when used for hedging will, after the first year, put on 15–20cm/6–8in each season and attain a height of 2m/6½ft to full hedge width after about ten years. A free-standing tree of the normal species will reach about 2 × 1–1.5m/6½ × 3–5ft after ten years, 4 × 2.5–3m/13 × 8–10ft after twenty years, and perhaps 30 × 20m/100 × 65ft after anything from 200 to a thousand years.

Taxus baccata

Thuja FALSE CEDAR

These are perhaps the important garden conifers least known by the majority of gardeners, who might dismiss them as simply cypresses. In fact, both as specimen trees for the larger garden and as hedging plants, I find them superior. They are also less demanding in their site requirements, and give off a pleasant fragrance when clipped.

SOIL Always best on deep, moist soils, but tolerant of most.

SITUATION Full sun to light shade; *Thuja* is more tolerant of wind exposure than cypresses, although it will still be browned by constant salt spray.

WATERING AND FEEDING Until well established mulch in autumn and spring, and apply a general fertilizer in mid-spring.

PRUNING None. When grown as a hedge, clip twice, the first time around midsummer, the second in early autumn; or clip once only in late summer, although this will give a tidy appearance for a shorter time. Some gardeners are allergic to the foliage of *Thuja*, which can produce a slight skin rash when handled. It is wise to wear gloves when clipping hedges, therefore.

COMMON PROBLEMS None.

PROPAGATION Hardwood cuttings in winter.

TROUBLESHOOTING Should not be necessary. Damaged trees will regenerate slowly if only cut back into wood younger than about eight years old.

SIZE The species most likely to be seen, and the one sold for hedging, is *T. plicata*, the Western red cedar, which will reach 4 × 1.5m/13 × 5ft in five years, 8–9 × 4m/26–30 × 13ft in ten years, and ultimately a height of up to 40m/130ft in favourable sites.

Thuja plicata 'Aurea'

Tsuga HEMLOCK

Although the full-grown western hemlock, *T. heterophylla*, makes a stately specimen coniferous tree with a characteristically drooping main shoot, it is a big and uncommon plant, and not one I would include here were it not that it makes a superb and very dense hedge.

SOIL Most, but usually best on free-draining, slightly acidic soils.

SITUATION Full sun to moderate shade; *Tsuga* is very tolerant of wind exposure.

WATERING AND FEEDING Until well established mulch in autumn and spring, and apply a general fertilizer in mid-spring.

PRUNING None. When grown as a hedge, clip twice, first around midsummer and again in early autumn; or alternatively clip once, hard, in early autumn.

COMMON PROBLEMS None.

PROPAGATION Not feasible from cuttings.

TROUBLESHOOTING Should not be necessary, although trees damaged for any reason will regenerate slowly if cut back into moderately old wood.

SIZE Free-standing trees will attain 4 × 1.5m/13 × 5ft in five years, 8–9 × 4m/26–30 × 13ft in ten years, and ultimately a height of up to 40m/130ft in favourable sites.

Tsuga heterophylla

TREE FRUIT

One of the commonest criticisms levelled at the authors of gardening textbooks is, 'My tree doesn't look like the one in your pictures', for every tree is an individual and will branch and produce its buds slightly differently from its neighbours. Pruning diagrams always show idealized trees, but I have tried in the plant entries to cover individual variations in position of buds and so forth. Adhere as closely as you can to my advice, but if your tree is more or less vigorous or has some other growth quirk, don't worry; a few centimetres variation in the position of a pruning cut will not make the difference between success and failure.

While there are general similarities between the cultivation of fruit trees and ornamental trees, there are also a number of differences. These can perhaps be summed up by saying that fruit trees need considerably more care and attention in the early years and a little more throughout their lives, but the better you look after them when they are young the simpler they will be to care for later on.

Though it is possible to obtain a fruit crop of sorts from a wide range of soil types, the best will always come from deep, well-manured and fertile loams. Very acid, very alkaline and very cold wet soils are those least likely to give satisfactory results. But I must stress the importance of feeding fruit trees, of not forcing them to compete with surrounding grass or other vegetation, especially in their early years, and of paying careful attention to watering and mulching. The greater bulk of any fruit is in fact water, and only by ensuring that the soil remains moist through mulching will your trees, young trees especially, be able to obtain enough water to swell the fruit and prevent premature drop.

Like many ornamental trees, most fruit trees that you buy have been grafted: a fruiting variety, carefully bred or selected over the years for its cropping qualities, has been grafted on to another, the rootstock variety, bred for its rooting efficiency. With most tree fruit, there is little choice in rootstock variety but apples are a notable exception. Here, the rootstock exerts an influence on the overall size of the tree, irrespective of the fruiting variety. It is possible, therefore, to grow apple trees appropriate to the size of your garden, but it is not always appreciated that the more dwarfing the influence of the rootstock, the better must be the growing conditions. The most dwarfing of all apple rootstocks, known as M.27, while very useful in allowing a small apple tree to be grown in a container, must be planted in a high quality soil-based potting compost and fed annually throughout its life. Dwarfing rootstocks also require permanent staking and are too weakly anchored for exposed sites.

With certain exceptions, fruit trees will crop better (some will otherwise not do so at all) when grown in combination with others of a compatible variety. The reason for this is simply that most apples, pears and to a lesser extent plums, cannot be fertilized by their own pollen. The choice of the best pollinating variety may vary from district to district, so take advice from the nurseryman from whom you buy your plants. The problem does not arise with sour cherries, the most popular modern sweet cherry ('Stella'), peaches, nectarines, apricots or figs, all of which are self-fertilizing.

The need for a pollinator variety of apple or pear may create difficulties for gardeners with limited space. But there are ways around the problem. The first is to grow your trees as cordons (single stems producing fruiting spurs), which take up very little room, or to choose a 'Ballerina' or similar columnar variety. The latter require no pruning but the range of trees of this type is very limited and they barely approach the traditional varieties in flavour. Another possibility is to grow a single, family tree. This is a plant in which more than one fruiting variety has been grafted on to a single rootstock: one plant, and a range of eating and cooking apples over a period of several months, is an attractive proposition.

PRUNING AND TRAINING

The most important difference of all between fruit and ornamental trees is that fruit trees will not crop to their full potential unless they are trained or pruned in an appropriate manner. Training is essentially the shaping of a tree so that it conforms to the space around it and, in the case of a fruit tree, so that its crop may be picked with ease. Pruning falls into two categories: formative, which is the pruning carried out during the first few years in order to train a young tree, and maintenance, which is the

How a tree produces fruit

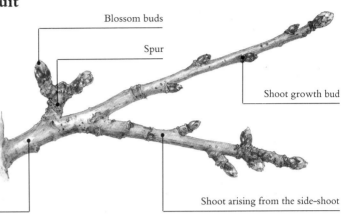

Blossom buds

Spur

Shoot growth bud

Side-shoot from main trunk

Shoot arising from the side-shoot

▶ **SPUR-BEARING VARIETIES** Most apples and pears produce their fruit on short branches called spurs. The spurs form naturally, but part of the aim of pruning is to encourage the tree to produce a greater number. Clearly evident in early spring are the fat blossom buds in clusters on the spurs, and the flat growth buds that will break to form non-flowering leafy shoots.

◀ **FLOWERING TIME** Flowers and then fruit are borne in clusters at the bases of the side-shoots or spurs. Much pruning of apples and pears involves cutting back to a prescribed point relative to this basal cluster, which encourages the spur to branch and so produce more buds the following year, while restricting the amount of leaf growth the tree makes relative to the fruit produced.

▶ **TIP-BEARING VARIETIES** Some types of apple and pear produce fruit at the tips of the branches. 'Irish Peach' and 'Worcester Pearmain' are tip-bearers, and 'Blenheim Orange', 'Bramley's Seedling', 'Discovery' and 'Lord Lambourne' are partial tip-bearers. On these forms, prune half the branches in alternate years.

annual pruning of a trained tree in order to maintain its cropping efficiency. Techniques of both formative and maintenance pruning vary according to the type of fruit tree in question, and I describe them under the separate entries.

There are, however, a number of more general points that are best discussed here. First, in order to grasp the principles of pruning, it helps to understand the means by which fruit trees bear their fruit. Generally, the bud that develops at the base of a leaf in any given year will do one of two things. Either it grows out to form a long leafy shoot or it forms a short shoot or spur bearing a blossom bud (or

fruit bud as it is called). Sometimes the bud at the leaf base remains dormant for one or more years and sometimes it forms a blossom bud straightaway, without undergoing a second season's growth. If a tree is growing vigorously, most of the buds grow into leafy shoots; if it is growing more weakly, most tend to become plump blossom-bearing spurs. Pruning tends to encourage shoot growth and so hard pruning will reduce cropping; yet without pruning the whole plant will soon become a tangled, unkempt mass of branches. Very hard or very light pruning should therefore be avoided for the best results. The aim is to

Tree Fruit

Fans: plums, apricots, peaches, nectarines, cherries, figs

Fans can be grown trained against horizontal wires arranged free-standing in fence style, but it is very much better for them to be grown with the support and shelter of a wall. Shown here is the basic method for establishing a fan, with variations for peaches and nectarines. The pruning of each tree is described under the individual entries.

Arrange a series of horizontal wires spaced 60cm/2ft apart. Plant the young tree or feathered maiden in suitably prepared soil in autumn or late winter.

▲ **I THE SPRING AFTER PLANTING** Cut the main stem just above a bud positioned about 60cm/2ft above soil level, choosing one that has at least two other buds below it, one facing left and one facing right. (If the plant is a feathered maiden with side-shoots, likewise cut above two oppositely facing side-shoots.)

▲ **2 THE FOLLOWING SUMMER** Tie in the side-shoots to the wires at an angle of 45°, using canes to give added support (these side-shoots will form the lowest ribs of the fan), and cut the main stem back to the point immediately above where the uppermost side-shoot emerges.

▲ **Peach/nectarine** Treat as described left, but in addition cut all side-shoots emerging from the ribs at a point just above one leaf from their bases.

▶ **3 SPRING, 2ND YEAR** Cut back the two ribs to just above a bud about 40cm/15in from the base of each rib, leaving the rib with at least four buds on it.

produce a proper balance between shoot growth and blossom bud development.

For tip-bearing apples, see previous page. Plums bear all of their fruit on one- and two-year-old shoots, and should be pruned as little as possible because they respond very vigorously, producing masses of leafy shoots. Among other stone fruit, peaches and nectarines fruit mainly on one-year-old wood whereas sweet cherries fruit only on two-year-old shoots. Their prun-

ing methods should therefore be adjusted.

Trees that are growing too vigorously and producing too much leafy growth in proportion to fruit can be slowed down not only by pruning but also by tying down some of the branches to below the horizontal; this will limit sap flow and often induce fruit buds to form instead of leaves. With apples, although free-standing trees are normally pruned in the winter, summer pruning (as is usual with

Tree Fruit

▲ 4 SUMMER, 2ND YEAR

Choose three side-shoots emerging from each rib – one from below, and two, spaced about 10–15cm/4–6in apart, from above. Cut back any other shoots to one leaf. Tie the selected shoots to the support wires so they radiate outwards in a fan.

▲ 5 SPRING, 3RD YEAR You

will now have eight ribs to your fan, and in this spring cut each back to a point above an upward-facing bud, leaving about 75cm/2½ft of the previous season's growth.

◄ 6 THE FAN IN SUMMER

Tie in the extension growth on these ribs to the support wires and also tie in new shoots systematically to fill in the spaces between the ribs. Follow further training and pruning methods as described under the entries for each tree.

cordons, page 226) will also restrict growth by removing a proportion of the foliage and so limiting the supply of nutrients to the roots.

PROBLEMS AND DISEASES

A common problem with fruit trees is a tendency to biennial bearing, in which a crop is produced only every other year. Some apple varieties such as 'Blenheim Orange', 'Crispin', 'Ellison's Orange', 'Fortune', 'Newton Wonder' and 'Rev. W. Wilks' are inherently prone to biennial cropping, whereas the condition may be induced in others by stress. If a tree that has hitherto cropped annually begins to do so biennially, it can sometimes be restored to its previous habit by careful feeding and watering and by pruning only lightly.

Fruit trees are subject to rather more than their fair share of pests and diseases and often little can be done to prevent attacks. Tar oil should be sprayed on the dormant plants as a regular routine in winter to kill eggs and adults of pests overwintering on the bark and, of course, damaged or dead branches should be cut away promptly. Damaged fruit within reach should be removed before the inevitable decay fungi become established on them. But, while I believe that young trees should be given protection from aphids, mildew, scab and other problems, old-established trees can by and large be left to their own devices. Even canker, the most serious disease on most types of tree, can be tolerated in moderation, although badly affected branches should be removed.

Tree Fruit

Bushes: apples, pears, plums

Plant the young tree or feathered maiden in suitably prepared soil in autumn or late winter.

▲ 1 THE SPRING AFTER PLANTING Cut the main stem just above a bud. The height of this bud depends on the type of tree being planted, and more information is given under the individual entries. The chosen bud should have three or four other buds or side-shoots below it on the stem; these will develop into the main branches.

▲ FEATHERED MAIDEN If the plant already has side-shoots, in the spring after planting cut the main stem at a point above three or four principal side-shoots. Cut these back by about half for an **apple** or **pear**, two thirds for a **plum**, to a point just above an upward-facing bud. Cut off all other side-shoots flush with the main stem.

▲ 2 NEWLY PRUNED The feathered maiden will look like this.

◀ 4 APPLES AND PEARS In subsequent winters, cut the previous season's extension growth on the main branches back by half, and cut side-shoots to just above four buds from their bases. Remove any shoots emerging from the main stem.

▶ 3 THE NEXT WINTER Cut back the most vigorous of the shoots by half to two thirds of the previous season's growth, just above an upward-facing bud. Cut inward-pointing shoots hard back to very short lengths. Remove new shoots emerging from the main stem. For a **plum**, pruning and training is now complete.

◀ 5 AFTER ANNUAL PRUNING The tree will look quite sparse, with very short side-shoots.

Apple

The most popular garden tree fruit, the easiest to grow, available in the greatest number of varieties and with the widest range of size, form and pruning options. There are libraries of books on apple culture, so I have restricted myself to those aspects that I believe to be of relevance to the majority of gardeners.

SOIL Most, but least successful in very heavy, cold and wet clays, and in extremes of acidity or alkalinity.

SITUATION Full sun to light shade, although the best – and best-ripened – crops will always be in full sun. In cold and windy gardens, especially at altitudes of above about 200m/650ft, some shelter will be needed, and it may be more convenient to grow the trees as cordons or in another restricted form.

WATERING AND FEEDING Modern trees on restricted rootstocks should be fed and mulched at least until well established, and preferably permanently. In early spring apply a balanced rose or other potash-rich fertilizer and a mulch. Old and long-established trees should be self-sufficient, if cropping satisfactorily.

Espaliered apple

PRUNING Old trees producing adequate crops should be pruned as little as possible, because any cutting back will stimulate masses of twiggy growth which will itself then require pruning. The occasional cutting out in winter of damaged and crossing branches should be all that is required on old trees. Even cankered branches may be left, unless there are young and unaffected trees nearby, or if old trees are very seriously diseased, for many old varieties are highly canker-prone and yet still crop satisfactorily.

Pruning is very important, however, on young trees and varies considerably depending on the growing system employed. There are three main training and pruning methods widely applicable in gardens: the restricted systems of cordon and espalier and the free-standing bush. Once a restricted form is established, the tree will need regular annual pruning to maintain its shape; this pruning is described here under cordons, but applies to other restricted forms too. In general it is better to be a little late rather than early with the regular pruning, as there may be considerable further growth which will itself need pruning in early autumn.

BUSHES Follow the steps opposite, noting that in step 1 the height of the first cut varies with the rootstock used: trees grafted on the dwarfing rootstocks M.27 or M.9 should be cut above a bud about 60cm/2ft above soil level; those grafted on rootstocks M.26 or MM.106 should be cut above a bud about 75cm/2½ft above soil level. The pruning regime for trees trained as bushes is less precise than for the restricted forms; in general, the shoots on very vigor-ously growing trees should be pruned by slightly less than half, those on weakly growing ones by slightly more.

CORDONS Follow the steps illustrated overleaf. When the main stem has reached about 15cm/6in above the limit of its allotted space, cut off the tip in early summer just above a conveniently placed bud. Thereafter prune it annually in late summer to leave about 1cm/½in of the current season's extension growth.

As well as cordons, there is also available a type of upright apple tree that may be confused with them, the 'Ballerina' tree and its

Apple

Cordons: apples

Establish a system of horizontal support wires spaced 60cm/2ft apart. Plant the tree in prepared soil in autumn or late winter.

▶ 1 NEWLY PLANTED

Immediately after planting, tie the main stem at an angle of 45°, and prune all side-shoots longer than 10cm/4in to a point just above the third bud from their bases.

▲ 2 REGULAR PRUNING

Thereafter every year in late summer prune the side-shoots as follows. Cut side-shoots longer than 20–25cm/8–10in and growing directly from the main stem at a point just above the third leaf above the basal cluster.

▲ 3 AT THE SAME TIME, cut

shoots arising from the side-shoots at a point just above the first leaf beyond the basal cluster.

variants. These trees have been developed from naturally short-branched mutants; they do not form elongated branches, but retain their telegraph-pole appearance and require no pruning.

ESPALIERS Follow the steps opposite, repeating the stages to train further pairs of arms until the required height is reached. Once it is reached, prune the tip of the main stem as described for that of a cordon. At the same time (late summer), prune all the side-shoots on the espalier arms exactly as described for pruning cordons (steps 2 and 3).

Some nurseries offer apples trained as 'step-over' trees for growing alongside paths or to edge vegetable patches. These are, in effect, single-arm espaliers and should be pruned as for cordons (steps 2 and 3).

COMMON PROBLEMS Scab; mildew; canker; fruit rots; honey fungus; bitter pit; aphids; woolly aphid; codling moth.

Espaliers: apples

Establish a system of horizontal support wires spaced 60cm/2ft apart. Plant the tree in prepared soil in autumn or late winter.

▶ **1 NEWLY PLANTED**
Immediately after planting, cut the main stem: the place for the cut should be slightly higher than the first wire to come both just above a bud, and also a short distance above where two other buds, positioned facing left and right, occur close together.

◀ **2 THE NEXT SUMMER** Tie the shoot that arises from the top bud vertically. Tie the shoots arising from the two other buds at angles of 45° (not at this stage horizontally). Cut all side-shoots to a point just above six leaves from their bases.

▶ **3 THE FOLLOWING WINTER** Untie the first pair of 'arms' and pull them down to retie them horizontally along the lowest wire. Repeat step 1, cutting the main stem to form a second pair of arms in the same way. Cut all side-shoots pruned the previous summer to a point just above three buds from their bases. Once the espalier is formed, prune the side-shoots as described for cordons opposite (steps 2 and 3). Prune the tip as described for the tips of cordons (page 225).

Apple – Pear

PROPAGATION Impossible from cuttings.

TROUBLESHOOTING Old apple trees are best left to their own devices, if possible. If branches must be removed through disease or storm damage, make clean cuts to just above the basal collar to aid the healing process, for apples are particularly prone to invasion by wood rotting fungi. They are also very prone to honey fungus attack and when a tree is felled, the stump should be removed or ground out if feasible.

Trees that are cropping inadequately may be affected by a variety of factors. If blossom is produced in quantity, poor pollination is the explanation and this may be because of the lack of a suitable pollinator variety nearby (or perhaps one has recently been removed); or because the site is very windy and exposed, and the pollen and pollinating insects are being blown away. Provision of some shelter may help. If blossoming is also poor, then some pruning may help, especially if the tree is highly congested. The best plan is, in summer, to cut out entire branches rather than trim away pieces from the periphery, and then gradually establish a suitable pruning regime.

Trees growing in lawns may be suffering from competition with the grass; remedy this by cutting out a circular area approximately 1m/3ft in diameter, and then apply a rose or other potash-rich fertilizer and a mulch in early spring. Conversely, an over-vigorous tree – especially one producing abundant foliage but little fruit – may be suppressed by grassing up to the base of its trunk.

RATE OF GROWTH AND ULTIMATE SIZE While old trees are likely to be growing on their own roots and to attain various, largely unpredictable sizes, modern trees are all grafted on selected rootstocks which dictate their ultimate height regardless of variety. The commonest rootstocks and the approximate sizes the trees will attain are: M.27 2m/6ft; M.9 2.5–3m/8–10ft; M.26 3–3.5m/10–11½ft; MM.106 5m/16ft. In general, the more dwarfing the rootstock, the better the soil and growing conditions it requires, the longer it will require staking, and the earlier it will reach its maximum height. Rootstocks M.27 and M.9 require permanent stakes.

Pear

With some justification, pears are generally thought to be more difficult to grow than apples, and take longer to come into full cropping. As trees, they are certainly more tender but growing them as cordons or espaliers offers them wall protection, and they are very responsive to these forms. And while there are no rootstocks as dwarfing as those of apples, the modern pear tree is much more manageable than its forebears and quicker to mature.

SOIL Most, but least successful in very dry or waterlogged soils, and in extremes of acidity or alkalinity.

SITUATION Full sun to light shade, although the best – and best-ripened – crops will always be in full sun. In cold and windy gardens, especially at altitudes of above about 100m/330ft, some shelter will be needed and it may be more convenient to grow the trees as cordons or espaliers.

Pear 'Conference'

WATERING AND FEEDING Modern trees should be fed and mulched at least until well established and preferably permanently. Apply a balanced rose or other potash-rich fertilizer and a mulch in early spring. Old and long-established trees should be self-sufficient if cropping satisfactorily.

PRUNING Pears are pruned in the same ways as apples.

COMMON PROBLEMS Scab; mildew; canker; fruit rots; aphids; leaf blister mite; pear midge.

TROUBLESHOOTING See Apples. When attempting to solve the problems of poor pollination, it is often overlooked that the popular pear variety 'Conference', although self-fertile, will crop very much more satisfactorily if a pollinator variety is also present.

RATE OF GROWTH AND ULTIMATE SIZE While old trees are likely to be growing on their own roots and may attain a very large size (up to 15m/50ft tall), modern trees are usually grafted on the rootstock 'Quince C'; although on poor soils, the slightly more vigorous 'Quince A' should be chosen. These will each give plants approximately 4–6m/13–20ft tall.

Plum 'Victoria'

Plum

Plums are not difficult to grow, provided you can offer them a sunny situation and good soil. Some of the best garden varieties are self-fertile, so only one tree is required; against that must be set the fact that no truly dwarfing rootstock is available. Damsons and gages may be grown similarly.

SOIL Most, but least successful in very dry soils; tolerant of fairly heavy soils, provided there is no tendency to waterlogging.

SITUATION Full sun to very light shade; warmth is essential for good ripening, so training the trees as fans against a warm wall is an ideal method of cultivation.

WATERING AND FEEDING Modern trees should be fed and mulched at least until well established and preferably permanently. Apply a balanced rose or other potash-rich fertilizer and a mulch in early spring; give only a very light dressing for wall-trained plants. Old and long-established trees should be self-sufficient, if cropping satisfactorily.

PRUNING All pruning of plums must be performed in spring, not in autumn and winter when pruning wounds are liable to be invaded by the fungus causing silver leaf disease. In general, established plums need very little pruning for they will simply respond by producing masses of dense twiggy growth. The occasional cutting out of damaged and crossing branches in spring should be all that is required on old trees. Pruning young trees is very important, however, for at least a few years. Of the several training methods possible, I shall restrict myself here to the free-standing bush and the fan, these being the most useful for gardens. On all types of tree, regularly cut out any suckers that may arise.

BUSHES Follow steps 1–3 on page 224. In step 1, cut the main stem above a bud about 1m/3ft above soil level. By step 4 the shape is established, and the side-shoots will become the main branches. From then on little pruning should be done other than occasionally thinning out the tree in spring if necessary.

Plum

Fans: plums, apricots, sweet cherries

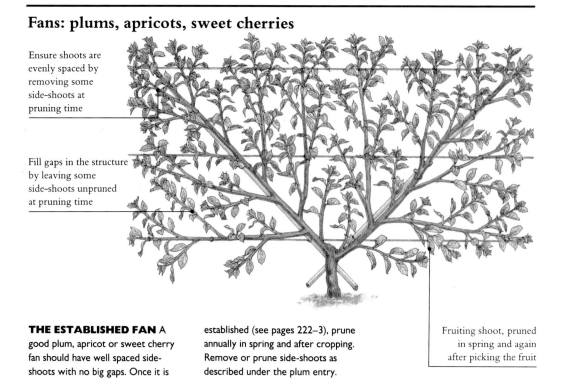

Ensure shoots are evenly spaced by removing some side-shoots at pruning time

Fill gaps in the structure by leaving some side-shoots unpruned at pruning time

Fruiting shoot, pruned in spring and again after picking the fruit

THE ESTABLISHED FAN A good plum, apricot or sweet cherry fan should have well spaced side-shoots with no big gaps. Once it is established (see pages 222–3), prune annually in spring and after cropping. Remove or prune side-shoots as described under the plum entry.

FANS Follow the steps on page 222. Once the fan is established, annual pruning is as follows, and takes place in spring. Cut out any shoots facing directly towards or directly away from the wall. Cut out excess side-shoots to leave spaces of about 10cm/4in between each one. Cut the side-shoots remaining at a point just above six leaves from their bases (unless there are significant gaps in the fan structure, when these side-shoots may be allowed to elongate to form more ribs).

After picking the fruit in late summer, cut back further those side-shoots already shortened, to three leaves from their bases. Tie in any unsupported shoots.

COMMON PROBLEMS Silver leaf; fruit rots; rust; bacterial canker; aphids; plum fruit moth.

PROPAGATION Impossible from cuttings.

TROUBLESHOOTING No matter how old and gnarled, mature plum trees should be pruned as little as possible. Simply remove any dead or severely damaged branches by cutting them back to their bases in spring. As with apples, over-vigorous trees may be induced to produce less foliage and more fruit by grassing up to the base of the trunk. The wood of plums is brittle and readily breaks with the weight of fruit, so it is sensible to support wide-spreading branches of old trees with wooden props. Trees showing signs of silver leaf disease should be left for at least two seasons, for they often recover. If the disease is spreading, however, and especially if its effects appear on suckers, the tree should be felled and destroyed. For other problems, see Apple.

RATE OF GROWTH AND ULTIMATE SIZE While old trees are likely to be growing on their own roots and of unpredictable size, modern garden trees are almost invariably grafted on one of two selected rootstocks, 'St Julien A' or 'Pixy', which will produce trees 6–7m/20–23ft or 4m/13ft tall respectively.

Peach, Nectarine, Apricot

These three relatives of plums all have a reputation for being tender, the apricot especially so because of its early flowering and consequent exposure to late frost. I am convinced, however, that these trees – although benefiting from shelter – are much tougher than generally reckoned and worth trying in many gardens.

SOIL Most, but best in moist, deep, rich loams – preferably slightly alkaline for apricots, slightly acid for peaches and nectarines.

SITUATION Full sun to very light shade; warmth is essential for good ripening so training the trees as fans against a warm wall is an ideal method of cultivation.

Peach 'Peregrine'

WATERING AND FEEDING Modern trees should be fed and mulched at least until well established and preferably permanently. Apply a balanced rose or other potash-rich fertilizer and a mulch in early spring; give only a very light dressing of fertilizer for wall-trained plants. Old and long-established trees should be self-sufficient, if cropping satisfactorily.

PRUNING All pruning must be performed in spring, because in autumn and winter the pruning wounds are liable to be invaded by the fungus causing silver leaf disease.

PEACHES, NECTARINES AND APRICOTS, BUSHES Train the plant as described on page 224. Thereafter, each spring, cut out any overcrowded or crossing branches and up to one quarter of the two- and three-year-old wood, cutting in each case back to the point of emergence of a young, vigorous shoot. This ensures a supply of healthy new shoots on which the fruit will be borne.

PEACHES AND NECTARINES, FANS Follow the steps on pages 222–3, noting that in step 2 all side-shoots emerging from the ribs should be cut to a point just above one leaf. Once step 6 is reached, continue as follows. During that summer, side-shoots will arise from the ribs. Select one shoot for about every 10cm/4in of rib, and leave this unpruned until it reaches about 45cm/1½ft; then pinch out the tip. All other side-shoots should be cut back to one leaf. The framework of the fan is now established, and regular annual pruning is as described overleaf.

As fruits form during the summer, pinch out some of them every year to leave one for approximately every 20cm/8in of shoot length. If possible, peg back the foliage to allow the ripening fruits maximum exposure to the sun.

APRICOTS, FANS Train as for peaches, following the steps on pages 222–3 and the notes above. Once the fan is established, prune annually in spring as for a Plum.

COMMON PROBLEMS Silver leaf; fruit rots; aphids.

TROUBLESHOOTING See Plums.

RATE OF GROWTH AND ULTIMATE SIZE See Plums.

Peach, Nectarine

Pruning fans: peaches, nectarines

▶ **1 SPRING** Identify the shoots to be pruned. These will be shoots made the previous year, and at pruning time they will be bearing flowers. If you are confident of what you are doing, leave the leading shoots unpruned (although they will also be bearing flowers); if not, prune all shoots bearing flowers.

Shoot to be pruned

Leading shoot

Main rib

Growth bud left at base of shoot

Shoot to be pruned (as shown below), flowering

Main rib

Flower buds

Growth bud left in centre of shoot

Growth bud left at tip of shoot

◀ **PINCH OUT GROWTH BUDS** Ignore the flower buds, but pinch out the *growth* buds (clusters of young leaves) on these shoots to leave one at the tip, one at the base, and one in the centre. Once side-shoots have developed from the growth buds, pinch them out to a point just above six leaves from their bases. This restriction of new growth concentrates the plant's energy into producing a crop of fruit.

▶ **2 LATE SUMMER** After picking the fruit, cut back each fruited shoot to just above its lowest side-shoot: this will then form the replacement fruiting shoot for next year's crop.

Main rib

Shoot to be pruned the next spring, as described above

Elongated shoot from growth bud, now fruited

Cherry

There are two main groups of garden cherries. The warmth-requiring sweet cherries need protection from birds, and are now very much easier to grow than formerly with the introduction of self-fertile varieties (most notably 'Stella'), which can be accommodated in a large fruit cage. The hardier acid cherries are ideally grown fan-trained against a north-facing wall.

SOIL Most, but least successful in very dry soils; tolerant of fairly heavy soils, provided there is no tendency to waterlogging.

SITUATION SWEET CHERRIES Full sun to very light shade; warmth is essential for good ripening so training the trees as fans against a warm wall is an ideal method of cultivation.

ACID CHERRIES Full sun to moderate shade, ideally trained against a north-facing wall.

WATERING AND FEEDING Modern trees should be fed and mulched at least until well established and preferably permanently. Apply a balanced rose or other potash-rich fertilizer and a mulch in early spring; give only a very light dressing for wall-trained plants. Old and long-established trees should be self-sufficient, if cropping satisfactorily.

PRUNING As with plums, all pruning of cherries must be performed in spring and summer, not in autumn and winter when the pruning wounds are liable to be invaded by the fungus causing silver leaf disease. On all types of tree, regularly cut out any suckers that arise from the rootstock.

SWEET CHERRIES, BUSHES Train and prune as for Plums.

SWEET CHERRIES, FANS Train the tree as for a Peach, following the steps on pages 222–3 and the additional notes under the Peach entry; then prune it as for a fan-trained Plum (see pages 229–30).

ACID CHERRIES, FANS Train the tree as for a Peach, following the steps on pages 222–3 and the additional notes under the Peach

Cherry 'Morello'

Pruning fans: acid cherries

LATE SUMMER After cropping, cut back the fruited shoots to just above a new side-shoot close to its base. Tie this side-shoot to the support wires; this will form a replacement shoot to bear the next year's crop.

Side-shoot on which next year's fruit will be borne

Fruited shoot

entry. Once the fan is established, prune as follows. In spring, cut out any shoots growing directly towards or away from the wall. Remove shoots to leave one for every 8–10cm/3–4in of rib, and tie the shoots remaining to the wires. Fruit will form on these shoots during the summer, and side-shoots will develop. After cropping, cut back each fruited shoot to just above a side-shoot close to its base. Tie in this side-shoot; it will form a replacement shoot to bear the next year's crop.

COMMON PROBLEMS Silver leaf; bacterial canker; aphids; birds.

PROPAGATION Impossible from cuttings.

TROUBLESHOOTING See Plum.

RATE OF GROWTH AND ULTIMATE SIZE Old trees are likely to be growing on a rootstock such as 'F12/1', a selection of the wild *Prunus avium*, which is perfectly capable of producing a tree 12–15m/40–50ft tall. On the rootstock 'Colt', a bush tree rarely exceeds about 6m/20ft.

Fig

Although there are other, tender species of *Ficus*, it is the moderately hardy, deciduous, fruiting fig that is commonly grown as a small garden tree.

SOIL Most, but for a good crop a poor soil is needed and the plant is best confined within a bottomless cube. Line a 1m/3ft square pit with concrete paving slabs and fill this with a mixture of half and half by volume garden soil and limy rubble.

SITUATION Full sun or very light shade. Figs benefit from wall protection in most areas and are most easily managed when fan-trained against a south- or south-west-facing wall.

WATERING AND FEEDING Mulch in autumn and spring. Feed with a very light dressing of balanced rose or other potash-rich fertilizer in mid-spring. Water copiously during the summer.

PRUNING Free-standing plants require no pruning other than the

Figs

WINTER In northern climates figs will not ripen within a single season, but overwinter as tiny embryo fruits borne at the tips of the shoots. In the autumn some of the half-formed fruits shrivel and drop off, but by midwinter many more are evident on the plant, and will mature the following summer. Pruning in mid-spring has to be a balance between removing enough shoots to encourage new growth, yet not cutting off too many of the growing figs.

removal in spring of damaged shoots and the occasional cutting out of diseased or overcrowded branches. Wall-trained plants do need pruning annually, and in a northern climate this is best performed in spring and early summer.

There are two principles behind the pruning of fan-trained figs. The first is that, unlike the other fruits discussed where a main framework provides a permanent structure, the fig's ribs need to be renewed gradually, ideally over a five- to six-year cycle. The plant will produce strong new main stems either from its base or from the main trunk, and a proportion of these should be retained each year and the oldest removed. The aim is a fan of five to eight main stems per plant.

The second principle of pruning is that in northern climates figs will not ripen within a single season, so those that mature in one summer passed the previous winter as tiny embryo fruits borne towards the shoot tips (see below left). Pruning is therefore directed towards maintaining the fan shape, encouraging new shoots to arise, without cutting off too many embryo fruits.

Fig trained against a wall

Train the fan initially as for a Peach, following the steps on page 222–3 and the additional notes on page 231. Once established, prune the fan in mid-spring: cut damaged side-shoots and any growing directly towards or away from the wall back to one bud above their bases. Then cut alternate side-shoots back to one bud from their bases, selecting those with the fewest embryo fruits as the shoots to remove. Tie in the remainder to the support wires, leaving a spacing of at least 15cm/6in between adjacent side-shoots to allow for the growth of the very large leaves.

In early summer, shorten the newest side-shoots (with no fruits yet) to five or six leaves from their bases. This will stimulate the production of more, potentially fruit-bearing, side-shoots. At the same time, tie in one or two strong new main stems arising from the base or main trunk, to make a maximum of five to eight.

On plants mature enough to have their full quota of main stems, each year in mid-spring cut back one or two of the oldest main stems to the main trunk or the base of the plant. Also remove up to one quarter of the oldest side-shoots, cutting them back to their bases. Prune alternate side-shoots as before. It may be necessary to retie several of the main stems and older side-shoots to ensure that both old and new are spaced as equidistantly as possible, and that all contribute to the structure of the fan. Prune and train the plant in early summer as before.

COMMON PROBLEMS Coral spot.

PROPAGATION Semi-ripe cuttings in summer.

TROUBLESHOOTING Old and misshapen free-standing plants will regenerate very satisfactorily if cut back to the base in spring, although if the entire plant requires renewal, the work should be spread over two years. Neglected fan-trained plants may have eight or more stems arising from the base. One or two should be removed and the plant progressively renewed.

SIZE A free-standing fig tree not seriously cut back by frost will reach about 3×2–$3m/10 \times 6\frac{1}{2}$–10ft after five years, and perhaps $5 \times 5m/16 \times 16ft$ after twenty. Wall-trained plants are pruned within these limits according to the space available.

ACKNOWLEDGEMENTS

The publisher thanks the following photographers and organizations for their kind permission to reproduce the photographs in this book:

Eric Crichton: 5, 28, 34 above, 36 above, 38, 39, 44 below, 47, 49 below, 50, 55, 58, 61, 70 above, 77 below, 85, 87, 91, 98, 104, 105, 110, 119 above, 123, 125, 126 above, 129, 130, 132, 140, 142–3, 146 above, 150, 153 above, 154, 172, 176 below, 180–181, 186, 187 below, 197, 199, 208, 212–5, 219, 225.

Derek Gould: 29 above, 124.

Andrew Lawson: 27, 31, 32, 41, 49 above, 54, 60, 66, 72 below, 74, 92, 107, 111, 115, 117, 121 above and centre, 126 below, 131, 135, 137 above, 138, 155, 157, 159, 163 below, 164, 169, 171, 174, 176 above, 178, 184, 203, 206, 216–7, 233, 235.

S & O Mathews: 2–3, 4–5, 12–13, 29 below, 34 below, 36 below, 42, 43, 46, 57, 59 below, 72 above, 80–1, 95, 100–1, 109, 112, 121 below, 127–8, 133, 147, 156, 161, 166–7, 173, 179, 187 above, 190–1, 211.

Tania Midgley: 75.

Philippe Perdereau: 46 below, 51, 77 above, 146 below, 198, 201.

Photos Horticultural: 26, 33, 37, 67, 69, 70 below, 71, 108, 118, 119 below, 134, 137 below, 149, 153 below, 162, 163 above, 170, 175, 177, 185, 188, 210, 228–231.

Harry Smith Collection: 53.

The publishers would like to thank Valerie Buckingham, Wendy Dallas and Margaret Daykin for editorial help; Sally Powell for design assistance; Judith Harte for proofreading; Capel Manor Horticultural and Environmental Centre for help providing reference for the illustrations.

Index compiled by Indexing Specialists, Hove, East Sussex BN3 2DJ